Architectures of Poetry

79

Internationale Forschungen zur Allgemeinen und Vergleichenden Literaturwissenschaft

In Verbindung mit

Dietrich Briesemeister (Friedrich Schiller-Universität Jena) - Guillaume van Gemert (Universiteit Nijmegen) - Joachim Knape (Universität Tübingen) - Klaus Ley (Johannes Gutenberg-Universität Mainz) - John A. McCarthy (Vanderbilt University) - Manfred Pfister (Freie Universität Berlin) - Sven H. Rossel (University of Washington) - Azade Seyhan (Bryn Mawr College) - Horst Thomé (Universität Kiel)

herausgegeben von

Alberto Martino
(Universität Wien)

Redakteure:
Norbert Bachleitner & Alfred Noe

Anschrift der Redaktion:
Institut für Vergleichende Literaturwissenschaft, Berggasse 11/5, A-1090 Wien

Architectures of Poetry

Edited by
María Eugenia Díaz Sánchez
and Craig Douglas Dworkin

Amsterdam - New York, NY 2004

Cover: Torre Galatea, Salvador Dalí

Le papier sur lequel le présent ouvrage est imprimé remplit les prescriptions
de "ISO 9706:1994, Information et documentation - Papier pour documents -
Prescriptions pour la permanence".

The paper on which this book is printed meets the requirements of " ISO
9706:1994, Information and documentation - Paper for documents - Requirements
for permanence".

ISBN: 90-420-1892-5
©Editions Rodopi B.V., Amsterdam - New York, NY 2004
Printed in The Netherlands

Contents

Craig Dworkin

Introduction: Against Metaphor (construye en lo ausente)

Amas la arquitectura que construye en lo ausente ...
Federica García Lorca

Architecture is the simplest way of articulating time and space;
of modulating reality; of making people dream.
Ivan Chtcheglov

Stanzas: little rooms for words.

A few years ago, among poets, all the talk was about architecture. A trend, perhaps, and not without some obvious attractions — developments in the field of architecture had brought together the artistic credentials of the creative arts with an increasingly sophisticated critical literature *and* commercial success. Smart and hip and stylish and able to buy the drinks — what more could poetry ask?

But one might still ask of poetry: why *architecture* rather than some other field? The soul of poetry has transmigrated before; in recent memory it fled from the corpse of verse to the body of critical and theoretical writing (one might think of Jacques Derrida's *Glas*, Susan Howe's poetical essays and investigatory poems, the verse essays of Charles Bernstein and Bob Perelman, or the philosophical inquiries of Lyn Hejinian, for just a few examples), and after that metempsychosis it shows signs of what is at least a new infatuation with haunting the virtual body of the internet and digital media. Were those architecturally attuned poets simply following a trajectory of intellectual interest that has kept a tradition of critical poetry restlessly on the move and in search of new proving grounds?

In asking these questions, I do not want to imply that poetry and architecture have ever been too distant or estranged. There are obviously a number of traditions that have long negotiated between the two spheres. From the imagined structures at the heart of the classical art of memory to the minor genre of the Elizabethan country-house poem, architecture has informed poetry to a greater or lesser extent. One need only recall Pound's *tempio*, Rilke's *Kathedrale*, Blake's tabernacle, or Crane's bridge to recognize the important role that architecture can play *within* the poem, or think of Ruskin's treatise on poetry and architecture, the forms in Keats' Hyperion poems, or the dialogue between Buckminster Fuller and John Cage to remember that the conceptual and theoretical discourse of the sister arts has a long history of correspondence between the poem and the building. Indeed, all of those intellectual movements with interconnected concerns — the baroque and the gothic, cubism and futurism — have left buildings and blueprints in dialogue with contemporaneous linguistic structures and manuscripts. Less direct affinities might also be sketched between the distinctly urban poetry that emerged from Charles Baudelaire's Paris and Vladimir Mayakovsky's Moscow. Like many, Mayakovsky was also impressed with the architecture of New York City, which had made a similarly strong imprint on the work of the Romantic

Romantic writer Sousândrade (pen-name of Joaquim de Souza Andrade [1833-1902]), in his extraordinary "O inferno de Wall Street [Wall Street's Hell]," and which might be felt as well in the work of the native contemporary Walt Whitman — not to mention subsequent revisions in its guise as the capitol of the 20th century by Federico Garcia Lorca, Louis Zukofsky, and Frank O'Hara among many others.

Beyond such thematics, architecture has also served as the "metaphoric" model for structuring poems, from the inclusive urban and suburban imaginative spaces of William Carlos Williams' *Paterson* to the organization of Ronald Johnson's *Ark*, another late modernist long poem in which individual cantos take the part of "beams" and "ramparts," "spires" and "foundations." That metaphorical valence has also gone further to shape the structure of the poem itself, as in works as varied as George Herbet's *Temple* and Vasily Kamensky's *zhelezobetonny*: [ferro-concrete] poems, which modeled their hard-edged constructivist inspiration on advances in steel-reinforced concrete building material. Moreover, projects like Fiona Templeton's 1988 *You, The City* and the *Streetworks* events organized by the Architectural League in the late 1960s pushed the text closer to street-theater by actually incorporating the city as a integral aspect of the realization of the written work itself.[1]

One could multiply examples along any of these lines, but what strikes me about the essays in this collection are the degree to which they refuse to take "architecture," or "poetry" for that matter, in a merely figural sense.[2] At their best, they work to investigate the quite literal architectures of poetry. The literalization of metaphor can be the model for a methodology: a willingness to take the unintended suggestions of language as reality and to pursue a figural and subjunctive hypothesis with a quite literal, demonstrative logic. Such a methodology — what we might call the literal wager — is an investigatory strategy familiar from the *plateaux* of Gilles Deleuze and Félix Guattari, and one played out in many of the essays included here. Such a speculative extrapolation, in fact, is one way to understand the three essays that formed the kernel from which this collection grew: all written by participants at "Transgressing Boundaries: Strategies of Renewal in American Poetry," a conference held at the University of Salamanca in the summer of 2000, and all focusing on the work of Shusaku Arakawa and Madeline Gins.

Recognized as integral to the canon of 'conceptual art,' the work of Arakawa and Gins applies a distinctly phenomenological torque to conceptual art in order to gain a purchase on the body's relation to the systematicity of knowledge — its cleaving function of simultaneous states of separation and unification. In the process, they have undertaken sustained

---

[1]   Although Templeton's project was presented as a dramatic work (an "intimate play"), and the various street-works projects were pursued under the sign of the nascent genre of performance art, it is worth noting that the documentation of Templeton's work was published by a poetry press (NY: Roof Books, 1998), and that the 1969 streetworks were documented in the final number of the journal *0-9*, which was edited by the poets Vito Acconci and Bernadette Mayer.

[2]   One might recall Guy Debord's caution to those interested in a free architecture that the new buildings would not be founded on "poetic" forms, in the sense that contemporaneous painting was considered to be "lyrically" abstract ("Rapport sur la construction des situations et sur les conditions de l'organisation et de l'action de la tendance situationniste international [Report on the construction of Situations and on the International Situationist Tendency's Conditions of Organisation and Action]" (privately circulated, 1957); translated in Ken Knabb, *Situationist International Anthology* (Berkeley: Bureau of Public Secrets, 1981), pp. 17-25.

critical explorations of the indexical thrust by which we understand and navigate a world shot through with signs, and the ways in which categories of knowledge are shaped by language. To a degree equaled only perhaps by Adrian Piper, theirs is a decided *philosophical* practice of art and architecture, or an architectural art which provokes and records a philosophical investigation. Working out to architecture from the degree zero of the "I" in much the same way that the grammarians of The Port Royal worked out the ontology of the *je* from the mere inscription of the copulative verb "to be" in a sentence such as "Le ciel est bleu [The sky is blue]," Gins and Arakawa have developed a linguistic phenomenology.[3] In part, their work is a study of "the area of perception created, located, and demonstrated by the combining (melting) of languages."[4]

There is obviously much more to be said about the seriously playful language games of Arakawa and Gins' collaborations, and the essays at the center of this volume argue eloquently for the importance of their work. Since there is not space in this brief introduction for the extended discussion that would be necessary to give other aspects of their work the attention it deserves, I want to instead briefly note one topic that has been conspicuously *absent* from the critical discussion of their architectural interventions. Where Arakawa and Gins pitch their conceptual geographies toward philosophy, such investigations could equally incline toward politics, as demonstrated by the "new urbanism" integral to the Situationists. Moreover, the constructed situations and psychogeography of the Situationists resonates — sometime harmonically, and sometimes with telling patterns of interference — with the roughly contemporaneous work of Arakawa and Gins. Both remind us that we are not simply given a world, but that we construct one, and that any system — perceptual, cartographic, classificatory, architectural — can be used in other ways. The philosophical precedent for such propositions can be found in Ludwig Wittgenstein's later writing, where "the point is," in mathematics, for instance, that "we can think of more than *one* application of an algebraic formula," and where the insistence falls again and again on "the fact that there are other processes, besides the one we originally thought of."[5] But the political force of such realizations should not be elided; even before any hint of an assertion that the world *should* be otherwise, they manifest the revolutionary force of remembering, quite simply, that the world *could* be otherwise.

More specifically, one might compare the goals of Gins and Arakawa's "reversible destiny" with Guy Debord's "reversible connecting factor":

Reprendre ainsi le radicalisme implique naturellement aussi un approfondissement considérable de toutes les anciennes tentatives libératrices. L'expérience de leur inachèvement dans l'isolement, ou de leur retournement en mystification globale, conduit à mieux comprendre la cohérence du monde à transformer — et, à partir de la cohérence retrouvée, on peut sauver beaucoup de recherches partielles continuées dans le passé récent, qui

---

3   For more on the implications of the "je," see Louis Marin's discussion (*passim*) of Antoine Arnauld and Émile Benveniste in the first part of *Détruire la peinture* (Paris: Éditions Galilée, 1977); for the statement on the architectural implications of the "I" see Arakawa and Gins, 'The Tentative Constructed Plan as Intervening Device (for a Reversible Destiny)', *A + U* 255 (Tokyo: December, 1991), 48.

4   'Notes on My Paintings: What I am Mistakenly Looking For', *Arts Magazine* 44: 2 (November, 1969), 29.

5   Sections 146 and 140: *Philosophische Untersuchungen/Philosophical Investigations*, trans. by G. E. M. Anscombe, 3rd ed. (New York: Macmillan, 1968).

accèdent de la sorte à leur vérité. L'appréhension de *cette cohérence réversible* du monde, tel qu'il est et tel qu'il est possible, dévoile le caractère fallacieux des demi-mesures, et le fait qu'il y a essentiellement demi-mesure chaque fois que le modèle de fonctionnement de la société dominante — avec ses catégories de hiérarchisation et de spécialisation, corollairement ses habitudes ou ses goûts — se reconstitue à l'intérieur des forces de la négation.

[To revive radicalism naturally also involves considerable research work, with a view toward all the earlier attempts at freedom. The experience of their failure, which ended in isolation or fell back into global mystification, leads to a greater understanding of the continuity in the world that must be changed — and by means of this understanding it is possible to salvage many of the partial results that the most recent research has obtained and which can thus be verified. This understanding of the reversible connecting factor in the world exposes — to the extent that it exists and is possible — the false character of halfway measures, and the fact that there are essentially only half-measures each time that the model of the functioning of the dominant society — with its categories of hierarchy and specialization, correlating its habits and its tastes — constructs itself at the center of the forces of negation].[6]

Even before the urbanist critiques of the Situationists and what Guy Debord would come to term their "architecture sauvage [wild architecture]," the radical artistic left was taking the architecture of poetry quite literally.[7] In opposition to the functionalist New Bauhaus and Hochschule für Gestaltung in Ulm, Asger Jorn and Giuseppe Pinot-Gallizio formed The International Movement for an Imaginist Bauhaus, taking as their founding inspiration Constant Nieuwenhuys' urbanist interventions and declaring: "for the first time in history, architecture shall become an authentic art of construction […] It is in *poetry* that life will be housed."[8] Similarly, the Lettrist International (which had split from the Lettrists in part because they believed that Isidore Isou's group focused too exclusively on language as such) argued that rather than use the modern urban condition as a model for revolutionizing linguistic experience, the lessons of language would be brought to bear on the urban environment and the revolution of architectural consciousness.[9] Recognizing, as Gins and Arakawa would, that "architecture is a tool that can be used as writing has been, except that it can have a far more extensive range of application" the Lettrists pursued a 'writing from the street' (in the sense that one might conceive of a 'writing from the body').[10] "Poetry," they could flatly assert "is in the form of cities," and Constant Nieuwenhuys would predict that "the new urbanism will find its first facilitators" in the domain of poetry.[11]

---

[6] "Les Situationnistes et les nouvelles formes d'action dans la politique ou l'art," originally published in *Destruktion af RSG 6* (Galerie EXI: Odense, Denmark, June 1963); republished in *Mille et une nuits*, La Petite Collection, n° 300 (Paris: September 2000); emphasis supplied.

[7] Guy Debord, 'De l'architecture sauvage,' in Asger Jorn, *Le Jardin d'Albisola* (Torino: Edizioni d'Arte Fratelli Pozzo, 1974).

[8] A. Alberts, Armando, Constant, Har Oudejans, 'First proclamation of the Dutch Section of the SI,' *Internationale Situationniste* #2 (December 1959); emphasis supplied.

[9] See Simon Sadler, *The Situationist City* (Cambridge: MIT Press, 1998), pp. 95-6.

[10] Arakawa and Gins, "Dear Neverending Architectonic Reflective Wherewithal," an open letter to Jean-François Lyotard, in *Reversible Destiny: We Have Decided Not To Die* (NY: Guggenheim Museum, 1997), p. 12.

[11] 'Réponse a une enquête du groupe surréaliste belge,' *Potlatch*, 5 (Paris: July 1954; and also as a special issue of *La Carte d'après Nature* [Brussels, January 1954].; reprinted in *Potlatch 1954-1957* (Paris: Editions Lebovici, 1985), pp. 37-38; Constant Nieuwenhuys, 'Report to the Munich Conference,' *Internationale Situationniste* #3, (December 1959). An anonymous essay on "Poésie" (*Potlatch* 24 [Paris: November 1955]; reprinted in *Potlatch 1954-57*, 183) connects contemporary poetry and the dissolution of fixed poetic form with the dis-

With that understanding of an urban poetry "written on the faces of adventures," the Lettrists required a legible semiotics of the city.[12] They asked themselves: "what sign could we recognize as our own?" The answer: "certain graffiti, words of refusal or forbidden gestures inscribed with haste."[13] Indeed, the proto-situationist interventions could be quite literal; the *L. I.* wrote in chalk on the streets themselves to "add to the intrinsic meaning" of street names, and graffiti flowered over the walls of Paris during the Situationist-inspired revolution of May '68 as Lautréamont's dream of a poetry made by all was reiterated, in paint, by those who simultaneously realized it.[14] The architecture of the city was reconfigured in that summer of 1968 with decidedly *poetic* ends; with the paving stones pried loose from the street and piled to form barricades, or hurled at police vans, one of those graffiti slogans read: "sous les pavés, la plage [beneath the paving stones: the beach]."

With those stones replaced and our streets now reconstructed as "information highways," this collection is an attempt to catch a glimpse of another — more recent and less politicized — moment when poets once again dreamt architecture. With no pretense to anything like a complete documentation, or even a representative sampling, and with many obvious figures absent, this volume is a snapshot of a skyline that has already, irrevocably, changed. Perhaps the attraction of architecture for poets was always girded by the knowledge that for all its sketches and plans and theories — and for all the disdain that the most interesting architects have had for actual buildings — architecture was, in all senses of the phrase, a serious business. It will be interesting to watch how the architectural turn taken by poetry develops in the work written after September 11, 2001, and whether the newly palpable sense of the literal force of architecture will provoke a strengthened commitment to pursuing the architectures of poetry, or a chastened and sobered backing off.

With all the melancholy of *temps perdus*, Guy Debord ended his extraordinary artists' book *Mémoires*: "Je voulais parler la belle langue de mon siècle [I wanted to speak the beautiful language of my century]."

Hasn't that always been the dream of poetry? And hasn't that — in the towers it raised and demolished over the twentieth century — been the surprising success of architecture?

"The event preceded the architecture and the poem was the mediator. The story is clearly delineated; poetry and architecture are talking to each other forever."[15]

Language cameras, with little room for words.

---

solution of fixed urban forms in modernity. The article suggests, accordingly, that the creation of worthwhile literature, architecture and politics would be found in fluid and dynamic forms.

[12] 'Réponse a une enquête du groupe surréaliste belge.'

[13] Raoul Vaneigm, 'Commentaires contre l'urbanism', *Internationale Situationniste*, 6 (Paris 1961), 33-37.

[14] Anonymous, 'De rôle de lécriture', *Potlatch*, 23 (Paris: October, 1955); reprinted in *Potlatch 1954-1957*, p. 176-177.

[15] Carlos Brillenbourg, qtd. in David Shapiro, 'Poetry and Architecture, Architecture and Poetry', *Bomb*, 41 (1992), 20.

Jed Rasula

"When the mind is like a hall": Places of a Possible Poetics

With a broad range of both historical and theoretical referents, this essay explores the intricate set of relations between poetic inspiration and space. From Latin American avant-gardes to Symbolism, French Surrealism to video art, the essay reads our modern literary hertiage in terms of phenomenological, psychoanalytical, and architectural theory. Beginning with the specificity of site in Rilke's writing and edning with Krzysztof Wodiczko's video installations, the essay charts the poetics of architectual form and the imaginative burden that structures such as the pyramid, skyscraper, and labyrinth can bear.

Poetic inspiration has had a particular affinity with place since the episode recounted in Hesiod's *Theogony*, in which a shepherd tending his flock on the slope of Mount Helikon is visited by the Muses. The place is important in that the site of the visitation is not flat, but precipitous. With Hesiod's fable, poetry might be thought of as undergoing initiation as a *site-specific* art.

Consider the specificity of site in the case of the 20ᵗʰ century's most famous instance of fraught inspiration: Rilke's *Duino Elegies*. Initiated in a Trieste castle perched on a cliff over the Adriatic, further work on the Elegies stalled in the miasmic locales of Paris and Munich, and they were only completed ten years later (along with the unexpected *Sonnets to Orpheus*) in a tower in the Swiss Alps. (*Duino Elegies* is a book that needed a passport.) The Elegies and the Sonnets, taken together, affirm the poetic legacy of the vertical axis.

Rilke belongs to a tradition of encounters with mountains. Petrarch is credited with being the first to reach the summit of Mont Ventoux in France. Neruda's visit to cloud swept ruins of the ancient Incas resulted in *Las Alturas de Macchu Picchu*, and his fellow Chilean Vicente Huidobro wrote an epic invocation to verticality in *Altazor, or A Voyage in a Parachute*. Eugene Jolas made a program of verticality, first in the vertiginously polylingual *Secession in Astropolis* (1928), then in the 1932 manifesto "Poetry is Vertical." *Vertical* finally blends with *integral* in his 1936 manifesto "Vertigralism," drawing on a rich vein of prepositional inversions: to go in is to go out, as above so below. Sidereal motion is terrestrial event. The poetry of the stars is written in geology. So a host of earth-besotted figures (Vallejo, Neruda, Césaire) join alchemical hands with the aeronautical poets. When García Lorca says "the duende climbs up inside you, from the soles of the feet" he neglects to say that it might as well go right up on through the crown of the head.[1] It appears that, viewing Mallarmé's unique typography in *Un coup de dés*, Paul Valéry

---

[1]   Federica García Lorca, *Deep Song and Other Prose*, ed. and trans. by Christopher Maurer (New York: New Directions, 1980), p. 43.

encountered something like an astral duende. "He has undertaken finally to raise a printed page to the power of the midnight sky."[2] In this realm, where up and down swap roles,

> There is no Space or Time
> Only intensity,
> And tame things
> Have no immensity.[3]

Architectural verticality is usually associated with skyscrapers, but Bruno Taut jettisoned the gravitational field of earth altogether in *Alpine Architecture*, in which fanciful visions of glass palaces in the mountains eventuate in Sternbau or star-building. The interplay of terrestrial recess with stellar orbit is fully realized in "Grottenstern mit schwebender Architektur" (cavern star with suspended architecture) [Figure 1]. For poetics, a comparably vertigral orientation is memorably rendered in an Ostyak tale about a golden pole atop the Nail of the North, with a very wise tomcat who climbs up and down the pole. When he climbs down, he sings songs; when he climbs up, he tells tales.[4] Here again is acknowledgement of poetry as precipitous. Going down in order to sing the song: Orpheus' descent is a basic trope, rendered in epic by Odysseus and Aeneas, who make their narrative progress up the golden pole accelerate by dipping down into lyric sufferance — as, in fact, Francis Ponge advises: "Poets should in no way concern themselves with human relationships, but should get to the very bottom. Society, furthermore, takes good care of putting them there, and the love of things keeps them there; they are the ambassadors of the silent world. As such, they stammer, they murmur, they sink into the darkness of logos — until at last they reach the level of ROOTS, where things and formulas are one."[5] *Where things and formulas are one:* what better definition of architecture can you come by? The irony is that this is an ideal. The ideal is an idea bearing the pretence of the real, as the real material deal.

Bernard Tschumi calls this "the paradox of the Pyramid of concepts and the Labyrinth of experience, of immaterial architecture as a concept and of material architecture as a presence."[6] The paradox cannot be resolved, it can only be teased with the chopsticks of divergent expectations. "*Like eroticism,*" says Tschumi, "*architecture needs both system and excess.*"[7] Architecture rarely gets concrete realizations of system amalgamated to phantasm — Gaudí's Sagrada Familia, the postman Chaval's Palais Ideal in Hauterives, and Simon Rodia's tower in Watts are rare examples — but poets specialize in bringing out the excess of systems, as in Baudelaire's "Correspondences" with its vision of nature as a temple, "in which living pillars sometimes utter a babel of words; man traverses it through a forest of symbols, that watch him with knowing eyes [La Nature est un temple où de vivants pil-

---

[2]   Paul Valéry, *Leonardo Poe Mallarmé*, trans. by Malcolm Cowley and James R. Lawler (Princeton: Princeton University Press, 1972), p. 312.

[3]   Mina Loy, *The Lost Lunar Baedeker*, ed. by Roger L. Conover (New York: Farrar, Straus & Giroux, 1996), p. 3.

[4]   Giorgio de Santillana and Hertha von Dechend, *Hamlet's Mill: An Essay on Myth and the Frame of Time* (Boston: Gambit, 1969), p. 96.

[5]   Francis Ponge, *The Voice of Things*, ed. and trans. by Beth Archer (New York: McGraw-Hill, 1972), pp. 109-110.

[6]   Bernard Tschumi, *Architecture and Disjunction* (Cambridge: The MIT Press, 1994), p. 47.

[7]   Tschumi, p. 50.

GROTTENSTERN

mit schwebender Architektur

iers/Laissent parfois sortir de confuses paroles;/L'homme y passe à travers des forêts de symbols/Qui l'observent avec des regards familiers]."[8] Verticality prevails even here, in the vocalizing pillars and the voyeuristically disposed symbols — trees endowed with flânerie (as if shedding leaves were leave-taking).

Rendered architecturally, the forest of symbols becomes Walter Pater's vision of an interrogative structure: "The very place one is in, its stone-work, its empty spaces, invade you; invade all who belong to them [...] seem to question you masterfully as to your purpose in being here at all."[9] Not that this can't be said of poems as well. Poetry can seem to materialize in the somatic unconscious just as a building slinks off into a flavor deep in the blood. Addressing the potentially anomalous topic of subjectivity in architecture, Robert Harbison evokes the specter of "buildings gnarled like inner experience, even vanishing, like thoughts."[10] He finds in one example that "there can be no rest or relaxation but a kind of mental circling like that of a bird looking unsuccessfully for a perch."[11]

Henry James anatomizes such an experience in "The Jolly Corner," in which an architect returns to New York after a life and career abroad, and has the rare opportunity to revisit his childhood home, finding it "immense, the scale of space again inordinate; the open rooms [...] gloomed in their shuttered state like mouths of caverns; only the high skylight that formed the crown of the deep well created for him a medium in which he could advance, but which might have been, for queerness of colour, some watery under-world."[12] What James depicts is not the usual trope of a haunted house, but a person haunted *by* a house. In *The Notebooks of Malte Laurids Brigge*, Rilke charts a comparable experience, in the narrator's recollection of a childhood home never seen again after age thirteen. "As I find it in the memories of my childhood, it isn't a complete building; it has been broken into pieces inside me; a room here, a room there, and then a piece of a hallway that doesn't connect these two rooms, but is preserved as a fragment, by itself. In this way it is all dispersed inside me [...] It's as if the image of this house had fallen into me from an infinite height and shattered upon my ground."[13]

In 2001 Americans had to absorb the image of a great collapse, even as it was inverted into a feverish worksite of ideological construction. Not since Pearl Harbor has wreckage sprung so nimbly into action as the insignia of political resolve. Diana Agrest identifies the skyscraper as "an empty signifier that can assume and attract different meanings."[14] In linguistics, the category for the empty sign is *deixis*, consisting of words whose indication is context specific, and the tacit context is a dialogue. But can you enter into an intersubjec-

---

[8]   Charles Baudelaire, 'Correspondances', in *The Modern Tradition*, ed. by Richard Ellmann and Charles Feidelson, Jr. (New York: Oxford University Press, 1965), pp. 59-60.

[9]   Ellen Eve Frank, *Literary Architecture: Essays Toward a Tradition* (Berkeley: University of California Press, 1979), p. 37.

[10] Robert Harbison, *Eccentric Spaces* (New York: Knopf, 1977), p. 160.

[11] Harbison, pp. 172-3.

[12] Henry James, *Eight Tales from the Major Phase:* In the Cage *and Others*, ed. by Morton Dauwen Zabel (New York: Norton, 1969), p. 341.

[13] Rainer Maria Rilke, *The Notebooks of Malte Laurids Brigge*, trans. by Stephen Mitchell (New York: Vintage, 1990), p. 25.

[14] Diana I Agrest, *Architecture from Without: Theoretical Framings for a Critical Practice* (Cambridge: The MIT Press, 1991), p. 87.

tive exchange with a building? There's obviously a dialogical rapport established by the very functionality of a building you enter. Points of orientation to interior possibilities are inherently solicitous. But what about a building you don't enter, and may never even see except in souvenirs or photographs? The deictic summons of the skyscraper was made evident in the collapsing World Trade Center towers, the image of which also collapsed the random and the anonymous into the personal, as if a built structure could only hit the ground, but the interior building might keep on falling unchecked forever. And this is precisely what happens in poetry, a limitless descent. Part of the impact of rereading "Tintern Abbey" or *Tender Buttons* is to reaffirm a certain vertigo, to register the work itself as an event *still falling*, as a kind of invited catastrophe.

Gaston Bachelard has an applicable theory: "The *fall*, even before any moral metaphor intervenes, is a constant psychic reality. This psychic fall can be investigated as an aspect of poetic and moral physics. The *psychic slope* changes constantly. The *general tonus* — that dynamic fact that every consciousness grasps at once — becomes *immediately a slope*."[15] In the same book, *Air and Dreams*, Bachelard supplements the model of the "psychic slope": "The poetic image," as he defines it, "is a sudden salience on the surface of the psyche."[16] A salience is a highlight, a distinction; it's also associated with sudden movement, and with something that protrudes at a striking angle. It's a distress that stresses the point. Image, as such, is disaster — quite the opposite of Pound's model of image as cod-liver pill for pumping iron in the blood. Djuna Barnes, in *Nightwood* (that great castanet of aphorisms), pithily says "An image is a stop the mind makes between uncertainties."[17] This evokes for me an image — as if to prove Barnes's point — and the image is that of a railway station. If uncertainty is motion, image is a station: image marks the spot where you get off or climb aboard the vehicle of your mobilized uncertainty.

The crossroads of the vertical axis and the horizontal axis is memorably pinpointed on a railway platform in *Party Going* by Henry Green. Elliptical as it sounds, this is how the novel opens:

> Fog was so dense, bird that had been disturbed went flat into a balustrade and slowly fell, dead, at her feet.
>
> There it lay and Miss Fellowes looked up to where that pall of fog was twenty foot above and out of which it had fallen, turning over once. She bent down and took a wing then entered a tunnel in front of her, and this had DEPARTURES lit up over it, carrying her dead pigeon.[18]

But for the patently English fog, Miss Fellowes might be heading for the same railroad car young Marcel takes to Balbec in Proust's vivid demonstration of train travel as a species of mobilized architecture. Marcel catches a glimpse of sunrise ("a necessary concomitant of long railway journeys"), but the train rounds a bend, plunging the car back into darkness, and "the morning scene gave place in the frame of the window to a nocturnal village, its roofs still blue with moonlight [...] and I was lamenting the loss of my strip of pink sky

15   Gaston Bachelard, *Air and Dreams: An Essay on the Imagination of Movement*, trans. by Edith R. and C. Frederick Farrell (Dallas: Dallas Institute of Humanities and Culture, 1988), p. 11.

16   Bachelard, p. 248

17   Djuna Barnes, *Nightwood* (New York: New Directions, 1946), p. 111.

18   Henry Green, *Loving. Living. Party Going* (London: Picador, 1978), p. 384

when I caught sight of it anew, but red this time, in the opposite window which it left at a second bend in the line; so that I spent my time running from one window to the other to reassemble, to collect on a single canvas the intermittent, antipodean fragments of my fine, scarlet, ever-changing morning, and to obtain a comprehensive view and a continuous picture of it."[19] To dream of a continuous picture is also to glimpse the fugitive totality of your own life, never present all at once but like Proust's train curving out beyond one horizon after another. Yet the tantalizing prospect of biological destiny achieving fruity circumference is realized in another image, this time from Fritz Kahn's medical textbook *Man in Structure and Function* [Figure 2], the caption of which reads: "If the blood corpuscles of a human body (25 million in number) were joined together to form a chain, they would pass four times around the globe. Their surface covers an area of 4,900 square yards."[20] In another diagram [Figure 3], the labor required of the heart as a pump is illustrated in the vertical field: "In the course of a day the heart is theoretically capable of filling three tank cars with ten thousand litres of blood, and in seventy years it pumps 250 million litres of blood, a quantity sufficient to fill the cubic area occupied by a modern skyscraper."[21]

Kahn's enticing imponderables demonstrate the power of analogy to insist on a habitat, some dwelling space commensurate with the power of thought, in calculable ratios. There are limits of *ratio*, naturally, and the early Greek philosophers were intent on estimating where sensation vanished, giving way to cogitation — or *cogito* to agitation. "Whatever occupies time must always be becoming older than itself, and 'older' always means older than something younger. Consequently, whatever is becoming older than itself, if it is to have something *than* which it is becoming older, must also be at the same time becoming younger than itself."[22] Henri Bergson, trying to come to terms with Plato's *sprawl*, suggests as summary formula: "*The affirmation of a reality implies the simultaneous affirmation of all the degrees of reality intermediate between it and nothing.*"[23] The meltdown of the thinkable is not only a daily event, but an everyday necessity, it turns out. The genius of Plato (and Bergson) inheres in this: *we like to think these things — and think this "liking" to be a need of likeness.* The genius of Plato (and Bergson) inheres in this: *we like to think these things — and think this "liking" to be a need of likeness.*

In the domain of resemblance, especially under the pressure of Plato's enigma of a contracting expansion or expanding contraction, the operative principle is *multum in parvo*, much in little. Regarding vastness, the mind rapidly closes in on particulars; *things* become blockades against the infinite, and the miniature emerges as an extravagant investment in the power of reduction. Something is gained, and something else lost, in the process, as

[19]   Marcel Proust, *Remembrance of Things Past, Vol. I*, trans. by C. K. Scott Moncrieff, revised by Terence Kilmartin (New York: Random House, 1981), pp. 704-5.

[20]   Fritz Kahn, *Man in Structure and Function*, Vol. I., trans. by George Rosen (New York: Knopf, 1943), p. 208.

[21]   Kahn, p. 180.

[22]   Plato, *Parmenides*, in *The Collected Dialogues, Including the Letters*, ed. by Edith Hamilton and Huntington Cairns (New York: Pantheon, 1961), pp. 934-935 [141:a-b].

[23]   Henri Bergson, *Creative Evolution*, trans. by Arthur Mitchell (New York: Modern Library, 1944), p. 351.

136. Four times around the globe! If the blood corpuscles of a human body (25 million in number) were joined together to form a chain, they would pass four times around the globe. Their surface covers an area of 4,900 square yards.

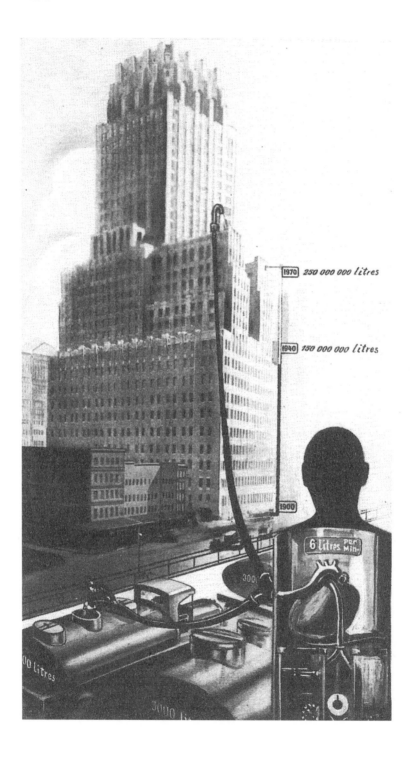

illustrated in the tale of Orpheus and Eurydice. The condition of the Orphic descent to retrieve Eurydice from the underworld is that he lead her out without looking to see if she's behind him. He looks, and she vanishes. So it's not a familiar tale of lost and found, for Eurydice is lost when found. The instantaneousness of it is most poignant, for it suggests a kind of ontological impertinence in the very desire to see the unseeable, to know with daytime vision what has to stay in the dark. *You can know, but you can't see*, the parable says; and yet we go on equating knowing with seeing ("I see what you mean"). Joseph Cornell's boxes can be thought of as labyrinthine models of Orpheus' descent, inviting a gaze into *bewilderment* as if that were the name of a specific site. In these wonder cabinets, to be lost is to risk being found out — that is, to have one's desires put on parade in a box. The boxes, filled with fetishistic relics, are like portals onto a space paradoxically vast with narrowness. The mind darts around, leaving the body behind like Eurydice in the underworld. So pregnant is the implied dynamic between the inanimate objects that they practically thump with cardiac potential. They could be three-dimensional love letters tipping over like a jug of milk into the galaxy, except that the falling or draining is stationary, arrested in, or *as*, a scene. The name of this enchantment is *vertigo*, and it has to do with the blood-tide spoken of in antiquity as the Ouroboros, the serpent biting its own tail (and going around in circles brings on dizziness). So is it "negative capability" (in Keats's sense) that's at work in you, trusting your heart (your box) will keep pouring you into the abyss that is your life, the beginning and end of which are lost in obscurity, so that it seems to be poured into the middle and spreads outward in rings into past and future alike? In any case, it's a capacity of the heart to split in the imagination (as a conceptual reminder of the physical organ's two chambers?) into the physical agitation in the chest — the pulse of emotion — and the calm, nurturing visage of compassion. The heart makes places work, as appearance and as labor. The heart works contrasts up into the open in an ongoing alchemical manifesto. For, as James John Garth Wilkinson memorably says, "the heart is a self-supplying knot of affirmations" — at work "in a bed of structural desire," no less, for "the heart love[s] its own blood, which it squeezes hot and naked with its ruddy fingers."[24] "For the heart is a proposition that never goes beyond a bare statement, but pumps through us the substance of self-evidence."[25] Wilkinson calls imagination "the heart-house," sedulously worked by desire, "the dilating, opening, or cavity-making facility."[26]

To the poetics of ingress and egress elaborated in Wilkinson's treatise *The Human Body* — audaciously subtitled "and its Connexion With Man" — I would add Grant Hildebrand's anatomically sensitive deliberations from *The Origins of Architectural Pleasure*:

> Any architectural project worth doing entails, of necessity, decisions about the three dimensions of its spaces, the opening or closing of spaces to one another, the presence and absence of transparent and opaque bounding surfaces, the availability, location, and character of vistas, the composition of paths of movement [...] Con-

24 James John Garth Wilkinson, *The Human Body*, 2nd ed (London: Chapman & Hall, 1860), pp. 172, 175, 178.
25 Wilkinson, pp. 183-4.
26 Wilkinson, p. 196.

cepts of prospect and refuge, enticement, and peril are simply ways of providing a certain kind of information for such decisions.[27]

Hildebrand's *prospect* and *refuge*, *enticement* and *peril* are conceptually intimate with Bachelard's *psychic slope*. To be in motion is to have an appointment with slippage; every banana skin peels the thought of secure progress; the world comes alive with "Secret staircases, frames from which the paintings quickly slip aside and vanish," André Breton exclaims in *Nadja*, "buttons which must be indirectly pressed to make an entire room move sideways or vertically, or immediately change all its furnishings; we may imagine the mind's greatest adventure as a journey of this sort to the paradise of pitfalls."[28] As this passage reveals, Breton wanted to write a book that could be left "ajar, like a door."[29] Breton's aspiration may have been most memorably met in *Nightwood*, which is like a painting by Remedios Varo or Leonora Carrington achieved in wax (except the wax is words, whose apparent stability perpetuates their melting): a cabinet of curiosities most of which, being words, disclose nothing to the eye but everything to the nasal instinct. No wonder the main character ends up on all fours in olfactory reverie with a dog.

A book ajar not only allows the reader go into it (the usual experience), but lets emanations from the text creep out. The result is a honeycomb of wandering phantasms, for which *prospect*, *refuge*, *enticement* and *peril* are terms rendering palpable the sense that the reader and writer cohabit an apparition. The haunting (the hunting) is mutual. "Curious," says the narrator of Sándor Márai's novel *Embers*, "that in Hungarian our words for killing and embracing echo and heighten each other" [*ölés* and *ölelés*]).[30] A text, like a room, is a place of coming and going, embracing and hunting. In a poem, a stanza is a room, and nobody lavishes more attention on the architectural principles of the stanza than Mandelstam writing about Dante: "The step, linked to breathing and saturated with thought: this Dante understands as the beginning of prosody [...]. In Dante philosophy and poetry are forever on the move, forever on their feet. Even standing still is a variety of accumulated motion; making a space for people to stand and talk takes as much trouble as scaling an alp."[31]

A stanza accumulates motion, growing as congested as the psyche. Poetry is a kind of architecture enabling a certain dislocation of experiential luggage, a site where the benign and the monstrous can be reapportioned as if subject to culinary techniques. Enticingly, an architect might speak of "a bundle of walls" as if leeks or asparagus impinged on the drafting table.[32] Volumetrics struggle to emit haptic diversity. Architectural codes can act as surrogate zoning laws — eat here, sleep there, defecate yonder — but the great Freudian

27   Grant Hildebrand, *The Origins of Architectural Pleasure* (Berkeley: University of California Press, 1999), p. 147.
28   André Breton, *Nadja*, trans. by Richard Howard (New York: Grove Press, 1960), p. 112.
29   Ibid., p. 156.
30   Sándor Márai, *Embers*, trans. by Carol Brown Janeway (New York: Vintage, 2002), p. 126. Márai's haunting reciprocity evokes (and isomorphically mimics) Agamben's observation that "poetry possesses its object without knowing it while philosophy knows its object without possessing it" (Giorgio Agamben, *Stanzas: Word and Phantasm in Western Culture*, trans. by Ronald L. Martinez [Minneapolis: University of Minnesota Press, 1993], p. xvii).
31   Osip Mandelstam, *Selected Essays*, trans. by Sidney Monas (Austin: University of Texas Press, 1977), p. 6.
32   Zaha Hadid, *The Complete Buildings and Projects* (New York: Rizzoli, 1998), p. 130.

discovery confounds this, finding an archaeological law prevailing in the psyche, a law stipulating the collapse of all structures in the fullness of time. Insofar as poetry solicits — as polyvalent possibility — an archaeological rapport with shards and rubble, architects are envious.

The Soviet visionary architect Konstantin Melnikov designed a "Laboratory of Sleep" which he punningly called "Sonata of Sleep" (or *SONnaia SONata*, which plays on the Russian word for sleep, *son*).[33] Sleepers were to be assuaged by precisely controlled aromas and sounds, and Melnikov even provided for a gentle undulation of beds. The beds, intriguingly, were arranged in a common space so that the recumbent workers' dreams would interpenetrate into a thoroughly socialized collective unconscious. Party planners in Moscow didn't understand how sleep could be a form of labor, so Melnikov's design was never realized.

Architects have often set to work as if dreaming, visiting a site of overlapping claims, obligations, and potentialities that can only be declared through a congested corridor of sketches and models bearing little resemblance to structures of any sort. (Look at the shapes taken by crumpled paper in an architect's waste basket and then look at the assemblages on the drafting table: what's the difference?) Commenting on the role of gesture in architectural design — the calligraphic infusion by means of which a building is the yield of a trace — Zaha Hadid speaks of "chromasomatic origin points for the disposition of the project."[34] Her "Paper Art" installation at the Leopold-Hoesch Museum filled the two story space below the cupola with metallic streamers, as if a rhythmic gymnast's ribbon might somehow achieve structural integrity in its descent and, rather than crumpling on the ground, retain the arrested poise of zero gravity. Scrutinizing Frank Gehry's concept sketch for the Guggenheim Museum in Bilbao, which Roger Connah calls "one of the most published scribbles of the last decade of the twentieth century," it's understandable that the achieved project be thought of as "the *Tristram Shandy* of twentieth-century architecture."[35] "By looking at the innumerable Bilbao Guggenheim drawings and models, it seems that the architect designs many buildings in one go. All of these could be smaller or larger versions of yet another building. Knowing when to stop the building and let another come out will be part of the architect's not inconsiderable talent"[36] Connah might just as well be describing Ponge's exquisite draft tableaux for *Le Pre*, or Ezra Pound's labors on *The Waste Land*.

As for Gehry's own description of his process: "I'm looking through the paper to try to pull out the formal idea [...] it's like somebody drowning in paper."[37] As with certain compositional practices (I think of a poet like Clayton Eshleman who exudes a heap of drafts like entrails), the poet and/or architect "incessantly raids his own departure," as Connah remarks of Finnish architect Reima Pietilä. "It is a form of writing that balloons out from the gestalt sketch" — which brings to mind Lacan on the gaze: "Imagine a tattoo traced on

33   S. Frederick Starr, *Melnikov: Solo Architect in a Mass Society* (Princeton: Princeton University Press, 1978), p. 179.
34   *Architecturally Speaking: Practices of Art, Architecture, and the Everyday*, ed. by Alan Read (New York: Routledge, 2000), p. 217.
35   Roger Connah, *How Architecture Got its Hump* (Cambridge: The MIT Press, 2001), pp. 87-8; 161.
36   Connah, pp. 163-4.
37   Connah, p. 89.

the sexual organ *ad hoc* in the state of repose and assuming its, if I may say so, developed form in another state."[38] Elsewhere, Lacan compares instinct to "the 'messenger-slave' of ancient usage, the subject who carries under his hair the codicil that condemns him to death [who] knows neither the meaning nor the text, nor in what language it is written, nor even that it had been tattooed on his shaven scalp as he slept."[39]

Lacan might be describing bats, creatures whose architectural destiny is negotiated by echolocation. In one of his Adagia, Wallace Stevens evokes the poetic corollary of echolocation: "When the mind is like a hall in which thought is like a voice speaking, the voice is always that of someone else."[40] Stevens here revisits an episode from Valéry's dialogue "Eupalinos, or the Architect," in which Socrates asks Phaedrus "what is your own thought?" and Phaedrus replies, "I no longer know how to grasp it. Nothing contains, everything implies it. It is within me, like my own self."[41] Implication activates complicity in this dictum by Maurice Blanchot: "To write is to make oneself the echo of what cannot stop talking."[42]

Resorting to a mechanical model in his small essay "On the Gradual Fabrication of Thoughts While Speaking," Kleist suggests that "Speech is not a fetter, then, like a drag chain on the wheel of the mind, but a second wheel running parallel to it on the same axle."[43] But he slips the noose of this particular analogy in favor of another. "For it is not *we* who 'know'; it is rather a certain condition, in which we happen to be, that 'knows'."[44] The uncanny dimension most evident in architectural circumstance reflects Kleist's sense that our *placement* does much of our thinking for us — almost as if *we* were there to prompt some divulgence latent in the view from a window, or half surmised in the shadows of a

---

[38]   Roger Connah, *Writing Architecture: Fantômas Fragments Fictions, An Architectural Journey Through the 20th Century* (Cambridge: The MIT Press, 1989), p. 96. Jacques Lacan, *Écrits* (Paris: Éditions du Seuil, 1966), p. 803.

[39]   Lacan, *Écrits*, 302. The exquisite case of neurologist Geoffrey Sonnabend is to the point here. Recovering from a nervous breakdown in the hinterlands of Paraguay, the scientist attends a Lieder recital by Madalena Delani, whose voice was "steeped in a sense of loss" (said one critic). It's not clear whether Sonnabend was aware of speculations that the singer "suffered from a form of Korsakov's syndrome, with its attendant obliteration of virtually all short- and intermediate-term memory, with the exception, in her case, of the memory of music itself" (Lawrence Weschler, *Mr. Wilson's Cabinet of Wonder* [New York: Vintage, 1996], p. 5). In a sleepless night following her recital, Sonnabend conceived his multi-volume opus *Obliscence: Theories of Forgetting and the Problem of Matter*, outlining his conviction that memory was illusory, since forgetting was the sole outcome of experience: "We, amnesiacs all, condemned to live in an eternally fleeting present, have created the most elaborate of human constructions, memory, to buffer ourselves against the intolerable knowledge of the irreversible passage of time and irretrievability of its moments and events" (Weschler, p. 6). The saga of Delani and Sonnabend is from the unpublishable but ever imminent *Repertoire of All Possible Creatures*, under localized curatorial anaesthesia at sites like the Museum of Jurassic Technology in Santa Monica, California.

[40]   Wallace Stevens, *Opus Posthumous.* ed. by Samuel French Morse (London: Faber & Faber, 1959), p. 168.

[41]   Paul Valéry, *Dialogues*, trans. by William McCausland Stewart (Princeton: Princeton University Press, 1956), p. 77.

[42]   Maurice Blanchot, *The Space of Literature*, trans. by Ann Smock (Lincoln: University of Nebraska Press, 1982), p. 27.

[43]   Heinrich von Kleist, *An Abyss Deep Enough*, ed. and trans. by Philip B. Miller (New York: Dutton, 1982), p. 221.

[44]   Kleist, p. 222.

corridor. As Heidegger suspected, poetry and dwelling speak volumes. And "When I speak I do so only for the purpose of casting a spell."[45]

In his cultural history of ventriloquism, Steven Connor observes that "the voice always requires and requisitions space"; but "the voice is not merely orientated in space, it provides the dynamic grammar of orientation." This is clearly an architectural model, with implications: "As I speak, I seem to be situated in front of myself, leaving myself behind. But if my voice is out in front of me, this makes me feel that I am somewhere behind it." Connor finds the power of the voice commensurate with its frailty. "My voice can bray and buffet only because it can also flinch and wince. My voice can be a glove, or a wall, or a bruise, a patch of inflammation, a scar, or a wound."[46] To make such a scar visible is an aspiration of Krzysztof Wodiczko's "Xenology" project — xenology being "the art and science of the stranger" as well as "the immigrant's art of survival [...]. Xenology is the art of refusal to be fused."[47] Among the several "immigrant instruments" Wodiczko has designed as xenological tools is the "Porte-Parole," a cyborgian mouthpiece that positions a video monitor directly in front of its wearer's mouth (like a gag, he insists), producing hypergraphic images of the lips, morphing them into rubbery funhouse contortions, turning the corporeal agents of speech production inside out, as it were, so that the lips become an exterior *display* of the laboring buccal cavity.[48] The Porte-Parole is designed to "spread the communicable (contagious) process of the exploration of one's own strangeness."[49]

Wodiczko's "Mouthpiece" specifies the point at which poetry and architecture merge — where "Perplexity can only be met with complexity" — much as Luis Fernández-Galiano sees architecture as an intermediate dimension situated between construction and combustion, or more evocatively for poetics, "between mud and breath."[50] In doing so, his referential axis accommodates a central problem of architecture, which is the dialectic of creation and destruction. As Valéry memorably puts it, "Destroying and constructing are equal in

---

[45] Andrey Bely, *Selected Essays*, ed. and trans. by Steven Cassedy (Berkeley: University of California Press, 1985), p. 103.

[46] Steven Connor, *Dumbstruck: A Cultural History of Ventriloquism* (New York: Oxford University Press, 2000), p. 105.

[47] Krzysztof Wodiczko, *Critical Vehicles: Writings, Projects, Interviews* (Cambridge: The MIT Press, 1999), p. 131.

[48] Wodiczko, pp. 132, 118. Wodiczko's Porte-Parole, especially in its ambulatory applications, suggests a distant kinship with the Bomarzo Gardens created by Pier Francesco Orsini in the sixteenth century (which Robert Harbison thinks was designed "to memorialize an intense disgust," "to preserve bitter and fugitive sensations" [Harbison, *Eccentric Spaces*, p. 10]). Long since overgrown, the remaining statuary is all the more monstrous for being obscured by vegetation. Mouth images abound, from the table with teeth for seats to the gaping mouth of the ogre (with steps leading up to it) bearing the inscription "Ogni pensiero vo" (every thought flies) (Miller, p. 51).

[49] Wodiczko, p. 120. Wodiczko subsequently redesigned the Porte-Parole so that the mouthpiece could sit adjacent to the face, thereby doubling the volume of available lips. Another xenological instrument is the Aegis, with a set of screens that rise up from the wearer's back like wings, projecting multiple pre-recorded images of his or her face. The Aegis projects the appearance of the stranger, emphasizing that "contemporary strangers intentionally or unintentionally perform an angelic or prophetic mission in today's migratory and alienating world" (p. 133).

[50] Wodiczko, p. 133. Luis Fernández-Galiano, *Fire and Memory: On Architecture and Energy*, trans. Gina Cariño (Cambridge: The MIT Pres, 2000), p. 3.

importance, and we must have souls for the one and the other."[51] "Destroying and constructing," enthused Wenzel Hablik, participating in the Crystal Chain circle instigated by Bruno Taut, "are the radio stations and aerials of cells with a telepathic, primordial, spatial and temporal volition that creates living buildings." Accordingly, he declares Utopia "the form nearest to nature of all artistic and architectural energy."[52]

It's in this spirit that *Walden* is appears to be an architectural manifesto. Thoreau claims much more on behalf of subtraction than addition. "No yard! but unfenced Nature reaching up to your very sills," he enthuses. "Instead of no path to the front-yard gate in the Great Snow, — no gate — no front-yard, — and no path to the civilized world!"[53] Likewise, Whitman proclaims "Unscrew the locks from the doors!/Unscrew the doors themselves from their jambs!" — an exhortation that tacitly includes the construction of the very thing it's then necessary to dismantle.[54] Giorgio Agamben adopts a similar principle, envisioning critical investigations that would not discover an object but ensure "the conditions of its inaccessibility."[55] Agamben and Whitman would recognize Hablik's credo: "I believe that 'art' in every form is the subjective life and death of the millennia in one's own body — and therefore cannot be taught. One can only practice writing it down, and even that demands the expansive sense of cosmic, innate lust. Transmigration of body and soul until the point of recognition is reached."[56] At which point, "the mind is like a hall in which thought is like a voice speaking," and "the voice is always that of someone else" — to which the final words of Lambert Strether lend an air of exquisite deferral to finality: "Then there we are!"[57]

---

[51]   Valéry, *Dialogues*, p. 70.

[52]   *The Crystal Chain Letters: Architectural Fantasies by Bruno Taut and His Circle*, ed. and trans. by Iain Boyd Whyte (Cambridge: The MIT Press, 1985), p. 133.

[53]   Henry David Thoreau, *Walden and Resistence to Civil Government*, ed. by William Rossi, 2nd ed (New York: Norton, 1992), p. 87.

[54]   Walt Whitman, *Leaves of Grass*, ed. by Sculley Bradley and Harold W. Blodgett (New York: Norton, 1973), p. 52.

[55]   Agamben, *Stanzas*, p. xvi.

[56]   Whyte, *Crystal*, p. 133.

[57]   Henry James, *The Ambassadors*, ed. by Christopher Butler (New York: Oxford University Press, 1985), p. 438.

Gregg Biglieri

Sublime Façade: Borromini's Oratorio and the Presentation of Radical Exteriority

In this poetical essay, the baroque façade of Borromini's Oratorio becomes a space with which to frame the philosophical implications of a set of terms: concavity, folds, and above all the sublime. From the perpective of the Oratorio, we can gain a clearer view of the relation between the varieties of "radical exteriority" theorized by Immanuel Kant, Gilles Deleuze, and Theodore Adorno. Ultimately, the Oratorio opens onto a phenomenology of language, providing an occasion to exemplify what it means to inhabit the space of words.

For a building to be motionless is the exception; our pleasure comes from moving about it so as to make the building move in turn, while we enjoy all the combinations of its parts, as they vary: the column turns, depths recede, galleries glide; a thousand visions escape from the monument, a thousand harmonies.
Paul Valéry

One looks at Bernini's buildings with the eyes; one feels Borromini's with the whole body.
Anthony Blunt

Borromini observed precisely all the rules for displeasing the eyes. ... [a]nd yet, even in his greatest freaks there is something undefinably grand, harmonious and subtle, which reveals his sublime talent.
Franceso Milizia

the façade, an outside without an inside
Gilles Deleuze

It may be possible for us to imagine a radical exteriority that would not be the opposite of an interiority.
Bernard Cache

Nature is on the inside
Paul Cézanne

The word "image" is in bad repute because we have thoughtlessly believed that a design was a tracing, a copy, a second thing, and that the mental image was such a design, belonging among our private bric-a-brac. But if in fact it is nothing of the kind, then neither the design nor the painting belongs to the in-itself any more than the image does. They are the inside of the outside and the outside of the inside, which the duplicity of feeling [le sentir] makes possible and without which we would never understand the quasi presence and imminent visibility which make up the whole problem of the imaginary.
Maurice Merleau-Ponty[1]

---

[1] The sources of these epigraphs are as follows: Paul Valéry, *An Anthology* (Princeton: Princeton Univ. Press, 1977), p. 81; Anthony Blunt, *Borromini* (Cambridge: Harvard Univ. Press, 1979), p. 23; Francesco Milizia, qtd. Blunt, *Borromini*, p. 219; Gilles Deleuze, *The Fold: Leibniz and the Baroque* (Minneapolis: Univ. of Minnesota Press, 1993), p. 28; Bernard Cache, *Earth Moves* (Cambridge: MIT Press, 1995), p. 37; Paul Cé-

PART I: FAÇADES

Façade #1

Inside the face. [F *façade*, fr. It *facciata*, fr. *faccia*]. A form forms from within with a force that thrusts the projection of the façade outward. If this force is recognized as the dominant impetus of the movement, then that which appears on the exterior as a sweeping concave can be seen as the inner rim of a projected convexity whose other plane is that of the atmospheric space beyond it. The concavity which appears "welcoming" [*accogliente*] is really the product of two equally opposing forces — one pushing out invisibly from within and the other the pressure of the void, atmospheric space against which the thin, extending curve of the façade visibly projects. If it all depends on the position of the observer then the outside of the building is separated and projected from an invisible inside, and yet this inside is turned (inside-out) into an outside. Perhaps this is what Harrison describes as Borromini's "countergesture which paradoxically advertises privacy."[2]

The unfolding of within from without, the enfolding of without from within. Exteriors which expressively display interiorities; interiors which fold from within and, paradoxically, by folding within seem to dilate in ever contracting space, and which appear to invite an exterior reading while presenting an interiorized text.

To develop out of this embedded node, rather than having the essay develop into it; to act neither as envelope or container, but as façade. The sequencing of an argument which keeps on the inside looking in and on the outside looking out. An interiority that *subjects* itself to the various inflections upon a surface of radical exteriority. The notion of reflection (or self-reflection) is torqued and so distorts a mimetic model of mirror writing which would postulate an exact correspondence between the viewer and the object viewed. The viewing subject is already inflected by "objective" projections received from the object which mediate his own "subjective" projections.[3] The work of the artwork occurs in that zone of "radical exteriority" between subject and object and, in an architectural context, the façade appears as that part of the building that works and is worked upon by opposing forces; it functions as the threshold or membrane through which the enclosed space inside the building and the void space outside the building (both zones of indeterminacy) are mediated; thus, the façade is the site where determined particulars manifest themselves in the arrested and contested convexities and concavities that texture the surfaces of its planar projection. The buckle effect evident in the sculpted niches and bulging convexities of the façade, therefore, nuances what only appears to be a single sheet outstretched along a temporal continuum. The zone of indeterminacy is what is produced by the sublime experience which, in turn, reproduces it. In order for the subject to be transformed, he does not have to transcend this world, but rather end his entrancement with it by passing through a moment

---

zanne, qtd. Maruice Merleau-Ponty, 'Eye and Mind', *The Primacy of Perception and Other Essays* (Evanston: Northwestern Univ. Press, 1964); Merleau-Ponty, *Primacy*, p. 165.

[2]   Robert Harbison, *Eccentric Spaces* (Boston: Godine, 1988), p. 72.

[3]   And with another twist of the screw, the process of reciprocal mediation completes the "dispossession": "Pale terror siezd the Eyes of Los as he beat round/The hurtling Demon. Terrifd at the shapes/Enslavd humanity put on he became what he beheld/He became what he was doing he was himself transformd" (William Blake, *The Four Zoas*, in *The Complete Poetry and Prose* [NY: Doubleday, 1988], p. 338).

of opacity, which not only reflects itself, but also must be reflected upon: "As reflection increases, content itself becomes ever more opaque."[4] Thus, one does not simply translate material sight into immaterial vision, but instead focuses on the opacity, distortion or blindedness constitutive of optics in order to even begin to think that which cannot be clearly seen — to think the unpresentable. This recalls us to the Kantian recoil which provides one definition of the sublime: "sublime is what even to be able to think proves that the mind has a power surpassing any standard of sense."[5]

In order to think the nonvisual, one's seeing itself must pass through the a moment of opacity, rather than attempting to resolve the unfocused blur either into a single, static picture, or a concept of reified, hypertrophied sight. Kant directs us back inside the mind, to the detriment of the empirical existence of the "object," in order to locate the sublime: "hence what is to be called sublime is not the object, but the attunement that the intellect [gets] through a certain presentation that occupies reflective judgment."[6] In contrast, Adorno directs us back to the constitutive opacity inside the artwork in order to crystallize his notion of "second reflection," which puts renewed emphasis on the artwork because this particular concept is germinated in it, rather than arbitrarily applied as a purely philosophical concept which would be generated by a determinative judgment: "second reflection lays hold of the technical procedures, the language of art in its broadest sense, but it aims at blindness."[7] Any viable concept of aesthetics must perform its work in a darkness commensurate to the artwork's opacity.

So, if we twist Kant's claim that "inadequacy itself is the arousal," we can apprehend the necessity of maintaining an opacity in vision when confronted with an object, the empirical fact of an object or artwork that one cannot resolve into focus by improvising a capacity for a higher powered lens which would mechanically make one's vision more acute.[8] It devolves upon the mind as deflector and receptor to attempt to think this inadequacy of vision which is stimulated by vision's blindedness. So we need a concept of the artwork (an aesthetics) that mediates between the blindness of the work and the clarity of philosophical thinking. We need to produce a knowledge of artworks: "the knowledge of artworks is guided by their own cognitive constitution: they are the form of knowledge that is not knowledge of an object. This paradox is also the paradox of artistic experience. Its medium is the obviousness of the incomprehensible."[9] The capacity for vision turns upon the incapacity of imagination to present an Idea of the whole. What I am arguing is that, through Adorno's concept of "second reflection," it is possible to translate this incapacity of the sense of sight into the artwork's own constitutive opacity ("incomprehensibility"). It is only by "aim[ing] at blindness" that we might actually be capable of thinking about what we can't see in the artwork as it exists before our eyes. Through the mediation of the artwork the faculty of reason in its "instrumental" function is checked; similarly, the sense of vi-

4   Theodore Adorno, *Aesthetic Theory*, trans. Robert Hullot-Kentor (Minneapolis: University of Minnesota Press, 1997), p. 26.

5   Immanuel Kant, *Critique of Judgment* (Indianapolis: Hackett, 1987), p. 106.

6   Kant, p. 106.

7   Theodore Adorno, *Aesthetic Theory*, p. 26.

8   Kant, *Critique*, p. 106.

9   Adorno, *Aesthetic Theory*, p. 347.

sion/imagination is blocked out, or blinded. But if we focus on the opacity of the artwork and think reflectively on the unthinkable as manifested in the concreteness of the artwork, we have a means of accessing what has neither been seen or thought previously; i.e., an aesthetics of the sublime: "what is essential to art is that which in it is not the case, that which is incommensurable with the empirical measure of all things. The compulsion to aesthetics is the need to think this empirical incommensurabilty."[10]

extrinsic[/]intrinsic explicit[/]implicit external[/]internal

explanation [fr. L *explanare*, lit., to make level][/]explication[L *explicare*, lit., to unfold].

That is, the discursive project is to perform both operations (to flatten out and unfold) on the same level and at the same time — the curved plane of the text is a façade. The interior, subjective force of writing extends not only from *within* the subject (as architect of the text), but as if from beneath the page, pushed up from underneath to meet, oppose and mediate its incipient inscription on the plane of the page. From this subject position, the vanishing point falls on the interior of the building; so that if the perspective is reversed, the objective interiority of the building would project outward toward the position of multiple subjectivities. This dynamic of mutual mediation is played out on and in the façade of the building and on the surface of the page. The page is marked from its obverse, interior side by the negative, or void space which remains unseen from one's position outside the text (building). The pen that inscribes the surface of the page acts as a writing "eye" that produces marks (visual perceptions/visual inscriptions) which work in resistance to these invisible forces (which are in the process of emerging from the other/interior side), marks which also work against the resistance of the medium of the linguistic material in itself, remaining radically exterior to the subject's/writer's own subjective interiority. Thus, the page become the permeable membrane which negotiates the boundary between inside/outside in the same way as the façade of a building mediates the opposing forces of the interior and exterior zones of indeterminacy which push against it.

Deleuze: on the monad

> the 'unilaterality' of the monad implies as its condition of closure a torsion of the world, an infinite fold, that can be unwrapped in conformity with the condition only by recovering the other side, not as exterior to the monad, but as the exterior or outside *of* its own interiority: a partition, a supple and adherent *membrane* (italic mine) coextensive with everything inside.[11]

Façade #2

The outside, or façade, is not the supplement, the essence, or the excess of the inside. Its closure is open and welcoming; and yet its openness in its function as an entrance to the building is a gesture which simultaneously cuts it off from the space in front of it. It is an outward thrust, a blockage and obstacle and inhibition [*Hemmung*] — and this denial of access, this breaking against and breaking through, provokes the sublime.

---

[10]   Adorno, p. 335.
[11]   Deleuze, *Fold*, p. 111.

You cannot move *into* what is already an *inside*: you cannot move out of what you are already outside of. Ingress and exit are denied. There is only the return of the recessed.[12]

You are outside but you are drawn into, brought closer to, "welcomed" by this experience of alienation. This outside seems to contract inside you as you become increasingly dilated within yourself. You imagine yourself projected and made externally visible to yourself and yet the notion of your own subjectivity vanishes in its reduction to this external reflection. And you are "subjected" (reflex action) to the reflecting, deflecting, flexing surface of the façade. Self-portrait in a convex/concave context. The vision of self-reflection has been revised by being turned inside-out — eversion as the experience of the sublime.[13]

Potential Movements:

> Borromini's architecture is an architecture of movement and aspires to a condition of dynamic equilibrium. Movement is evoked by a series of compositional operations reconstructible in the final image, and such as to provoke in the observer at various times the impression of movement taking place, an imminent movement, or a completed movement.[14]

Blunt posits that Borromini borrowed from Michelangelo this concept of "a building as related to a body in movement and in action rather than static."[15] Thus the initial movement occurs in the nerves and sinews of the building, and its sinusoidal lines generate a sequence

---

[12] The allusion to Freud is not fortuitous. Freud himself speaks of the *façade* of a dream: "like the façade of an Italian church in having no organic relation with the structure lying behind it. But it differed from those façades in being disordered and full of gaps, and in the fact that portions of the interior construction had forced their way through into it at many points" (Sigmund Freud, *The Interpretation of Dreams* [New York: Avon Books, 1965], p. 245). I am arguing that those "gaps" referred to by Freud are precisely those gaps which appear in Borromini's façades — the apparent disorder manifested in their torsions of convexity and concavity. The reference to the "portions of the interior construction [forcing] their way through" the membrane of the façade also points to the discussion above concerning the forces emerging from the other side of the page. For a more complete analysis of Freud's notion of the façade and its relation to the work of "secondary revision," see Judovitz.

[13] Peter De Bolla speaks of "eversion" in a discussion of an unpublished fragment of Coleridge's which describes his experience "within" a Gothic cathedral: "This shapeless form inhabits the infinite shapeliness of the interior of the church: the external has become the boundary delimiting the possibilities for the internal. In terms of the relations between the discourse of analysis and the experience described, what we are witnessing is the eversion of the discourse on the sublime so that its boundaries become internalized within the limits of the experiential, while its interior becomes the substance of the experience" (Peter De Bolla, *The Discourse of the Sublime* [Oxford: Blackwell, 1989], p. 47).

[14] Portoghesi, *Rome*, p. 386.

[15] Blunt, *Borromini*, p. 51. For the particular description of the façade of the Oratorio itself in relation to the body (an analogy the import of which I will elaborate upon and invert later in the essay) I am referring to this citation: "For Borromini the essential link between architecture and nature was, I believe, through mathematics, but on one occasion he refers to a different theory, the familiar idea that architecture was based on the human body. This occurs when he is discussing his design for the curved façade of the Oratory, which, he says, is like a man stretching out his arms to welcome the faithful, and he pursues the parallel further to say that the central bay, which is convex on the lower storey, represents the chest, and the wings are the arms, each wing being composed of two sections at different angles, like the human arm" (Blunt, p. 51).

of nonlinear, potential, reversible (counter)movements in a series of subsequent (re)actions as (con)sequences: motion in the wandering eye of the observer as it moves over surfaces (its tensions not relieved, but in relief, and therefore accentuated and textu[r]ally significant), and a concomitant commotion (agitation) in the mind of the observer which provokes the sublime.[16]

PART II(a): Descriptions of the Façade of the Oratorio/Blunt, Portoghesi and Argan

> As a result of these careful dispositions the façade of the oratory is entirely different from that of S. Carlino. Instead of being a mass of masonry curving in and out, it has the springiness of a sheet of metal which has been slightly curved under pressure. It is totally unmonumental but is maturely Baroque in that it forces the eye of the observer to move across it along determined lines.
>
> The façade is planned on a single, very slow curve, which is interrupted in the middle section by a projecting convex bay for the door and a concave niche for the balcony to the library.[17]

In these descriptions I would like to point out three points of convergence: (1) the lean curve ("curva dolce") of the façade, and the "springiness" of its "yielding plane;" (2) The force and impact of the façade upon the eye of the observer, the pressure, the agitation (*mosso*) and the dilation of vision; (3) The "point of inflection" of the *cardine* (pivotal point) of the middle section which creates an interior relation of convex/concave upon the plane of the façade. The coffered bay within the central concave niche of the second storey with its slight recession, its scooped out depth within a depth which, paradoxically, emphasizes the continuous plane of the façade *as* the single, dominant surface or superficial plane.

> Una veduta frontale, invece, l'artista aveva previsto per la fronte del Convento dei Filippini; ma proprio qui, dove lo spazio era piú ampio e accogliente, i risalti si spianano, i vuoti affiorano, i contrast luministici giuocano in una gamma attenuata, *il ritmo si fa piú mosso e piú fluido. Tutto la fronte si svillupa in una curva dolce, sembra quasi ritrarsi dallo spazio antistante ...*
>
> Il diverso andamento ritmico dei due ordine è coordinato sull'asse della fronte: in basso è un breve piano convesso, che fa da *cardine* alle due ali della fronte; in alto la conca appiattita del nicchione, che apre e dilata i piani luminosi.[18]

---

[16]   We must begin the process of provisionally defining the sublime somehow, or else we risk prescribing an inhibition upon any exhibition of it. Thus: "The sublime can be described thus: it is an object (of nature) *the presentation of which determines the mind to think of nature's inability to attain to an exhibition of ideas*" (Kant, *Critique*, p. 127). For a succinct gloss on this description of the sublime, and for an incipient analytic which can be derived from it I am indebted to this passage from Weiskel: "Kant is concerned exclusively with the natural sublime, holding as he does the rather inadequate and conventional view that the sublime of art is 'always restricted by the conditions of an agreement with nature.' For Kant's *Gegenstand (der Natur)* we may substitute *any* object (a line of poetry [and, I would add, a façade of a building], for example), which leads us to a formulation something like this: We call an object sublime if the attempt to represent it determines the mind to regard its inability to grasp wholly the object as a symbol of the mind's relation to a transcendent order" (Thomas Weiskel, *The Romantic Sublime* [Baltimore: Johns Hopkins Univ. Press, 1976], p. 23).

[17]   Blunt, *Borromini*, pp. 93-4; italics mine.

[18]   Guiulio Carlo Argan, *Borromini* (Milano: Sansoni, 1996), p. 74; italics mine.

The agitated and fluid rhythm that Argan notes above dovetails nicely with Blunt's depiction of the pressurized "springiness" of the façade. In addition to mentioning the internal counter-rhythm of the concave/convex, Argan points out that the façade seems to withdraw from the void space which opens out in front of it. This notion expands upon, or "dilates" that internal rhythm of the façade outward to a play of its superficial exteriority in abutting against the open space in which the observer confronts the building.

> Borromini breaks up the plane by making it come forward in the center, thus gaining in curvature without loss of space, and guided by the same exigencies he inserts into the center the counterpoint of the convex projection. In this case the objective is not so much one of simply making the façade seem more concave or the balcony deeper, as it is one of satisfying that *tendency of vision "to dilate,"* as Serlio had already noted, and of *not confronting the observer with an inert screen but rather of offering him a yielding plane.*[19]

Finally, Portoghesi recapitulates the descriptions of Blunt and Argan, again focusing on the "counterpoint," or pivot of the middle section of the façade and calling attention to the "confrontation" of the building and the viewer through the medium and mechanics of vision. Here, it is important to note that by insisting that the façade is not to be seen as an "inert screen" but as a "yielding plane," Portoghesi implies that the façade itself is dynamic (as if it were a movie screen that was not fixed but expanded and contracted in a rhythm accorded by the projections of the filmic images and the projections of the observer's acts of vision). In other words, the façade itself has its own internal movements which extend to the alternative viewpoints and external movements of the observer and to the internal complexities of his own visual processes.

PART II(b): KANT WITH BORROMINI #1

> For if one stays too far away, then the apprehended parts (the stones on top of one another) are presented only obscurely, and hence their presentation has no effect on the subject's aesthetic judgment; and if one gets too close, then the eye needs some time to complete the apprehension from the base to the peak, but during that time some of the earlier parts are invariably extinguished in the imagination before it has apprehended the later ones, and hence the comprehension is never complete.[20]

You must be far enough away to get the sense of the dimension of the single curving plane (*curva dolce*), but close enough to see the incredibly thin bricks which contribute to the sense of its magnitude. The sheer number of the bricks (quantity): Borromini "had taken pains to get bricks which were very thin and regular and laid with so little mortar that the divisions are hardly visible."[21]

It is impossible to simultaneously comprehend that single concave curving plane and the countermovements of the middle section which is convex below and slightly concave

[19] Paolo Portoghesi, *The Rome of Borromini* (NY: Braziller, 1968), p. 58; italics mine.
[20] Kant, *Critique*, p. 108.
[21] Blunt, *Borromini*, p. 92.

above.[22] One's vision must constantly shift between the line of the overall curve and the pivot of its center (centrifugal/(*cardine*)/centripetal). The singularity of the curved plane and the folds within it at its center give it a paradoxical sense of both projection outward and withdrawal inward. A sense that the surface has been scooped out in the second storey niche, which in turn is indented by the another coffered recess (inside the inside) and the projection of the convexity of the lower storey that then initiates a counter rhythm. The single plane emphasizes the dominant effect of the surface while the interplay of forces in the central sections disrupts that surface by enfolding (an unfold) a withdrawal into itself and projecting a convexity which pushes out from that surface; both internal, inverted, antithetical movements belie the single *curva dolce* of the façade as a whole and both aspects (the concept of the façade as a whole and its internal disruptions) cannot be comprehended at the same time.

Here, with respect to the pyramids, Kant introduces the notion of temporality into the experience of observing the object. Since these perceptions cannot take place at the same time but only partially, "the comprehension is never complete." Later, Kant returns to the notion of temporality in terms of succession and simultaneity and if one is to attempt to somehow bypass his notion of the spectacles of space and time, one must confront the absolute interiority of time inherent in his "vision":

> On the other hand, comprehending a multiplicity in a unity (of intuition rather than of thought), and hence comprehending in one instant what is apprehended successively, is a regression that in turn cancels the condition of time in the imagination's progression and makes simultaneity intuitable. Hence, (since temporal succession is a condition of the inner sense and of an intuition) it is a subjective movement of the imagination by which it does violence to the inner sense, and this violence must be the more significant the larger the quantum is that the imagination comprehends in one intuition.[23]

That is, there must be a way of dealing with that double interiority of time that is re-marked by the internal parentheses in the above quotation. In order to do this one would need to have recourse to "a pure temporality which we can't accede to as subjects," as Cache suggests:

> For that temporality is unlike Kantian interiority; it is the opposite, or worse than that. If indeed we stick to Kantian concepts, time, as a form of interiority, is contrasted with space, which is a form of exteriority. However, it may be possible for us to imagine a radical exteriority that would not be the opposite of an interiority.[24]

---

[22]   Cf. Bernard Cache's argument against the classical notion of architectural space "as a form of coexistence or simultaneity": "If we wish to define architecture as an operation on space, we must then define the nature of this space more precisely. Classical philosophy saw it as a form of coexistence or simultaneity. It was contrasted with time, which was seen as a form of succession. But architectural space is not this general form of simultaneity; it is a space where coexistence is not a fundamental given, but rather the uncertain outcome of a process of separation and partitioning. The wall is the basis of our coexistence. Architecture builds its space of compatibility on a mode of discontinuity" (Cache, *Earth*, p. 24).
[23]   Kant, *Critique*, p. 116.
[24]   Cache, *Earth*, p. 37.

Kant seems to posit that a perfect viewing point of the pyramids is possible (at least as an intuition). In regard to the façade of the Oratorio, the sequence of visual perceptions does not produce a compilation of perspectives as a totality. And it is because there is no pre-scription for a correct linear sequence of perspectives, that the observer must constantly shift between sightlines and contradictory movements producing a sense of disequilibrium. Thus there is a disjunctive, discontinuous rhythm between the contraction and dilation of space and, as it were, the contraction and dilation of the eye, and this shuttling is not fol-lowed sequentially but reverses itself, inverts and perverts the project of a totality while perpetuating the process.

PART III: THE EYE ALTERING ALTERS ALL: from EYE to MIND[25]

The mode of production, the architect creates a design, a blueprint to map out intentions [a travel agent versus a tour guide; setting up various possible itineraries; perspectives, forms which are not filled-in as with some prefabricated content] rather than fixed routes.

From "EYE" to "I"
The sublime then is stimulated "through" the eyes of the observer … [Beholder — as if by trying to "hold" the image in place, "static," the beholder's perception, and then imagina-tion are overwhelmed by the implicit force of the "sublime" which can be apprehended but not comprehended by the understanding. This condition forces the observer to change posi-tions, laterally and literally; to view the work from different perspectives, but also to reform the very constitution of his own subjectivity].[26] This "static" is actively produced by think-ing through the difficulty and thus is truly anti-static. This cognitive static, then, signals the transition from the eye to the mind and initiates the scenario which produces an experience of the sublime. The eyes are unable to focus, or settle upon, one particular perspective and this momentary condition of "blur" forces the viewer to refocus internally (in the mind's eye). But the viewer finds that the sense of disequilibrium is only intensified "here," and cannot be deflected. This experience actually accentuates the disjunction between eye and

---

[25] In Merleau-Ponty's fascinating essay "Eye and Mind" it seems to me that one could locate a conception of the "sublime" of the body at the level of perception, which would be attached neither to intuition or cognition. Though it is beyond the scope of this essay to develop the ultimate plausibility of that idea, one could at least point to the elision of the body in the Kantian sublime (see Terry Eagleton, *The Ideology of the Aesthetic* [Ox-ford: Blackwell, 1970], pp. 70-100). See also Slavoj Zizek, "the Sublime is no longer an (empirical) object in-dicating through its very inadequacy the dimension of a transcendent Thing-in-itself (Idea) but an object which occupies the place, replaces, fills out the empty place of the Thing as the void, as the pure Nothing of absolute negativity — the Sublime is an object whose positive body is just an embodiment of nothing" (*The Sublime Object of Ideology* [London: Verso, 1989], p. 206).

[26] From Fra Juan de San Bonaventura's long and detailed report on the building of San Carlino: "we see these people of different nations look about them without being able to leave or to say anything for a while, and what amazes them most is that when one continues to look at this church it makes one wish to look more and one seems to see it anew and is left with the desire to return to see it again. … This church, when it is seen by these people from different nations seems to disrupt their intellect, because for some time they are seen not to move … and after seeing it they look at it again." (qtd. Portoghesi, *Rome*, pp. 379-80).

mind and recapitulates the discord between the Kantian faculties of imagination and reason which causes the irruption of the sublime.

... who then moves (alters his physical position in relation to the work) and then is "moved" mentally and, in turn, in turning, internally provokes a break, gap, *Hemmung*, disruption, rupture, and confusion.[27] The subject's own subject dis-position comes into question and becomes dissatisfied of its own accord (or discord) of thinking itself to be the "all" and shifts, changes, "alters," passing through the cognitive static (which is *active* static as distinguished from stasis).

Still disconnected externally from the empirical phenomenon (the work itself in its materiality) and still outside of a position of the sublime (for one cannot inhabit the sublime; one can be inhibited by it and there seems to be a relation between the actual exhibition of nature and the internal commotion of mind in response to that stimulus which causes an initial inhibition followed by a flood which dislocates the subject from any specific position both externally and internally).[28] But this force also reinforces the fact that there is an impassable chasm between the external (nature) and the internal (mind):

> In this case the intuition of an architecture that is a fact of knowledge, a direct expression of man's appropriation of nature, is put forth in immediately verifiable and unequivocal terms. But the same dominant aim is reflected in a more general sense in all of Borromini's architecture, which strives to discover and investigate new possible relationships between man and space, between perception and the mental elaboration of spatial impressions.[29]

What is called for is a radical realignment of perspectives (outlooks), a shift of world-view and of subjective, cognitive orientation (insights — that an insight into the subject itself is caused by the inadequacy of outlooks, or "eyes." The eye must be altered — disabled or otherwise defocused in order to provide access to its blind side (its "other" force as the other side). First, the eyes as convex extensions of the mind must be blocked in order for "vision" to occur. The optic nerve is both the conduit through which visual information passes and is translated from eye to mind and the source of one's blind spot. By focusing on this constitutive blindness, one dethrones the eye and instead envisions (imagines) alternative relations between "seeing" and "knowing." The disabling of the eye is a precursor to the disabling of the "I." Without the dissonant, disorienting experience of this "rottura dell'equilibrio," there is no possibility of establishing a new orientation toward knowledge or knowing as taking place ("taking place" as an event, or movement in the sequence of time).[30]

The observer then is not only engaged in the passive absorption (receptive) of the work, but is an active agent (perceptive) in the transformative process of the work as value. The

---

[27]   "The sublime MOVES us, the beautiful CHARMS us" (Kant, *Critique*, p. 98).

[28]   "(the feeling of the sublime) is a pleasure that arises only indirectly; it is produced by the feeling of a momentary inhibition of vital forces followed immediately by an outpouring of them that is all the stronger" (Kant, *Critique*, p. 98).

[29]   Portoghesi, *Rome*, p. 379.

[30]   Argan, *Borromini*, p. 63.

work of art is then the external stimulus which causes internal affects. The frieze that un-freezes; the static picture that promotes dynamic response/action in the mind of the viewer.

I don't mean that architecture then should be seen as the material manifestation of a purely mental construction (or as a symbol of the mind) but as a site where a practice is processed (or process is practiced), where its turning itself inside-out provokes the viewer, in turn, to turning himself inside-out, shifting the burden of meaning from the focus of the eyes through the unfocused, disruptive movement of the sublime back to the register of the cognitive in the mind of the observer:

> ... the endowing of the structure with complex formal qualities that solicit from the mental activity of the ob-server, not an instantaneous judgment of quality, but a process of comprehension that endures, that is indeed continually nourished by the connotations received from each of the terms and from their various possible ag-gregations. The contemplation that synthetically grasps the absolute organicity of the image gives way to a gradual reading in which, by successive strata, qualities are continually revealed that are more intimate and hidden and which correspond to varying degrees of cultural initiation in the observer.[31]

It is important to realize that the intention of the artist cannot be directly mapped onto the response of the viewer. Though the mechanics of the cognitive process may be similar the results exist more as potentialities than as actual realizations. Thoughts swirl and exchange "places" (from producer to consumer) but take on different forms by alternate routes. The "eye" and the "I" have been altered, "all" has been altered. Universal concepts, as a conse-quence, achieve a new orientation only by acceding to the imperative — only particularize. "All" eyes must become "particular"-ized.

PART IV: BORROMINI WITH KANT #2

One of the Borrominian twists on the Baroque notion of the expansion of the form in space is that of his conception of the contraction of that same space. The focus is on the curves of Borromini:

> ma anche qui il Borromini è in contrasto con le preferenze barocche: che vanno decisamente alle superficie convesse, che suggeriscono un'espansione della forma nello spazio, o al collegamento di convessità e concavi-tà, come effetto combinato di capienza ed espansione spaziale. Le curve del Borromini, invece, no sone mai una concessione allo spazio atmosferico ... sono il prodotto di una flessibilità della materia serrata tra i rigidi risalti delle membrature. La risultante della flessione del piano non è mai di espansione, ma di contrazione spaziale: onde la tendenza delle membrature a uscire dal piano e a surrogarsi all funzione di sotegno dei muri. La curvatura dei piani è indicativa della concezione borrominiana dello spazio architettonico.[32]

Another way of articulating Borromini's inversion is to say that the play of the exter-nal/internal and concave/convex signals and extends a corresponding set of movements, possibilities, and inversions in the mind of the spectator. How the surface effects of the fa-

---

[31] Portoghesi, *Rome*, p. 380.
[32] Argan, *Borromini*, p. 65.

çade, twisting between concave and convex, simultaneously make folds, recesses, indentations, depths hollowed out of space within surfaces AND thrust out concave shapes that belie the otherwise flat, planar surface of the façade. So that the façade is not only seen as a permeable membrane, but as an absolute external and internal limit, an outside marked by and marked off from the inside and, as it were, pock-marked from without/outside by pockets of absent, void space. And this corresponds to the tensions and inversions between the external and the internal, between the "eye" and the "I", the "eye" and the "mind". The "slash" between the external/internal and concave/convex is not removed but complicated and implicated from within, and also intricately explicated from without. It is meant to be followed as a (dis)continuous, nervous, incipient transition (*segue*) at eye level and flattened between the levels of eye and mind. "L'occhio dello spettatore non afferra un misurato equilibrio di masse, un'ampia distribuzione di spazi articolati, ma segue la nervosa indicazione di moto delle strutture."[33] And this "slash" is the marker of the pressures placed upon it from both sides of the dichotomy; texturally, sculpturally and textually, it remains as the sacrificial scar upon an artificial empty space. The oppositions are not resolved, rather the tensions of either side are urgently intensified. It is not the sheer incomprehensibility of the removal of that dividing line which provokes the sublime, but rather the tension that is exhibited by the imminent rupture of what that architectural, diagonal mark signifies: that a building's shape might devolve upon a greater shapelessness; that the infinite folds of inside and outside might subvert the very notion of a sustained categorial dichotomy, provoke an infinitude on that single superficial plane of the façade, that *tortuous* membrane, twisting so close to *torturous*, the painful stretching point (sticking place) where the polarities become unfixed and margins are cleft from abandoned centers (centrifugal meets centripetal). The dividing line is essential to the *definition* (definite as opposed to indefinite) of the building.[34] Thus, the building can appear to be "unbounded" even though it is fixed in space as a monument because it provokes a moment that is dynamic, creates between its folds and twists an infinite plane, a nervous membrane, the fault line or zigzag boundary of fracture, and the façade as the marker of the shifting of a architectonic plate which defies its own solid constitution and forces the mind to reject any immediate satisfaction and pass through the stage of pain or displeasure in which the judgment of sense is inadequate to the powers of the understanding and then indirectly reflects, as an instantiation of reason, that inadequacy of the actual to its boundedness and hence of the power of imagination to sacrifice this instant of freedom in lieu of a greater power of reason: "the imagination thereby acquires an expansion and a might that surpasses the one it sacrifices; but the basis of this might is concealed from it; instead the imagination *feels* the sacrifice or deprivation and at the same time the cause to which it is being subjugated."[35]

---

[33] Argan, p. 70.

[34] See Blake: "the great and golden rule of art, as well as of life, is this: That the more distinct, sharp and wiry the bounding line, the more perfect the work of art" (*Complete Poems*, p. 550).

[35] Kant, *Critique*, p. 129. Recall Kant: "But the sublime can also be found in a formless object, insofar as we present unboundedness, either [as] in the object or because the object prompts us to present it" (Kant, p. 98). The link between the nervous, sinuous line and the sublime is grounded on the concept of "agitation." Cf. "In presenting the sublime in nature the mind feels *agitated* [...]. This agitation (above all at its inception) can be compared with a vibration, i. e., with a rapid alternation of repulsion from, and attraction to, one and the same

PART IV(b): INSIDE RADICAL EXTERIORITY

But can this be thematized as an inside/outside perspective of the baroque subject position vis-à-vis the architectural façade as an inner outwardness, or outer inwardness? Or is it the collision of these separate spheres which creates a new space to articulate the dialectical reinforcement (as a quasi-*Aufhebung*) of that dividing mark (the slash) of this dichotomy?[36] Can the collapsing of space, the filling of voids or the hollowing out of niches into still deeper concavities, be revealed as prefiguring, in a sense impelling, the Kantian sublime? Does this necessarily have to do with the inside/outside of the building? The reversible text of architecture — its texture? The façade is then not seen as the exterior of the building proper but, since it is conceived and executed as radically divided from the "body" proper of the building, as projecting "invisible" interiority (its radical exteriority) of the building. "Baroque architecture can be defined by this severing of the façade from the inside, of the interior from the exterior, and the autonomy of the interior from the independence of the exterior, but in such conditions that each of the two terms thrusts the other forward."[37]

If the body (of the building) were turned inside-out then the skeleton would show. This is the process of the endoskeletal becoming the exoskeletal. The inside-out also of the mind whose thoughts would be made visible in material form but twisted, inverted, convoluted, obstructing any notion of "pure" visibility but, as it were, pockmarked by aspects of its own invisibility — its unseen invention made visible in architectural shorthand, the building as the residuum of mind, an abbreviated, fragmentary, sculptural, articulation of an equally fragmentary thought. A stutter or necessary interruption. Thus, coming up against not only the interrupted world but also the interrupted thought. And then the sublime invoked because of the gap or fissure which signifies a break in the sensorium, the inadequacy of imagination's ability to represent, a presentation of the inability to represent in solid form without a certain absence corroding its contours.[38] And would all this mean, in the words of Merleau-Ponty, that "the proper essence [*le propre*] of the visible is to have a layer [*doublure*] of invisibility in the strict sense, which it makes present as a certain absence"?[39]

---

object" (Kant, p. 115) and "the feeling of the sublime carries with it, as its character, a mental *agitation* connected with our judging of the object" (Kant, p. 101).

[36] By "quasi-*aufhebung*" I mean that object of consciousness is not negated and preserved in a higher form (not "elevated" along a hierarchical vertical axis in the Hegelian sense), but rather negated and preserved *in the same form* (flattened along the horizontal axis).

[37] Deleuze, *Fold*, p. 28.

[38] The sublime is therefore the paradox of an object which, in the very field of representation, provides a view, in a negative way, of the dimension of what is unrepresentable. It is a unique point in Kant's system, a point at which the fissure, the gap between phenomenon and Thing-in-itself, is abolished in a negative way, because in it the phenomenon's very inability to represent the Thing adequately *is inscribed in the phenomenon itself* (Zizek, p. 203). "Sublime is what even to be able to think proves that the mind has a power surpassing any standard of sense" (Kant, p. 106).

[39] Merleau-Ponty, *Perception*, p. 283.

PART V: BREAKING THE WAVE/ THE WAVE BREAKING

wave #1: Argan's description of the façade of the Oratorio (#2)

> Cosí il vuoto delle finestre è spinto in alto e in avanti, oltrepassa perfino i capitelli, si spinge fin sotto il cornicione mediano. È qui che tutti gli accenti di moto concorrono, *come onde che si frangono all sponda*: e, incredibile <<licenza>>, le cornici vanno ad impostarsi al disopra dei capitelli, rompendo senza rimedio la coerenza statica dell facciata.[40]

wave #2

Thus the reference to the wave motif, the breaking of the wave, the breaking of the plane, the breaking of the frame [It. *cornici*, frame].[41] The unfurling cut, the line of force as the discrete materialization of a internal/external tension. The atmospheric space which the façade, especially of the building, confronts seems to become closed-off and enclosed, making the vibrating line of the façade more open, though a mere cleft or comma or fragment of articulated material. Thus the atmospheric space is hollowed out by the incision of the façade coming up against the now interrupted world. The paradoxical depth of the thought of the concept of the surface, or the façade, which does not break free of the plane, but projects from it the fact of its inability to break free of that plane.

[40] Agan, *Borromini*, p. 74; italics mine.
[41] Cf. Paul Goodman's notion of the sublime as "actual experience of a tendency of combinations to break the aesthetic surface" (qtd. Weiskel, *Romantic*, p. 21).

A. S. Bessa

Vers: Une Architecture[1]

This essay explores the architectural trope in concrete poetry by concentrating in one of its major sources of inspiration-the poetry of Stéphane Mallarmé. Departing from a small number of texts by Mallarmé on the condition of poetry (*vers*) during his life time, I attempt to demarcate his concept of verse; one that brings together both architectural as well as musical concerns. A considerable part of the essay consists of applying this concept to an analysis of Mallarmé's masterwork *Un coup de dés*.

> *Le futur vers se dégage*
> *Du logis très précieux*
> Stéphane Mallarmé

> *A arquitetura como construir portas,*
> *de abrir; ou como construir o aberto;*
> *construir, não como ilhar e prender,*
> *nem construir como fechar secretos;*
> *construir portas abertas, em portas;*
> *casas exclusivamente portas e tecto.*
> *O arquiteto: o que abre para o homem*
> *(tudo se sanearia desde casas abertas)*
> *portas por-onde, jamais portas-contra;*
> *por onde, livres: ar luz razão certa.*
> João Cabral de Melo Neto

> *As one can't get architecture or even mural stuff DONE one retreats to printed page.*
> Ezra Pound[2]

The concrete poetry movement attributes its radical experimentalism in language to the influence of Mallarmé's work, and although this influence has been perennially heralded, intriguing aspects of it have thus far been left unexamined. Chief among these is the pre-

---

[1]   The title of this essay refers to Le Corbusier's seminal text *Vers une architecture* (*Towards a new architecture*). By inserting a colon in Le Corbusier's title I intend to isolate the word *vers* and make its ambiguities resonate — in French, *vers* takes on several meanings according to the context in which it is presented: toward, verse and worm. Although the equation worm/verse is full of implications to the kind of writing I am interested in exploring — the "night worm" in Blake's *The Rose* comes to mind — I will use *vers* mainly in regard to its other two meanings.

[2]   In 1929, when inquiring whether Wyndham Lewis might be willing to design decorative initials for his Aquila edition of Cavalcanti, Pound observed, "As one can't get architecture or even mural stuff DONE one retreats to printed page." *Pound/Lewis: The Letters of Ezra Pound and Wyndham Lewis*, ed. by Timothy Materer (NY: New Directions, 1985), p. 168. I thank Richard Sieburth for bringing Pound's quote to my attention.

dominantly architectural bent of Brazilian concretism, which seems to taint the more nuanced elements that might have manifested from Mallarmé's influence. The concept of concretism elaborated by the Noigandres Group in their manifesto *Plano Piloto para Poesia Concreta* has given rise to an eminently architectural perception of concrete poetry, as opposed to the more musically oriented model proposed by Öyvind Fahlström in his *Manifesto for Concrete Poetry*; in Mallarmé's work, as we shall see, architecture and music coexist and are inextricably woven into the *vers* ("*ou ligne parfait*").[3]

For Mallarmé, the *vers* has the same fluid, protean meaning that the word carries in its definition — it means both "verse" and "toward." It is through (*à travers*) the *vers* that Mallarmé bridges the depths of the white page, moves over the gutter between pages, and ultimately structures the edifice of his oeuvre. The "toward" of the *vers* also points to the *futur vers*, the poetry to come, the *vers* being his connection to the past (for Mallarmé intends to "*laisser intact l'antique vers*") and to the future.[4] Like Nietzsche's, Mallarmé's work was preparing the ground for what was to come, bridging the gap between the poet of the past and the poet of the future. This future might not be a utopia, as he made clear in *Le Phénomène Future*, but, as Henry Weinfield points out, "the poets have not disappeared; at the end of the piece, they 'make their way toward their lamps, their brains momentarily drunk with an obscure glory, haunted by a Rhythm and forgetting that they exist in an age that has outlived beauty'."[5]

There are few examples of finished works by Mallarmé, the greater part of his oeuvre falls into the category of *vers de circonstance* — tributes to dead friends or colleagues, gifts, *envois divers*, and so forth. Even a poem such as *Un coup de dés* has to be considered in the context of the specific circumstances of a commissioned work. All this leads to the conclusion that Mallarmé was interested in the concept (of poetry) rather than in poetry itself and the *vers* is where this concept is formulated.

The microscopic lens Mallarmé applies to the *vers* can be glimpsed in an excerpt from a letter to Swinburne, dated 1876, in which he suggests minor changes to a poem Swinburne wrote in homage to Theophile Gautier:

> A peine si je préférais lire au second vers "Pour y cueillir qu'un souffle d'amour" au lieu de "Pour recueillir rien qu'un souffle d'amour" à cause de l'équilibre assez heureux dans le vers des deux monosyllabes *y* et *rien* et du moins grand nombre de fois qu'apparaîtra de suite la lettre *r* appuyée notamment sur une voyelle muette *e* dans *re* après avoir servi de finale à *pour*.[6]

The same method is, of course, applied to Mallarmé's own poetry, in which similar examples are abundant. The first line of *Le vierge, le vivace et le bel aujourd'hui*, for instance, has three *v*'s in its first half, counterbalanced by three *u*'s in its second half. The visual sharpness of the initial *v*'s is suddenly smoothed by the curvaceous *u*'s in the line's last words. This is a poem to be both read and seen: the eyes hear its music.

[3]   Stéphane Mallarmé, *Oeuvre Complètes* (Paris: Gallimard, 1992), p. 455.
[4]   Mallarmé, p. 456.
[5]   Henry Weinfield, *Collected Poems: Stéphane Mallarmé* (Berkeley: University of California Press, 1994), p. 242.
[6]   Berrtand Marchal, *Mallarmé: Correspondance: Lettres sur la poésie* (Paris: Gallimard, 1995), pp. 546-7.

In "On the Way to Language," Heidegger writes that a poet might "come to the point where he is compelled to put into language the experience he undergoes with language."[7] Mallarmé's fascination with words and letters of the alphabet, and their endless combinatory possibilities, is at the core of a poetic venture that can only be called an "experience with language." This notion of an experience with language, through which "language brings itself to language," has often been used to describe Mallarmé's unique rapport with poetry. Whether through the linguistic explorations in "Les Mots Anglais," the intricate meditations on poetry and art in his innumerable essays, his poems, or his Tuesday-night gatherings, the image one holds of Mallarmé is of a demiurge pouring out an all-encompassing system of discourse grounded in the nineteenth century, but reaching to both the past and the future.

The *vers* is the *way* (*la voi,* or *un envoi*), the path through which Mallarmé travels back and forth in space and time. This path, this ground, is also where he buries things, such as names. He frequently inserted his own name (*Stéphane*: "R*este* là sur ces fleurs dont nulle ne se *fane*") or friends' names (such as *Verlaine*: "Je te lance mon pied *vers* l'aine") in the verses of his poetry.[8] A typical Mallarméan text resembles a field with a variety of traps — ambush, trick, stratagem, maneuver, artifice. The relationship, in a *vers,* between names, space, and time is exemplified by *Les loisirs de la poste*, which also establishes the rapport between his *vers* and architecture.

In its entirety, *Les loisirs de la poste* works as a poetic mapping of Paris in space and time, with the names of recipients and streets mixed up with contemporary events, anecdotes, and miscellaneous elements. Rhyme is the main focus in each quatrain, thus conferring on the general plan an intrinsic musicality. This musicality is attained by the juxtaposition of urban elements — urban planning as music, music as planned urbanity. It is worth noting that at the time Mallarmé was conducting his alleged "assault on language," the city of Paris had just gone through major transformations under the direction of Baron Georges Eugène Haussmann. The opening up of rationally planned avenues and boulevards in the organic maze of the old city is an apt metaphor for the task Mallarmé set himself with regard to the French language.

The parallels between language and architecture are particularly evident in the study of Mallarmé's progress as a writer. The evolution of his prose texts, as methodically examined by Norman Paxton, exposes the kind of rational decisions Mallarmé adopted in order to achieve a high level of structural complexity in writing:

> This complexity forces the reader to go slowly and therefore to be more aware of the careful balance of the sentence, comprehending it only at the end, when he can look back and see the whole nebulous confection in suspension. The artistic construction of a sentence is almost an end in itself. In the *Préface à Vathek* there is a considerable step forward towards a sentence structure which shall give aesthetic satisfaction by the original beauty of its involved construction and also communicate a thought modified by the unexpected juxtaposition of its elements.[9]

---

[7]   Martin Heidegger, *Basic Writings: from* Being and Time *(1927) to* The Task of Thinking *(1964)*, ed. by David Farrell Krell. (New York: Harper & Row, 1977), p. 59.

[8]   Stéphane Mallarmé, *Oeuvre Complètes* (Paris: Gallimard, 1992), pp. 55; 82.

[9]   Norman Paxton, *The Development of Mallarmé's Prose Style*, (Geneva: Droz, 1968), p. 52.

Terms such as "construction" and "structure" per se already insinuate the architectural motif, and the image of the reader going "slowly" down the sentence further enhances the suggestion of the sentence as a *via* — the *vers* as a path, although at times the path leads the reader to nowhere or to an abyss. In innumerable reworkings of the same texts, Mallarmé often omitted entire sentences, thus abandoning the reader to his own musings. In *L'action restreinte*, for instance,

> After "*Écrire* —" Mallarmé had originally written "*A personne, sans savoir quoi; du fait de ne te adresser, un objet, tu le traites.*" This sentence was simply omitted in the revision, with the result that "*Écrire* —" is launched into the void much more than before; but even originally Mallarmé had implied the relative unimportance of communication — only we need the original to see just what is that he was saying.[10]

It is this sense of structure that captivated the Noigandres poets. After the extremism of the Miesian *beinahe nichts* in modernistic architecture, the concrete poets embraced "structure" as a means to reach "essence." The importance of the structure in concretism supplanted that of the *vers,* and gradually blended into the notion of design. The *vers* was blown up to a point at which it gradually disappeared, leaving behind only a word or even just a fraction of it. Such is the case in Decio Pignatari's 1960 poem *Organismo*:

O ORGANISMO QUER PERDURAR

O ORGANISMO QUER REPT

O ORGANISMO QUER RE

O ORGANISMO QUER

O ORGANISMO

ORGASM

OO

O

Thus the versatility of the Mallarméan *vers* is reduced by concretism to the point of extinction. What triumphs instead is a notion of structure that seems foreign to any reader of Mallarmé's work. The minimalism hinted at by some of Mallarmé's mature work was one of high intellectual concentration and skill. There is nothing mechanical or repetitive in his poetics, nothing that would justify mistaking it for a method or a process. Any attempt to emulate his achievements — visual display in *Un coup de dés*, for example — will forever fail, because he did not propose rules for the poetry to come, but only prepared the ground for it. Nevertheless, the Noigandres group found in Mallarmé a confirmation for their own architectural tendency; and emphasized this aspect to the detriment of the more subtle aspects of the *vers*. In Poesia, Estrutura, written in 1955, Augusto de Campos wrote:

> Mallarmé is the inventor of a process of poetic organization whose significance for the art of letters seems to us aesthetically comparable to the musical value of "serialism" created by the musical universes of a Boulez or a Stockhausen. This process can best be expressed by the word *structure*. We should add that the particular use, that we here make of the word *structure* has in mind an entity medularly defined by a gestaltian principle

---

[10]   Ibid., p. 79.

that the whole is more than the sole addition of the parts, or that the whole is something qualitatively diverse of each component, thus ever being misunderstood as an additive phenomenon.[11]

Although there is in this passage a reference to music, it is not intrinsically connected to structure, but only compared to it. It is important to emphasize that the structure in Mallarmé is both musical and mobile, like a fan (*"Rien qu'un battement aux cieux"*), pliable, adapting to various circumstances and ends.[12] Virginia La Charité writes that the fan is "a segment of a circle which is constructed with thin rods which move on a pivot; made out of silk, feathers or paper, it opens and closes, mystifies and reveals."[13] This deceptively simple structure in fact will be used to great profit in Mallarmé's hands, for the movement of constriction and expansion, the act of folding and unfolding, will on the one hand generate a bountiful source of verbal joy (*"de la cendre/descendre," "un frisson/unisson," "la flamme/l'âme," "le plumage est pris/mépris," "le vide nénie/dénie," "vole-t-il/vil," "las/les lilas," "glacier/l'acier," "lune/l'une," "de visions/dévisions," "se para/sépara," "désir Idées/iridées," "devoir/de voir"*), and, on the other, provide the final shape of poems such as *Soupir*, where a dash in the fifth line provides the sole visual mark where the poem will fold into two opposed movements, ascending and descending as one's chest might when emitting a sigh.[14] That's how subtle, Mallarmé seems to tell us, the sound can be, like the flapping of a wing. Nevertheless, music is embedded into structure to the same degree as letters: *"Je pose, à mes risques esthétiquement, cette conclusion: que la Musique et les Lettres sont la face alternative ici élargie vers l'obscur; scintillante là, avec certitude, d'un phénomè, le seul, je l'appelai, l'Idée."*[15]

The "Idea" manifests itself through letters and music, but Mallarmé's music will never reach the operatic dimensions of Wagner's, for he is more interested in the "music of the spheres," which is highly abstract, or in the music produced by everyday objects — the chiming of bells, the ruffling of skirts, the flapping of fans, the rocking of a cradle.

When in motion, the fan emits sound waves — delicately, imperceptibly. Its sound replicates a pulsation, or a palpitation. It speeds up or slows down according to the physical and/or emotional condition of the one who manipulates it. For Mallarmé, a poem offers this kind of flexibility — it is ultimately left to the discretion of the reader how to manipulate or unfold the poem, which thus becomes extremely objectified. In the particular case of the *éventails*, some of which Mallarmé actually wrote on fans, the object itself becomes the poem. "The conception thus involves the mysterious transformation of the animate to the inanimate, the concrete to the abstract, the material to the spiritual."[16] It has been noticed that from the final letters of *éventail* an *"aile* springs poetically" standing for the traditional symbol of poetic inspiration.[17] This circularity, a poem about a fan that stands for a poem, is

11   Augusto de Campos, "Poema, Ideograma," in *Mallarmé* (São Paulo: Perspectiva, 1974), p. 177.
12   Mallarmé, *Oeuvre*, p. 57.
13   Virginia La Charité, *The Dynamics of Space: Mallarmé's Un coup de dés jamais n'abolira le hasard*, French Forum Monographs, 67 (Lexington: French Forum, 1987), p. 16.
14   La Charité, p. 17.
15   Mallarmé, *Oeuvres*, p. 649.
16   Weinfield, *Collected*, p. 196.
17   Weinfield, p. 196.

the essence of Mallarmé's poetic meditation — a poem writes itself about itself, a thought thinks itself about a thought, *"un coup de dés jamais n'abolira le hasard."*

Un coup de dés is the work in which all the aspects addressed above regarding architecture, music, poetry, and idea are so finely tuned as to provide us with an ideal model for discussion. *"Vers* is the primary direction in the text," writes La Charité, underlining the main motif in the poem — the alexandrine verse. Hasard derives from Arabic for "the die," thus "a throw of the dice will never abolish the di[c]e," a tautological statement that reiterates that the poem is *not* about something other than itself. *"Un coup de dés*, as 'POÈME' is an authentic object which is at the same time its own subject."[18] There is no message to be found at the bottom of this shipwreck, but only the POÈME as it is written on the title page. "The poem is and confirms itself through the informative and descriptive declaration of the titular phrase."[19] We go down the *vers* (*à tavers*), between wonderment and stasis, only to be thrown back to the beginning of the poem. And we come up with nothing — no major revelation, everything still kept secret. The poetic experience is confined to its duration, not the acquisition of truth. The poet is a performer who sets the conditions for such experience. The poet titles the experience, and the title is the experience. *Un coup de dés* is the unfolding of its title, of its gesture, of its performance.

Un coup de dés is the most extreme of the fan-poems and also the first modernist architectural construction. Its extremely calculated use of space opens up a series of questions regarding the brokering of the printed page as a territory for action. This calculation is the inverse of ratiocination, for Mallarmé's intention is to restore the primacy of language (language that speaks itself) through the poem. Poetry will unveil, in space, the *"subdivisions prismatiques de l'Idée."*[20] Heidegger contends that poetry is in the neighborhood of thought, "but because we are caught in the prejudice nurtured through centuries that thinking is a matter of ratiocination, that is, of calculation in the widest sense, the mere talk of a neighborhood of thinking to poetry is suspect."[21] With *Un coup de dés*, Mallarmé inaugurates the page as a field of action — the poet ruling over the constraints of space. La Charité brings our attention to the material and utilitarian aspect of the printed page, and its inherent set of laws:

> The unit of the printed page is a utilitarian form which makes the word visible through a given assembly of words into lines and lines into stanzas or paragraphs. Rules dictate how parts (words, lines, paragraphs) fit together and deny authorial freedom. Certain two-dimensional limits are imposed on the text by the medium of its communication. The formal order of the medium directs the reader: sequential pagination, a certain balance of type and space. To reassert the original freedom of the language as an initiating experience, Mallarmé turns his attention to an art of space and the role of the reader.[22]

Utility, rules, limits, formal order constrict language in its movement to speak itself. "Only because in everyday speaking language does not bring itself to language but holds back, are

---

[18]   La Charité, *Dynamics*, p. 102.
[19]   La Charité, p. 59.
[20]   Mallarmé, *Oeuvres*, p. 455.
[21]   Heidegger, *Writings*, p. 330.
[22]   La Charité, *Dynamics*, p. 15.

we able simply to go ahead and speak a language, and so to deal with something and negotiate something by speaking."[23] In *Un coup de dés*, Mallarmé inveighs against this conform-
ism and undermines the rules of the game. Reportedly, the printer for the first edition of *Un
coup de dés* reacted strongly to Mallarmé's use of space, and this contretemps between
writer and printer raises a series of questions that are essential to understanding the signifi-
cance of the leap that *Un coup de dés* represents.

> A page is printed in signature sheets, the most common one being in multiples of four; signatures are then
> folded to page size, the largest signature being a folio. Pages appear as verso and recto. Hence, a page is a
> fixed framework which delimits the amount of words and lines which it can support. A page may be said to
> represent a unity of space, the place for the confrontation of printed elements, but the writer does not own at
> any time a whole page because of the dictum of printer space. Printer space is space owned by the printer, not
> the writer, to wit the first verso after a title is generally unprinted and each page is surrounded by dead, unus-
> able space or printer's margin. The margin frames or encloses the printed elements. Center margin or gutters
> further compromise the integrity of the page and create a columnar effect; as a result, the vertical always
> dominates the horizontal although the horizontal does not actually oppose the vertical, but is harmonious in its
> subordination to it. The restraints of a page impose spatial ordering. Every page in a given printed work begins
> and ends with a predetermined line length, a length further dictated by type selection and margin space, which
> is a function of line length.[24]

The promise of *"un livre qui soit un livre, architectural et prémédité, et non un recueil des
inspirations de hasard, fussent-elles merveilleuses [...]. Le jeu littéraire par excellence: car
le rythme même du livre, alors impersonnel et vivant, jusque dans sa pagination, se juxtapose aux équations de ce rêve, ou Ode"* is partly fulfilled in *Un coup de dés,* for the relationship of book to poem in this work is so closely knit as to render it impossible to unra-
vel.[25] *Un coup de dés* is a poem-book-object, hence the futility of trying to quote it: any
attempt to quote *Un coup de dés* will invariably be transformed into an illustration.[26] All its
parts are connected to such a degree that to select any cluster of words is utterly useless.
Furthermore, there are no *bons mots* in this work that justify their isolation from the whole.
The experience of reading it is one of movement in space and time. The reader scrutinizes
the page, downward, from left to right, making bridges through the white space, the eyes
squinting or widening to adapt to the changes in type size.

> The type visually expands the emission of the thought into the concrete object of dice, space is crossed and
> filled, presence replaces absence, contact is established, and the reading activity is the experience of creation,

---

23   Martin Heidegger, *On the Way to Language*, trans. Peter D. Hertz (San Francisco: Harper & Row, 1982), p.
     59.
24   La Charité, *Dynamics*, pp. 41-42.
25   Marchal, *Mallarmé*, p. 585.
26   Paradoxically, the worst printing of *Un coup de dès* is to be found in the Pléiade edition of Mallarmé's *Oeuvre
     complète*. This edition does not observe Mallarmé's specifications regarding page size, font, type, or align-
     ment. The general effect is thus of a miniaturized illustration of the 'real thing,' which as a matter of fact was
     never really materialized.

in which the text emerges as both object and subject: a perpetual coming into being. The text is the event and place of the communication.[27]

"Thinking is not a means to gain knowledge. Thinking cuts furrows into the soil of Being."[28] Likewise, there's no knowledge to be extracted from *Un coup de dés,* just a thinking act. In reading, seeing, and listening to it, the basic requirements of any *Gesamtkunstwerk,* we perform the act of thinking, and grasp the *"subdivisions prismatiques de l'Idée."* A *poème* does not refer to anything outside itself. *"Rien n'aura eu lieu que le lieu."* This is the site, here in these pages. "In thinking there is neither method nor theme, but rather the region, so called because it gives its realm and free reign to what thinking is given to think."[29]

It was necessary to construct this book, so carefully planned, in order to distinguish the *poème* from any other written text, thus revealing the *poème* as a "power book." *Un coup de dés* is the prototype of hypertext, in which highly sensitive words carry the power to remit the reader to other texts. And the units of this construction are the page and the printing process.

> Basically, print is static, inert, concrete, impersonal, and utilitarian. Print is what the reader reads; it bestows order in its linearity, sets points of convergence and divergence, establishes sequence and stratification (subordination), fixes the fiction by controlling groupings of words which in turn offer precision and concision in the determination of the restraints which bring about meaning and the communication of that meaning through the assembly of the words into lines. Print is a psychological framework for the reader, who goes forward, word by word, line by line, page by page, identifying figures and their relations, or he goes backward in order to reconstruct the events of the forward-motion of the narrative.[30]

Mallarmé subverts this order and, in so doing, exposes the invisible structure that upholds literature — linearity, convergence, sequence, stratification, *in summa*, all the "restraints that bring about meaning."[31] Through his exploration of typography and topology, Mallarmé emphasized the idea of language as an artifice, a construction — not a natural trait, but a technique to express ideas, or the idea. The problem with assertions such as this lies in the likelihood that it will always be taken for an absolute ("language as a construct"), after all the nuances have been brushed aside. Hence the emphasis, by the majority of concretists, on the architectural aspect of Mallarmé's enterprise.

But Mallarmé's architecture is diaphanous, or at least mobile. In the letter to Verlaine known as "Autobiographie," when he refers to "un livre architectural et prémédité," he writes that the pagination of this book "se juxtapose aux équations de ce rêve, ou Ode." Writing about Maeterlinck, for instance, he notes that "une symétrie, comme elle règne en tout édifice, le plus vaporeux, de vision et de songes." And referring to Hugo, he writes, "Monument en ce désert, avec le silence loin; dans une crypte la divinité ainsi d'une majes-

---

[27]   La Charité, *Dynamics*, p. 124.
[28]   Heidegger, *On the Way*, p. 20.
[29]   Heidegger, p. 74.
[30]   La Charité, *Dynamics*, pp. 84-85.
[31]   La Charité, pp. 84-5.

tueuse idée inconsciente, à savoir que la forme appellée vers est simplement elle-même la littérature." At the end of "Igitur," after nothingness has been conquered, "reste le château de la pureté." "Dream" and "vision" are terms often invoked by Mallarmé, alongside "symmetry," "edifice," "monument," and "tomb"; but above all, this impalpable architecture is always called upon to provide an image, a stage set:

> Exterieurement, comme le cri de l'étendue, le voyageur perçoit la détresse du sifflet. "Sans doute," il se convainc "on traverse un tunnel — l'époque — celui, long le dernier, rampant sous la cité avant la gare toute-puissante du virginal palais central, qui couronne." Le souterrain durera, ô impatient, ton recueillement à préparer l'édifice de haut verre essuyé d'un vol de la Justice.[32]

Mallarmé's architecture often has the ghostly quality of the tower William Beckford had built after his own design — an architecture that is already a ruin, a monument, a tomb. Or perhaps an architecture such as is seen onstage: suggestive, evocative, and easily dissipated. The "architecture" of *Un coup de dés* is mobile, like the screens in a Japanese home. The reader is never able to contemplate the entire "edifice," but each space opens onto the next, revealing chambers, niches, and staircases, never differentiating between inside and outside.

And while there has been excessive stress on the term "structure" with regard to Mallarmé's poetics, there is a general tendency to ignore his penchant for ornamental motifs.

> Il y a à Versailles des boiseries à rinceaux, jolis à faire pleurer; des coquilles, des enroulements, des courbes, des reprises de motifs. Telle m'apparaît d'abord la phrase que je jette sur le papier, en un dessin sommaire, que je revois ensuite, que j'épure, que je réduis, que je synthétise. Si l'on obéit à l'invitation de ce grand espace blanc laissé à dessein au haut de la page comme pour séparer de tout, le déjà lu ailleurs, si l'on arrive avec une âme vierge, neuve, on s'aperçoit alors que je suis profondeement et scrupuleusement syntaxier, que mon écriture est dépourvue d'obscurité, que ma phrase est ce qu'elle doit être et être pour toujours.[33]

The relationship between syntax and architecture is one that concrete poets also pursue, but they equate syntax with structure, never with ornament. One might find the justification for such misreading in early texts on modernistic architecture, such as the condemnation of ornament by Adolf Loos titled "Ornament and Crime." Modernistic architecture repudiated ornament and advocated the supremacy of structure over surface beauty. The architecture of concrete poetry is not the same as Mallarmé's: the tendency toward ornament in Mallarmé is not merely a figure of speech, but an important feature of his whole enterprise, ranging from the curlicues in his signature to the subtle variation of font styles and sizes in *Un coup de dés*. Above all, this tendency manifests itself in effects that are sometimes nearly imperceptible, such as this particular topological display in *Un coup de dés*:

> There is considerable verticality attained by the ascending kerns, especially d, l, b. The unit begins with "de la mémorable," and the ascending kerns point upward. Moreover, the layout demands that this group be placed so that the b of "mémorable" be over the f of "fût" and that the f be over the l of "l'évènement." The vertical

---

[32] Mallarmé, *Oeuvres*, pp. 371-372.
[33] Paxton, *Development*, p. 54.

kerns and the capital letters stabilize the space of 10v [page 10 verso]; contrary to the lexical meaning of the unit "RIEN" which dominates by size, it has identity.[34]

Several of the *tombeaux* already hinted at the confluence of architecture and writing, even though visually they do not resemble tombs. The fan is an architectural construct par excellence: awnings are based on the fan's principle of pliability. But the fan poems do not evince an architectural shape. So where is the architecture in Mallarmé to be *seen*? It is in the *vers* ("l'exact ligne") that one will find this architecture. *"Dans le genre appelé prose, il y a des vers, quelquefois admirables, de tous rythmes. Mais, en vérité, il n'y a pas de prose: il y a l'alphabet et puis des vers plus ou moins serrés: plus ou moins diffus. Toutes les fois qu'il y a effort au style, il y a versification."*[35] The *vers* is the bridge through which Mallarmé will transcend the non-materiality of the page. Before the *vers* there is nothing, only the white page. The *vers* creates a site where the eye and the mind can find shelter. In *Building Dwelling Thinking,* Heidegger discusses the nature of a construction and the creation of a site:

> The bridge swings over the stream with ease and power. It does not just connect banks that are already there. The banks emerge as banks only as the bridge crosses the stream. The bridge designedly causes them to lie across from each other. One side is set off against the other by the bridge. Nor do the banks stretch along the stream as indifferent border strips of the dry land. With the banks, the bridge brings to the stream the one and other expanse of the landscape lying behind them. It brings stream and bank and land into each other's neighborhood. The bridge gathers the earth as landscape around the stream.[36]

Heidegger is interested in the relationship of thinking to construction (*edificare, cultivare*), and therefore the proximity of architecture and language. Although its conciliatory and contrite tone (owing to the circumstances that informed the delivery of this lecture) is in sharp contrast with Mallarmé's style, Heidegger's exploration of the bridge image is an apt metaphor for some aspects of the concept of *Vers*.

> To be sure, the bridge is a thing of its own kind; for it gathers the fourfold in such a way that it allows a site for it. But only something that is itself a location can make space for a site. The location is not already there before the bridge is. Before the bridge stands, there are of course many spots along the stream that can be occupied by something. One of them proves to be a location, and does so because of the bridge. Thus the bridge does not first come to a location to stand in it; rather a location comes into existence only by virtue of the bridge.[37]

The *vers* is the organizing principle. It brings (metric) order and symmetry to the chaos of unelaborated ideas: it is through the *vers* that the "Idea" actually flows. The *vers* has the power to name things, rescuing them from the depths of memory. *"Je dis: une fleur! et, hors de l'oubli où ma voix relègue aucun contour, en tant que quelque chose d'autre que*

---

[34]   La Charité, *Dynamics*, p. 78.
[35]   Mallarmé, *Oeuvres*, p. 867.
[36]   Heidegger, *Basic*, p. 330.
[37]   Heidegger, p. 332.

les calices sus, musicalement se lève, idée même et suave, l'absente de tous bouquets."[38] ("Language is the flower of the mouth," as Heidegger paraphrases Hölderlin).[39] The *vers* inaugurates a space, opens up a possibility for this space, and baptizes it. "What appears on the page is real; it exists; it is both trustworthy and credible because it is so deliberately set, displayed, and constructed."[40] The *vers* is a landmark, a point of orientation, an organizing principle, it casts a new light on space and objects.

> Le vers qui de plusieurs vocables refait un mot total, neuf, étranger à la langue et comme incantatoire, achève cet isolement de la parole: niant, d'un trait souverain, le hasard demeuré aux termes malgré l'artifice de leur retrempe alternée en les sens et la sonorité, et vous cause cette surprise de n'avoir ouï jamais tel fragment ordinaire d'élocution, en même temps que la réminiscence de l'objet nommé baigne dans une neuve atmosphère.[41]

The *vers* creates out of the book a site. "For Mallarmé, the poet has the power to create with words, to go beyond the object by making an absolute out of language. The very act of writing on the page ordains the credibility of the text," writes La Charité. The conversion of the page into a site attests to Mallarmé's belief in the transcendent power of language and the tools and skills involved in its pursuit:

> Écrire —
>
> L'encrier, cristal comme une conscience, avec sa goutte, au fond, de ténèbres relative à ce que quelque chose soit: puis, écarte la lampe.
>
> Tu remarquas, on n'écrit pas, lumineusement, sur champ obscur, l'alphabet des astres, seul, ainsi s'indique ébauché ou interrompu; l'homme poursuit noir sur blanc.
>
> Ce pli de sombre dentelle, qui retient l'infini, tissé par mille, chacun selon le fil ou prolongement ignoré son secret, assemble des entrelacs distants où dort un luxe à inventorier, tryge, noeud, feuillages et présenter.[42]

There is a hopeful attitude in Mallarmé toward (*vers*) the progress of the *vers* — writing poetry as a philosophical practice, a practical manner of *thinking,* a science not confined to the restraints of the page and the printing process. The progress of the *vers* corresponds to the progress of the "Idea." Through (*à travers*) writing — and, among its various modes, poetry in particular — thinking takes form, expands, takes place. The author is a reader, a scribe, meticulously following the many unfoldings of the "Idea" and setting down on paper its every move. The *vers* is the unit of construction in this process — the micro that mirrors the macro, the encoding of a thought. The *Crise de Vers* is thus a constant crisis insofar as thought is constantly revolving, evolving, unfolding. *Crise de Vers* is the ever-present state of poetry, for the *vers* is always toward the poetry to come.

---

[38] Mallarmé, *Oeuvres*, p. 368.
[39] Heidegger, *On the Way*, p. 99.
[40] La Charité, *Dynamics*, p. 43.
[41] Mallarmé, *Oeuvres*, p. 368.
[42] Mallarmé, p. 370.

Tyrus Miller

Concrete Dialects, Spatial Dialectics:
Friedrich Achleitner as Poet and Architectural Historian

This essay considers the writing of Friedrich Achleitner, one of the original members of the post-war avant-garde "wiener gruppe" and a leading historian of Central European architecture. Seeking to establish the nature of the relation of Achleitner's architectural writing to his literary writing, the essay charts the signifcance of "concretness" and "construction" in his work. In the context of Achleitner's architectural essays, as well as recent theoretical writing on architecture, this chapter provides sustained close readings of Achleitner's dialect poems, as well as his extraordinary and unique *Quadratroman* and *Die Plotteggs kommen*.

Friedrich Achleitner, one of the original members of the "wiener gruppe," a provocative and controversial group of post-World War II avant-garde writers in Vienna, is also a major historian and critic of architecture and a professor at the Academy for Applied Art in Austria's capital. His activities as a literary figure include concrete poems, "montages" and "constellations," poems in dialect, cabaret performances, and prose texts of various sorts. He was also, along with Oswald Wiener and Gerhard Rühm, an inspirer and fellow-traveller of the slightly junior Vienna Actionist artists in their actions and publications of the late 60s and early 70s. In his scholarly work, Achleitner has published extensively on the architecture of Central Europe, combining a rich, detailed historical knowledge with an acute and engaged critical perspective sensitive to the peculiarities of the cultural cosmos that radiated outwards from Vienna during the past two centuries. It might, then, seem an obvious question to ask: in what relation do Achleitner's activities as an architectural critic and historian stand with his literary work, and vice versa?

Beyond the relatively banal observation that the strong presence in his work of "concrete" forms indicates his close attention to literary space and construction, the answer is not so immediately evident. In fact, although Achleitner's constructive impulse is far from irrelevant, I would suggest that the issue of "concreteness" or "construction" in Achleitner's writing might be misleading if we were to separate it from his interest in dialect. This conjunction might, at first glance, seem surprising. Achleitner's dialect poems, like those of other poets of the Viennese postwar avant-garde such as Ernst Jandl, H. C. Artmann, and Gerhard Rühm, seem linked to a distinct interest in performance, drawing on cabaret traditions and reveling in the colorful metaphorics and sounds of dialect. Yet in my view, these poetic practices should be seen as facets of a single complex of thoughts about language and its contextual realization, a conceptual and pragmatic framework that ultimately derives from the peculiar historical-political vicissitudes of language in Austria.

To put it bluntly, Achleitner's use of concrete forms is ultimately less concerned with formal construction as an aesthetic end in itself, than with the practical, situational, contextual, "dialectal" variability that may be demonstrated through such concrete forms.[1] Concrete forms do not for him stamp language with the abstract ideality of geometry nor lend it the transparent universality of a graphic idiom, as is the intention with some practitioners of concrete poetry. On the contrary, for Achleitner, using such forms pushes language into the uncoded or weakly coded realm of spatial arrangements, a domain shared by objects, landscapes, and architectures. In these fringe zones of the linguistic, the bonds that hold together signification begin to loosen, making language more readily available to pragmatic "dialectal" reappropriation and reshaping. In this sense, we could say that for Achleitner's poetic practice, construction sets up a framework for a more crucial moment — a moment of *finding* that activates, within the linguistically and graphically constructed frame, the implied contexts of meaning, thus realizing across a necessary *delay* a play of forces outside of and other than the formal aspects of language.[2]

This play, spanning spatial and historical contexts, is impelled by what Wittgenstein identified as the effective character of highly localized "forms of life," from which he derived the irreducible diversity of "language games." In keeping with the concerns of my essay, I understand the variability in usage investigated by Wittgenstein to offer a comprehensive picture of the more specifically linguistic variability involved in dialect. But throughout my essay, I move freely back and forth between these two scales of variability, emphasizing the blurry continuity between dialect and other "regional," contextual variations in usage.

As the space in which coded language and spatial constructions blend together, the quasi-linguistic zone of dialectal variability in space is also, for Achleitner, a conceptual pivot. For it is herein, rather than in the concept of construction, that lies the crucial point of contact between his poetic concerns and his architectural scholarship. If in his poetic writing, language reaches out — precisely through concrete form, through description, through his constructivist use of syntax — towards dialectal variability, in his architectural criticism Achleitner is especially attentive to how the peculiarly messy, schismatic politics of language in the Habsburg lands shaped Austrian and Central European architecture.

An example from Achleitner's dialect poetry can stand as a graphic diagram of this force field of space, performative language, and historical background. I quote in full the dialect text, which is followed by a standard English translation:

auf
auffö
auffö

schdaig

auffö

---

auffö   lomö
auffö

schdaig

auffö
auffö
auffö
          lomö

schdaig
          lomö
schdaig
          lomö
schdaig
          lomö

          owö
          lomö
          owö

          owö
          owö
          owö

up
up a
up a

stairs

up a
up a   let me
up a

stairs

up a
up a
up a
          let me

stairs
          let me

>   stairs
>   let me
>   stairs
>   let me
>
>   down
>   let me
>   down
>
>   down
>   down
>   down

The fragments of Wiener German, the simplified semantic focus, and the typography combine to give a powerful sense of bodily enactment to the poem, yet with the additional comic implication of a body that has stored up a few too many beers and smoked a few too many cigarettes to prevail against the forces of gravity. Kinesthetically, the poem wobbles on the page around its slightly asymmetrical pivot, as if a stumble or push could plunge the speaker down in free fall. More subtly, with his deceptively pared-down and literarily unencumbered text, Achleitner also participates in a specifically Viennese literary context, wherein space, language, and socio-political observations are closely intertwined. Suffice it to mention in this context the dramatic journalistic and corpus of Karl Kraus, who mapped such institutional spaces as the cafés, the pedestrian zones, the opera house, and the halls of government in terms of specific linguistic behaviors enacted there; and the novelist Heimito von Doderer, whose *Strudelhofsteige*, an enormously complex novel structurally modelled on a double spiral staircase in Vienna, could rightly stand as the maximalist counterpole of Achleitner's minimalist treatment of a staircase.

In what follows, I explore this relation between language, space, and dialectal variability in Achleitner's writing. I first give a brief sketch of his view of architecture and the way in which the language question affected architecture in the Habsburg Empire and the nations that emerged out of its collapse. Then, in light of the dialects/dialectics of space and language that Achleitner analyzes in architecture, I consider two post-Wiener Gruppe "poetic" texts by Achleitner: his "concrete" novel of the 1970s, *quadratroman* (Square Novel), and his recent "report" on plastic-wrapped hay bales in the Austrian countryside *Die Plotteggs kommen* (The Plot-eggs Are Coming), published in 1995. In all three cases — in his architectural criticism, his concrete novel, and his recent narrative writing — Achleitner confronts the legacy of the avant-garde's language-politics and implicitly raises the question whether the avant-garde's relative failure might not have resulted from its inability to deal effectively with problems of dialect and national/regional difference.

Architecture and the Semantic Mess

In their two-volume history of modern architecture, Manfredo Tafuri and Francesco Dal Co suggest that this history is marked by a major shift in the domain of questions about architecture's relation to language and more generally to "intellectual labor." Traditionally, they suggest, architecture was concerned with questions of how built structures could project collective ideas — ideologies — and suggest social ideals, especially in relation to the advancement of scientific and technological knowledge. In the latter part of the 19th century on, however, a new set of problems gradually emerged:

> [W]hat relationship is licit between the area of language and the extra-linguistic series? How can language become a means of economic valorization? And above all, what form of intellectual labor is the most adequate to enter directly into the sphere of productive work and transform its structure?[3]

Put somewhat differently, architecture — like other humanistic disciplines and practices such as philosophy, philology, literature, and the arts — found itself confronting a new welter of fragmentary, incommensurable, but socially effective idiolects emerging especially from the technical, scientific, and state-administrative domains.

Ever more urgent for the representatives of these traditional disciplines became the question of how to respond to the centrifugal forces on humanistic culture exerted by such rapidly evolving and proliferating idiolects. The stunning dynamism of modernist culture, and its often pathetic schizophrenia as well, derives from the vigorous and various attempts of humanist intellectuals to master these forces. Through conservative revivalism, through mythic reconciliation, through tough-minded appropriation and refunctioning, or through "negative dialectical" critique, modernist intellectuals tried to gain purchase on the reified but efficacious languages propelling intellectual labor in modern society. Two consequences follow from this general situation, in the view of Tafuri and Dal Co. First, language became an especial focus of attention, since it was perceived as the general medium in which the rifts opened by the proliferation of specialized idioms might be diagnosed, mediated, and healed. As Dal Co writes, "the problem is that of activating the 'author' so that he becomes capable of producing representations that render explicit, that bring forth 'on the stage of life' and within the systems of communication and consumption, the *potential forms* and *hidden interconnections* of contemporary civilization."[4] Second, attempts to employ language artistically in relation to these problems ended up torn between utopian evocations of their overcoming and mournful lamentation at their intractability. "The languages of modern art have a predominantly *evocative* quality," writes Dal Co, "whether in their avant-gardism they attempt to debunk the deceptions of traditional systems of representation and thereby awaken the public, the 'object' of their communication, to a vigorous state of awareness; or whether they limit themselves to meditating disconsolately on the decline

---

[3]   Manfredo Tafuri and Francesco Dal Co, *Modern Architecture I*, trans. by Robert Erich Wolf (New York: Rizzoli, 1976), p. 7.

[4]   Francesco Dal Co, *Figures of Architecture and Thought: German Architecture Culture, 1880-1920* (New York: Rizzoli, 1990), p. 104.

and poverty of aesthetic experience."[5] In either case, then, in Dal Co's view, the artistic evocation circles around its own center, leaving the schismatic field of language that occasioned the response peculiarly unaffected. From the point of view of architectural history, the implication of this view is that style is necessarily a reactive and ineffective phenomenon, at best serving as an index of historical forces situated elsewhere, at worst instantiating the blind ideologies of an obsolete discipline.

As an architectural historian and critic, Achleitner likewise sees the historical changes in Central European architecture as crucially shaped by questions of language. However, unlike Tafuri and Dal Co, Achleitner retains a more positive interest in the question of stylistic idiom, which for the Italian Marxists simply defers the necessary conclusion that any *architectural* solution to the social contradictions they diagnose must necessarily turn into an ideological blindness to the problem itself. Achleitner, however, puts more emphasis on the positive possibilities of style — even where that possibility was historically squandered or suppressed — because his linguistic focus is less on the languages of technology, science, and corporatist power than on the languages of everyday life.

Viewed from this everyday, public perspective in which buildings are put to use and experienced, the questions of style posed by architecture bear analogy to those posed by language in the strict sense, particularly in the Habsburg and ex-Habsburg lands. Which style is appropriate for building in a multi-ethnic, multi-lingual, but divided and hierarchical society, in which authority resides in a patchwork of overlapping competencies, became the pivotal problem, rather than a more immediate confrontation with the specialized languages of economics, material science, and social planning. Tafuri's and Dal Co's disciplinary critique of architecture extends outwards towards a general social critique centered on the new role of technical idiolects in the reproduction of capitalism in its most advanced form. Achleitner's history of architectural style, in contrast, points emphatically towards the anachronistic persistence of national-linguistic and regional-dialectal zones within the territories of a collapsing empire (and in the aftermath of its fall).

In his 1986 essay "Pluralism and Multi-lingualism in Viennese Architecture — or Doublecoding as Principle and Inclination," for example, Achleitner took his point of departure from the prominence of Vienna in discussions of postmodernism. He went on to consider the historical situation of Viennese architecture, which developed against the background of the multi-national, multi-lingual empire, as the basis for its anticipation of the more programmatic pluralism of architectural postmodernism. Of particular importance in Achleitner's analysis is the dialectical role of Otto Wagner and his universalistic, imperial modernism. On the one hand, Wagner himself strongly asserted the Greco-Roman idiom inherited from classicism, while updating it in light of technical progress. As such, despite the antagonism of some imperial elements to his innovations, Wagner's architecture ultimately functioned ideologically to make the empire more rationally acceptable to modern subjects, rather than representing a critique of empire from the point of view of a modernist rationalism. Yet his constitution of a Wagner "school," of which many of the adherents came from the non-German subject nations, had an unexpected outcome: it led to an exploration of

---

[5]   Dal Co, p. 104.

particular national (or nationalistic) idioms under the umbrella of Wagner's universalistic thought and practice. As Achleitner writes:

> Wagner's architecture was an imperial one insofar as it represented a kind of universal language that consciously excluded *foreign languages* or any *dialects*. But if one pursues the later careers of the followers of Wagner, precisely the question of national cultural identity, thus also the question of a national architecture, plays a major role.[6]

Achleitner here identifies in the later Wagner-school architects something of the same dialectics of imperial and "minority" language that Gilles Deleuze and Félix Guattari trace out in Kafka's writing. In Kafka, Deleuze and Guattari see a model of the way in which an artist of a subject population — Czech, Jewish, yet German-speaking in Prague — could *occupy* the imperial idiom, while turning that idiom into a space of appearance for particularistic, "minority" concerns. So too, adopting the terminology of these philosopher-critics, we could speak of the Wagner-school architects as rearticulating the master's imperial, "molar" architectural idiom to express minoritarian, "molecular" concerns and contents.

In his discussion of the canonical Viennese modernist architect, Adolf Loos, Achleitner is even more emphatic in his "linguistic" approach. He begins his discussion with a brief theoretical statement in which, implicitly referring to Wittgenstein's later philosophy, he situates the linguistic aspect of architecture in conventions of "usage." Although, he notes, architecture is of course not language, it can take on language-like traits through established usage:

> The linguistic aspect of architecture lives from the consensus about the use of determinate elements in a context made up of particular contents. Meanings can thus only exist in a conventional or conventionalized usage and are a priori bound to traditions.[7]

This latter point, the role of tradition in creating the possibility of stabilized usage and hence potential meanings in architecture, has a further implication for Achleitner: the relatively high degree of specificity of contexts necessary to allow this linguisticality of architecture genuinely to emerge and be put to knowing use by architects. Thus, on the one hand, he is able to view Vienna as a special context in which the semanticization of architectural elements for communicative purposes had a long and well-defined tradition. On the other hand, he identifies the weakness of postmodernism's vaunted use of "citations" and historical allusions as lying in their abstractness, their independence of any established "speech conventions" by which they might be "read," so that postmodernist allusion remains largely mute and ineffective as architectural communication.

Achleitner employs this basic theoretical framework to interpret the apparently paradoxical aspects of Adolf Loos's architectural idiom. Like the followers of Otto Wagner, Loos sought to overcome the arbitrary use of historical vocabularies that he perceived in the

---

[6] Friedrich Achleitner, ‚Pluralismus und Mehrsprachigkeit in der Wiener Architektur — oder Doppelkodierung aus Prinzip und Neigung', in *Wiener Architektur: Zwischen typologischem Fatalismus und semantischen Schlamassel* (Vienna: Böhlau Verlag, 1996), p. 18.

[7] Friedrich Achleitner, ‚Sprachliche Aspekte in der Architektur von Adolf Loos', in *Wiener Architektur*, 39.

eclectic forms of late historicism prominent in Viennese architecture in the latter part of the 19th century. His modernism thus partakes of the "longing for the perfection and endurance of a kind of architectonic 'high speech'" rooted in classicism.[8] Yet not only did this desire for a universal architectural idiom confront the intense critical sensitivity of Viennese intellectual life to questions of language generally, it also played out against its dialectical — and indeed, "dialectal" — opposite. As Achleitner writes: "a dialectical consequence of this romantic projection into a holy world of language was the discovery of 'modes of speech' (popular building forms), the language of the uneducated, the language living at the source."[9]

Loos, according to Achleitner, does not really resolve these two diverging but dialectically related responses to the late historicist linguistic confusion, but rather stabilized them at different levels of his practice, so that his work has been particularly subject to misunderstanding and misinterpretation. On the one hand, Loos famously pronounced that an architect is a bricklayer who has learned Latin. "Latin" implies the spiritual affiliation of the architect to the world of humanistic values and *Bildung*, but also a specific vocabulary of classical forms. For Loos, Achleitner argues, it was the classical form-language, the Latin of the architect, that guaranteed a context of conventions in which the semantic function of architecture could be secured. And it is this insistence on architecture's linguistic aspect that sets Loos's modernity off from the programmatic modernism of Functionalism and International Style.

At the same time, however, Loos's use of this vocabulary is not essential to him for its specific semantic content, but rather for its conventionality, its ability to guarantee the communicability of architectural content as such. Hence, Achleitner argues, one should not misunderstand even such spectacular deployments of the classical vocubulary as the gigantesquely magnified Doric column that Loos proposed in his entry for the Chicago-Tribune tower competition:

> With this project, it is certainly not for Loos primarily a matter of the Doric column. His problem was the challenge of noticeability, thus of unmistakability. To his thinking, informed by the logic of language, the decision was clear to employ a vocabulary that every person in the world knew; and to this, the ancient column happened to belong. Loos practically did not concern himself about the meaning of this vocabulary item. ... In the estrangement of scale he was really only interested in the effect of the polished granite surfaces in this new dimension.[10]

Herein lies the apparent paradox. At first glance, Loos seems to have insisted on the "Latin" architectonic idiom to ensure the semantic dimension of architecture. But once a background of conventions was formally guaranteed, he appears to have been only casually interested in the specific semantic contents these conventions entailed. For Achleitner, however, the paradox of Loos's architectural idiom becomes coherent when one follows out its analogy to language, to spoken language's interminable play of conventionality and vari-

---

[8]   Achleitner, p. 40.
[9]   Achleitner, p. 40.
[10]   Achleitner, pp. 42-3.

ability in use. Loos's strict conventionality was, Achleitner argues, a kind of stage for the less structured, "dialectal" play of architectural usage:

> The insistence on a linguistic level created a play of meanings, similar to the rules of Wittgensteinian language-games. That means, the element, the *vocabulary item*, does not express anything, and its meaning comes into being only in its constellation with other items. The expression becomes understandable only in context. Obligatoriness comes into being only through convention.[11]

The linguisticality of architecture thus exists in an irresolvable tension between the "grammar" and "vocabulary" of conventionalized archectonic elements on the one hand, and the dialectal modifications that may be operated on the architectonic code in the actual practice of building. Loos's greatness lies in having heightened this tension to its maximum, emancipating the dissonance within architecture's language and working out an exemplary modern theory and practice within this charged force-field.[12]

This interpretation of Loos stands behind Achleitner's attempt, again seemingly paradoxical, to find in Vienna's 19th-century historicism — the target of Loos's deepest scorn — precisely a precedent for the uncoupling of historical vocabulary and semantic content that also characterized Loos's architecture. Achleitner thus writes:

> Architecture is per se an ambivalent medium; its means can indeed refer to contents, but it is not in a position to express them concretely. There are no linguistically guaranteed architectonic elements — the classical column is a prominent example of this — that cannot be changed in another society or that would not take on a completely different role. On the other hand, it is well-known that meanings are read, understood, and even feared, otherwise religious or political buildings would never have been destroyed, built-over, dismantled, and their parts reused as trophies, bound into new systems, assimilated.[13]

In fact, Achleitner suggests, the seemingly static form language of classicism offers a stunning example of success in continually incorporating new ideological and political contents, up to and including, he notes, those of 20th-century totalitarian systems:

> The theme is thus here not the static form-system (with narrow breadth of variation), the use of a classical vocabulary, rather the context of contents in which it occurs. Indeed, the autonomy of architectural systems makes them capable of being taken up into arbitrary relations of content.[14]

---

[11] Achleitner, p. 43.
[12] Starting from a Heidegger-influenced meditation on dwelling, building, and the house, the philosopher Massimo Cacciari draws similar conclusions about these two dimensions of Loos's architectonic language. See Francesco Amendolagine and Massimo Cacciari, *Oikos. Da Loos a Wittgenstein* (Rome: Officina, 1975), and Cacciari, 'Adolf Loos e il suo angelo', in Adolf Loos, *Das Andere/L'Altro* (Milan: Electra, 1981). See also my review essay on Cacciari, *Architecture and Nihilism* and *The Necessary Angel*, in *Textual Practice*, 10/2 (Spring 1996), pp. 359-368, for a critical discussion of Cacciari's conjunction of Loos and Wittgenstein.
[13] Friedrich Achleitner, 'Das semantische Schlamassel, oder das historische Erbe der Donaumonarchie', in *Wiener Architektur*, p. 192.
[14] Achleitner, p. 194.

Achleitner goes on to sketch out an account of the internal transformation — and partial preservation in this form — of late 19th-century historicism, a historical narrative that puts in question a narrative of heroic, anti-historicist modernism fighting with the forces of feudalism and reaction in a dying empire. For it was the "cunning" of historicism itself that its represented contents became ever more abstract — "nation," "empire," "homeland," etc. — and ever more detached from historically concrete entities. "The historical detachment from history, impelled paradoxically precisely through historical interests," Achleitner concludes,

> led to a casualness, to an arbitrary exchangeablity and interpretability of elements. Not only did a resistance from outside historicism articulate itself through the changed economic, political, and cultural reality; but also through the practice of historicism, through its method's own dynamic, there appeared by itself a procedural critique that necessary led the way out of historicism.[15]

In other words, across the polemical abyss that seems to exist between late historicism and Adolf Loos, there is also a secret bridge. The semantic doubleness of architectonic convention and usage lends both historicism and anti-historicism a contextual elective affinity, a shared historical dialectic, in the Vienna of the early 20th-century.[16]

Achleitner's most synoptic and historically-rich account of the linguisticality of architecture in Vienna and Habsburg Central Europe is, however, his contribution to "Shaping the Great City," a recent exhibition in Vienna, Montreal, and Los Angeles on modern architecture in Central Europe, 1890-1937. Achleitner's essay is entitled "The Pluralism of Modernity: The Architectonic 'Language Problem' in Central Europe"; it surveys Central European architecture, from secessionism and (Otto) Wagnerian modernism to the various nationalist and revivalist styles to the avant-garde, against a background of the politics of language in the Austro-Hungarian monarchy. His general premise is that the Habsburg rulers' active suppression of direct challenges to their rule in the domain of language compelled a hothouse innovation in non-verbal artistic languages such as music and architecture, as well as lending impetus to a heightened sensitivity to problems of language across the disciplines. In this context, debates about architectonic languages took on, by analogy, some of the dissonant intensity of the broader language question that threatened to explode Habsburg society from within.

Achleitner's attempt to read the stylistic conflicts in the modern architecture of Central Europe as moves within a polyglot field of languages has two especially important consequences. First, historiographically, it entails a different form of historical narrative, or bet-

---

[15]   Achleitner, p. 199.

[16]   A conclusion also explored by Theodor W. Adorno in his 1965 address to the German Werkbund. Taking his point of departure from a dialectical decomposition of the opposition of useful and purpose-free arts and emphasizing the radical historicity of the "function" and "ornament," Adorno went on to ask whether Loos's criticisms of the ornamental might not have been misunderstood: "That which was functional yesterday can become its opposite; Loos was thoroughly aware of this historical dynamic in the concept of the ornament [...]. Critique of the ornament amounts to a critique of that which has lost its functional and symbolic meaning and is left over as the decaying organic, the toxic." See Adorno, 'Funktionalismus Heute', in *Gesammelte Schriften 10/1* (Frankfurt a. M.: Suhrkamp Verlag, 1977), pp. 376-377.

ter, the replacement of a narrative-chronological metaphor with that of a spatialized geo-linguistic field. As Achleitner notes:

> Viennese developments conformed only loosely to sequential periods. The 'polyglot' approach of architects (who generally employed two or more 'languages' or styles) and architectural schools bears a greater analogy to a network than to a chronological process. So it is a fundamental question of interpretation whether one focuses more on a linearity of developments or on a description of reciprocally influential forces.[17]

Second, it presents the radical avant-garde in a different light — more as an attempted escape from the force-field of polyglot languages than an effective historical intervention within it. Figures as diverse as Otto Wagner, Josef Frank, the Czech Cubists, Ödön Lechner, Károly Kós, Joze Plecnik, and Dusan Jurkovic had operated within the dialectical-dialectal space that compelled them to negotiate in complex ways the relations of empire and nation, universalistic language and particularistic dialect. The avant-garde that emerged after World War I, however, attempted to overcome the historical gains the earlier generation of modernists had made in articulating regional-national architectural languages with the ethnic-territorial divisions of the empire — or they simply failed to recognize the value of this task at all. Although, as Achleitner acknowledges, there remained significant regional differences among the various sectors of the avant-garde, the hard-won reference of architecture to national historical and social particularity nevertheless tended to be replaced by its putatively universal reference to the up-to-date achievements of modern technology and science. "One might even, with a touch of cynicism," Achleitner argues —

> maintain that hardly had these nations been given freedom with regard to their languages, or these languages been articulated as nations, when their best minds set out to develop a new universal language. The national aspect had ceased to be an existential theme. Architecture as a whole had been dismissed from the service of national identity; or, put differently, the representation of national progress shifted to the levels of technological, social, hygienic, and generally communitarian development.[18]

From this perspective, ironically, the avant-garde appears to pursue within the empire of the sciences what the Habsburgs had been unable to accomplish in their multi-national political empire: the definitive suppression of dialects and national idioms through a new postnational form-vocabulary of modern technology.

Concrete Dialects: *quadratroman*

This cautionary note in Achleitner's criticism of the architectural avant-garde might be extended to any too-hasty assimilation of his poetic work to a general context of post-World War II avant-gardism. Although in some respects, Achleitner's use of concrete forms and

---

[17] Friedrich Achleitner, 'The Pluralism of Modernity: The Architectonic "Language Problem" in Central Europe', in *Shaping the Great City: Modern Architecture in Central Europe, 1890-1937*, ed. by Eve Blau and Monika Platzer (Munich/London/New York: Prestel, 2001), p. 97.

[18] Achleitner, p. 105.

collage techniques, his minimalistic employment of vocabulary and narrative elements, and his constructivistic analyses of syntax find their complements in other theorists and practitioners of concrete poetry such as Eugen Gomringer and Max Bense, Achleitner's emphasis, I wish to suggest, lies elsewhere than with formal construction. Indeed, I read his book-length "concrete" work of the early 1970s (republished 1995), *quadratroman*, as both an epitome of concrete figural-formal inventiveness and a performative critique of the ideology of universal *Anschaulichkeit* (graphicness, clarity, vividness) implicit in the concrete poem's iconic showing-forth of its signified content.

The basic structure of *quadratroman* is fairly simple to describe: it is a book of about 180 pages (depending on how one counts), each page of which (excepting a title page and a copyright page, but including the front and back covers) contains a square outlined by a thin black line. Including the square on the covers and that of a second title page in the midst of the paratextual apparatus, there are 178 squares in all. The square (*quadrat*) that lends the book its basic form and its title is, like Loos's column, a "classical" vocabulary element. It finds, for example, its provenance in such avant-garde "classics" as El Lissitzky's utopian children's book *Of Two Squares*, in which two squares come to earth, fight against the forces of reaction, and impose their new constructivist geometry on the crooked timber of humanity. Yet unlike El Lissitzky's wholly abstract socialist science-fiction, Achleitner's book makes abundant use of verbal language and alludes to classic, highly conventionalized nineteenth-century narrative forms as well. Thus in the second square (counting the first as that of the cover), that which represents a title page, one reads:

> quadrat-roman
>
> von friedrich achleitner
>
> & andere quadrat-sachen
>
> 1
> neuer bildungsroman
> 1
> neuer entwicklungsroman
> etc. etc. etc.

This titling is equivocal in its attempt to designate the book's own closed, symmetrical figuralness. It claims to be a "novel" (*Roman*), but then indicates that some residual "other square-things" (*andere quadrat-sachen*) may be left over that do not really fit the square frame. The complications are multiplied by the implication of process, growth, organicity, and inexhaustibility in what follows: a new novel of education (*ein neuer bildungsroman*), a new novel of development (*ein neuer entwicklungsroman*), and the pleonastically iterated sign of iterability (*etc. etc. etc.*). Achleitner's square becomes a sort of stage for an unhappy marriage of Robbe-Grillet's new novel (*nouveau roman*), with its typically objectifying and spatializing registration of settings and shapes, and Goethe's *Bildungsroman*, with its representation of increasing inner maturation and individual complexity. Achleitner's chosen form, the square — favored by the classical avant-garde precisely for its non-anthropo-morphic rationality and refusal of narrative — reveals here more stubborn blockheadedness and unhappy misfortune (colloquial senses into which the particle *Quadrat-* can enter) than graphic clarity.

Achleitner subjects the square to a plethora of transformations and usages. On some pages, it functions as a frame for text or images. On others, it serves as a kind of double of the page itself, a page within a page. In some cases, it is a constitutive part of a depicted object or space, such as an signboard or a courtyard.[19] In others, it forms part of a second-order, depicted graphic *representation* of such an object or space, such as an architectural plan or a diagram of a chessboard.[20] In at least one instance, the graphic "representation" of the object is almost totally nominalistic, in the sense that were the label not present, the square would hardly be recognized as an icon of the object. Interestingly, Achleitner chooses architectural elements to exemplify this extreme nominalism and skepticism to-wards the iconic sign. The facing pages 86 and 87 contain squares that are unadorned ex-cepting their labels, respectively, "fenster (schematisch)" [window (schematic)] and "tor (schematisch)" [gate, door, or soccer goal (schematic)]. The next page contains a blank square, with a label below it suggesting a scale drawing, "boxing ring 1:60." This page is followed by a kind of concrete poem, in which the letters of the word "platz" (city square, piazza) are iconically arranged so as to suggest a street (the letters "pl") entering into the left side of a square (formed by 8 letters "a" arranged quadratically) and another street exit-ing from the right side of the square (the letters "tz"). However, in the context of the previ-ous square spaces, the point would seem to be that the "concrete poem" is not really any more definitely iconic than the openly nominalistic instances of labeling, since figurally it is really just another square that could be assigned a number of different labels. Finally, there follows on the next page another square containing a brief text that confidently asserts the contextual flexibility of the square as a spatial icon: "naturally this square can also be a meadow, a woods, a field, a city, or an american state."[21]

Some of the squares depict "objects" that are themselves already exclusively *graphic* or *printed* — for example, an invitation to an exhibition, a handwritten note, or a photograph — so that it is impossible to distinguish whether the figure in the square is a reproduction of the graphic object or a second-order representation.[22] In a few cases, finally, as on the page dedicated to the poet Reinhard Priessnitz, a cloverleaf-shaped crossword puzzle, or in the "sketch for a handwoven blanket," which is composed of densely intersecting vertical and horizontal lines, the square is fully occulted.[23] It persists only as a kind of afterimage car-ried over by the reader onto a page where the quadrat-figure is not manifest.

Achleitner also plays imaginatively with the square as a boundary marker, the function of bounding, of course, constituting a important point of contact between built structures and various sorts of verbal and non-verbal signs. Achleitner not only places things inside or

---

[19]   Friedrich Achleitner, *quadratroman* (Salzburg and Vienna: Residenz Verlag, 1995), pp. 127; 154.
[20]   Achleitner, pp. 97, 103; 155.
[21]   Achleitner, p. 90.
[22]   Achleitner, pp. 18; 65; 112.
[23]   Achleitner, pp. 153; 167.

outside of the square's containing shape, but also over and across its lines. Thus, on pages 21-23, he creates a sequence that dramatizes in rudimentary form the psychology of confinement, exclusion, and transgression. The first of these three squares has printed *within* the square a text that reads: "Here there is nothing else left to one than to stay outside."[24] The next page has a empty square, with the words printed above it: "or inside."[25] The last page of the sequence prints the text horizontally across the top third of the square, crossing its left and right verticals and continuing to the edges of the page: "One would perceive everything else as disorderly, almost anarchistic."[26]

Here the graphic conventions of reading and viewing open out upon an indefinite, but palpable allegorical dimension that extends Achleitner's "concrete" manipulations into a meditation on the hidden boundaries of architectonic, social, and discursive spaces. As he remarks in a square early in the book, "konkret ist hier viel los/de facto gar nichts [Concretely there's a lot going on here/de facto nothing at all]."[27] Far from making *quadratroman* an autotelic, autonomous formal artifact, Achleitner's "quadratic" reduction of theme and narrative to a concrete dimension allows its "de facto" emptiness to be read — concretized — at a variety of levels, in a multiplicity of contexts, and for a plurality of ends. It is worth referring briefly to Achleitner's essay from the "Shaping the Great City" exhibition, to suggest how he invites such allegorical extension through an expanded conception of reading. In justifying his linkage of the question of language in the Habsburg empire to the problem of architectonic "vocabularies," Achleitner observes: "[R]eading itself far surpasses the boundaries of verbal communication. [...] information can be derived from any organized or repetitive phenomenon. To this extent, architecture too can be 'read' in various ways and from the most diverse viewpoints."[28] So too the square unit of *quadratroman*.

On several pages, Achleitner exposes the reader's inescapable but arbitrary orientation of the square with respect to the printed space of the book, that horizontal and vertical directionality each square takes on by being placed on a page and assimilated through Western reading practices, trained on narrative and other forms of "linearized" discourse. One page, page 38, in particular seems to foreground the assumptions of directional reading, by directing the eye in a non-standard way up and down the page. Graphically, this page appears like a series of vertical bands within the square, alternating between a slightly wider and a slightly narrower band, for a total of nine "columns":

---

24   Achleitner, p. 21.
25   Achleitner, p. 22.
26   Achleitner, p. 23.
27   Achleitner, p. 11.
28   Achleitner, 'Pluralism', p. 94.

```
auf   ab   auf   ab   auf   ab   auf   ab   auf
auf   ab   auf   ab   auf   ab   auf   ab   auf
auf   ab   auf   ab   auf   ab   auf   ab   auf
auf   ab   auf   ab   auf   ab   auf   ab   auf
auf   ab   auf   ab   auf   ab   auf   ab   auf
auf   ab   auf   ab   auf   ab   auf   ab   auf
auf   ab   auf   ab   auf   ab   auf   ab   auf
auf   ab   auf   ab   auf   ab   auf   ab   auf
auf   ab   auf   ab   auf   ab   auf   ab   auf
auf   ab   auf   ab   auf   ab   auf   ab   auf
auf   ab   auf   ab   auf   ab   auf   ab   auf
auf   ab   auf   ab   auf   ab   auf   ab   auf
auf   ab   auf   ab   auf   ab   auf   ab   auf
auf   ab   auf   ab   auf   ab   auf   ab   auf
auf   ab   auf   ab   auf   ab   auf   ab   auf
auf   ab   auf   ab   auf   ab   auf   ab   auf
auf   ab   auf   ab   auf   ab   auf   ab   auf
auf   ab   auf   ab   auf   ab   auf   ab   auf
auf   ab   auf   ab   auf   ab   auf   ab   auf
auf   ab   auf   ab   auf   ab   auf   ab   auf
auf   ab   auf   ab   auf   ab   auf   ab   auf
auf   ab   auf   ab   auf   ab   auf   ab   auf
auf   ab   auf   ab   auf   ab   auf   ab   auf
auf   ab   auf   ab   auf   ab   auf   ab   auf
auf   ab   auf   ab   auf   ab   auf   ab   auf
auf   ab   auf   ab   auf   ab   auf   ab   auf
auf   ab   auf   ab   auf   ab   auf   ab   auf
```

This block might be seen to resemble graphically the black and white vertical stripes favored by the French conceptual artist Daniel Buren, another artist who has explored in sophisticated ways the complex relations of formal "vocabulary" and contextual "meaning."[29] But Achleitner's bands are only mediately "visual," for they are composed of vertical stacks of verbal elements, the words "auf" (up) for the wider bands and "ab" (down) for the narrower bands. If these words are taken to be imperative signs, however, directional instructions for reading the columns, then the page's "text" begins in the lower righthand corner of the square, and through a series of reversals up and down the page, ends in the lower left-

---

[29] See for example, Benjamin H. D. Buchloh's discussion of Buren, 'The Museum and the Monument: Daniel Buren's *Les Couleurs/Les Formes*', in Buchloh, *Neo-Avantgarde and Culture Industry: Essays on European and American Art from 1955 to 1975* (Cambridge, Mass.: The MIT Press, 2000), pp. 119-139.

hand corner. The spatial trajectory is fully dependent on language apprehension and *reading*. Its pathways, however, require a peculiar inversion of the positions to which the eye would "naturally" gravitate in reading a linear Western text (nor does it follow the reading orders of, say, Japanese or Chinese, Arabic or Hebrew, or archaic "boustrophodon" scripts).

Another square, in a complementary way, points up the ambiguity of linguistic markers of space ("shifters" or "deictics," in the technical terminology of Roman Jakobson). Terms such as right and left, up and down, over and under (and their equivalents in the order of time as well) depend on reference to an orienting perspective, whether that be provided by a living observer, a system of conventions (such as those already naturalized in reading a book or map), or an artificial code. Achleitner explores these issues in the square on page 20, in which the word "darunter" (below) is typed repeatedly in a band across the top half of the square, while the word "darüber" (above) is printed diagonally over "darunter" with a rubber stamp:

The spatial orientation, clearly, is to the square as an implied surface, with the typewritten text laid paradoxically over it, but beneath the rubber stamped text. It is the rubber stamp, the last overprinting, that governs the system of spatial orientation, not the square. Yet it may be that these words refer not to each other or to the printing surface, but to their own reiterations, providing a direction for reading. Thus "below" is written in a system of columns, which suggests a stepwise reading from top to bottom of the page, while "above" might be read in the opposite direction, rising from the bottom of the page to the top. Two other elements further complicate the spatiality of the concrete image, however. Just below the horizontal division of the square into top and bottom, there are another three shorter lines of typewritten text composed of the word "darunter" three times in each line. This "block" of three lines is graphically situated *below* the upper band of text, also composed of the repeated word "below." The bottommost element of the figure, however, is the word "above" stamped three times horizontally across the lower part of the square. Since it appears set off against mostly white space, it presents the reader with the question of whether the page should not be turned over entirely, setting "above" in its proper place with "below" sinking below it on the page.

Achleitner wittily invites his readers into two alternative and contradictory orders of reading, one discursive and generic, the other concrete and figural-abstract. This contradiction is embodied, above all, by the addresses to the reader on the front and back covers. On the front cover, he warns the reader that the book must be read in a strictly linear way, page by page from front to back, and that if, as is the reader's typical habit, she insists on flipping backwards from the end, then she will not be able to make much of the book. The author goes on to say, you are free to do as you please, but I have warned you already on the cover of the book and if you ignore my advice, then don't complain later. This text continues on the back cover in much the same vein, but unlike on the front cover, the text is printed above the square, rather than within its frame. Within the back cover's square is a hand-drawn diagram spelling out the word q-u-a-d-r-a-t from left to right at the top edge of the square, from top to bottom at the left edge, from right to left at the bottom edge, and from bottom to top at the right edge. Thus the word "quadrat" is composed into a four-sided square. From each of the letters, excepting those that form the corners of the square, arrows run in both directions, thus connecting the letters into a square matrix: "u" always being linked to the last "a," the first "a" always linked to "r," and "d" always linked to "d," "q" and "t" always being the free corner letters. Far from suggesting the directionality and organic growth of the *Bildungsroman*, however, this figure implies a closed combinatoric structure, with the characteristics of reversibility, iterability, and restriction of choice.

If the figural pattern of the "quadrat" seems to impose from the outset a comically infelicitous shape for a *Bildungsroman*, dooming it to repetition and non-linearity, so too the asymmetries of narrative and linear reading also continuously reinscribe the figure of the square in new contexts, denying its closure and geometrical transparency. For if Achleitner's *quadratroman* bears at best a schematic, abstract reference to the developmental structure of the novel, neither does it offer a heroic, avant-garde allegory of the defeat of outmoded literary conventions by graphic, concrete forms. If "Bildung" can be diagrammatized, reduced to a set of moves on a grid-matrix, then so too even as abstract a form as the square can be reshaped, through a practice of reading steeped in linear conventions, into narrative, anthropomorphic figures. Formulated in terms familiar from Achleitner's remarks on Adolf Loos: the abstractness and conventionality of the vocabulary item (the square) allows, indeed *invites*, its remotivation within multiple, changing use-contexts.

Yet Achleitner does not content himself with this circling of the square, but even allows contextual variability to sink all the way down to the fundamental structure of the vocabulary item itself, opposing, as it were, the aberrant *dialect* term to the authorized dictionary entry of the *Hochsprache*. It is in this light that we can interpret his final square of the book (excepting the back cover), in which he makes a comically agonized apology to the reader, the burden of which rests on the clichéd distinction between high German exactitude (technological *Hochsprache)* and low Viennese slovenliness (dialect):

> dear reader forget everything that you have read and seen at the end of the square novel a terrible error was discovered by the author nearly a catastrophe i want to state it short i don't want to torment you any longer short and painless it's said so beautifully in the german language in the language of the germans and of the proverbial german precision and I'd like to save my neck by saying typical viennese sloppiness and all that it didn't escape my precision that the squares used here are not squares at all they have here in the original naturally not in the somewhat reduced book that you have in your hand din a 4 [Deutsche Industrie Norm DIN-A-4] of the scale of one hundred twenty by 119 millimeters whereby the whole title and basis of the novel is withdrawn all that should as already correctly remarked have been called rectangular novel idiotic title and I have to take back the whole philosophy around the square the whole square philosophy it remains open to each to write without plagiarism a square novel but watch the typesetter the printer who makes the proofs quite closely once again a millimeter who h.[30]

It is as if the author had made the horrified discovery that his nice neat German square, shiny and fresh from a northern factory, had been crushed in its passage across the Austrian border, its edges irreparably bent out of shape by a southern dialectal mushing and rounding of its once geometrically crisp German vocables.

Vernacular Minimalism, or the Concrete Readymade: *Die Plotteggs kommen*

In 1995, the year in which *quadratroman* reappeared in print, Achleitner published another work, *Die Plotteggs kommen*, that explored the interpenetration of narrative and concrete form in a manner complementary, but opposite to that of *quadratroman*. In *quadratroman*, Achleitner set out from the formal, concrete presupposition of an abstract architectonic "vocabulary item," the square, and through contextual variation, drew it into the generic orbit of novelistic narrative. *Die Plotteggs kommen* from the outset exists in narrative form — it is subtitled "A Report" — but it revolves around the appearance of mysterious and disturbingly concrete forms in the Austrian landscape: "Plotteggs," or large, mechanically rolled and plastic-sealed hay bales. Here the conflict of concrete forms and narrative progress plays out not at the formal and generic level of the text, but within the fictive space of the narrative itself. The "Plotteggs" are in themselves as abstract and bare of hidden meaning as the square of *quadratroman*, yet they also foreground the sheer narrative pregnancy

---

[30]   Achleitner, *quadratroman*, p. 176.

of concrete form, as they consistute the "plot egg" of a kind of comical spy-mystery-detective narrative. Within this generic narrative, the allegorical confrontation of concrete and organic formal elements occurs in a highly specific regional space, in the *Steiermark* region of Austria.

In his "report" on an aborted holiday in the Styrian countryside, Achleitner amusingly conjures the "sinister" horrors concealed behind inexpressive blank forms that are the product of agricultural mechanization, a kind of found minimalist sculpture that has inexplicably begun to hatch within the vistas favored by the touristic *Wanderer* in search of authentic Austro-kitsch beauty. In this way, Achleitner evokes a number of topical contexts that have often formed the focus of his public interventions as an architectural expert, and which carry a profound political and cultural charge in present-day Austria. These include the aesthetics of tourism, regionalism vs. centralism, the relation of city and countryside, rural industrialization and the problem of landscape preservation, and the politics of public monuments and public art displays.[31] Although none of these themes may be explicitly peeled out of the white plastic wrap covering the Plotteggs, each is incubated within its ovular figure, precisely *so long as* their shell of allegorical opacity remains intact.

The book begins with the narrator in a typical Austrian pastoral scene, stumbling across the disturbing presence of Plotteggs in the midst of a meadow and at the edge of a woods. He goes on to describe the process by which hay is gathered into these "mini-silos," compressed, and sealed under four layers of translucent, taut plastic wrap. Through this process, they achieve a form "that expresses at once pressure and tension, formal resistance and the effect of power, an extreme productive form that to a certain degree through a dialectical mechanism turns into an expressive form."[32]

Achleitner conjures here a context of arguments, dating back to the mid-1960s, around minimalist sculpture and its post-minimalist offshoots in earthwork projects and land art. The box-like, reiterated metallic forms of Donald Judd's "specific objects," the grey-white cubes and L-volumes of Robert Morris, the site/non-site constructions and landscape interventions of Robert Smithson, and the analytic geometrical constructions of Sol LeWitt find their parodic, dialect-spouting Austrian counterparts in Achleitner's found agricultural objects, the Plotteggs. Moreover, Achleitner's description of them closely echoes the productivist bases of minimalist theory, especially that of Robert Morris. For example, in his essay "Notes on Sculpture, Part 3," Morris had argued that the three-dimensional work of the present (mid-1960s) would not base its forms on a tradition of sculptural art-forms (hence his placement of the term "sculpture" *sous râture*), but would rather draw upon the "cultural infrastructure" of industrial manufacture.[33] He writes:

There is some justification for lumping together the various focuses and intentions of the new three-dimensional work. Morphologically there are common elements: symmetry, lack of traces of process, ab-

---

[31] See, for example, the essays in Friedrich Achleitner (ed.), *Die Ware Landschaft: Eine kritische Analyse des Landschaftsbegriffs* (Salzburg: Residenz Verlag, 1977), and Friedrich Achleitner, *Region, ein Konstrukt? Regionalismus, eine Pleite?* (Basel: Birkhäuser, 1997).

[32] Friedrich Achleitner, *Die Plotteggs kommen: Ein Bericht* (Wien: Sonderzahl, 1995), p. 7.

[33] Robert Morris, 'Notes on Sculpture, Part 3', in *Continuous Project Altered Daily: The Writings of Robert Morris* (Cambridge, Massachusetts: The MIT Press, 1995), p. 38.

stractness, non-hierarchic distribution of parts, non-anthropomorphic orientations, general wholeness. These constants probably provide the basis for a general imagery. The imagery involved is referential in a broad and special way: it does not refer to past sculptural form. Its referential connections are to manufactured objects and not to previous art. In this respect the work has affinities with Pop art. But the abstract work connects to a different level of the culture.[34]

Morris thus signals minimalist sculpture's formal and material filiation to the industrial production of serial, stereotypical objects, hence also with the post-artistic "finding" practice of the readymade (as distinguished, in his view, from Pop Art's appropriation of media and commercial *imagery*). So too Achleitner sketches the comical dialectic of the Plotteggs, in which the forms and materials of Austrian agro-industrial production, the extreme negation of traditional artistic forms and media, dialectically generate a new expressive vocabulary and a late renascence of avantgarde provocation as well.

Morris's theoretical justifications for minimalist sculpture also had a strongly phenomenological component. His phenomenological concerns included the positioning and movement of the spectator within a three-dimensional space, the activation of experience in time through the encounter of spectators with the sculptural works, and the avoidance of pictorial arrangements of parts in favor of "whole gestalts" and "unitary forms." Achleitner wittily echoes this minimalist phenomenology in his description of the Plotteggs: "The Plotteggs are perhaps 1.3 meters high and have an identical thickness. That they nevertheless appear a bit higher is only an optical illusion; the deformed edges of the cylinder are more insistent in their appearance than the radii hidden in the volume."[35] (The Plotteggs, notably, are the precise phenomenological opposites of the pseudo-squares of *quadratroman*: the squares look symmetrical, but are really slightly uneven, whereas the Plotteggs look asymmetrical, but really are identical in height and breadth.)

At one level, one could understand Achleitner to be following to a logical conclusion the arguments that Morris and Smithson eventually developed from the minimalist point of departure. Once the special privilege given to art-forms and "art-perception" no longer could be sustained; once the traditional materials of painting and sculpture had lost their obligatoriness; once acts of finding readymades or commissioning industrially produced objects could be seen as artistic processes equivalent in value to those involving traditional craft; and once works of arts no longer needed to be produced and viewed in special "art" spaces such as the studio, the gallery, and the museum — then potentially any object, in any space, on any scale could be appropriated for what Rosalind Krauss would call "sculpture in the expanded field." Including, Achleitner asks with a grin, a field in the Steiermark with a hay bale in it, the sun glaring unpleasantly off its reflective plastic wrapping? Well ... lacking the visionary pathos or the monumentality of Smithson's and Morris's earthworks, Achleitner's Plotteggs are something of a comic *reductio ad absurdum* of the argument for earthworks and site-specific art. If up in Berlin, to widespread public outcry and international acclaim, the artistic genius Christo wraps in plastic the *Reichstag*, down in Austria it is just anonomous farmers wrapping up — stacks of animal feed. Achleitner's Plotteggs thus offer a profane, Austrian dialect response to the *Hochsprache* of post-minimalist art

34 Ibid., p. 27.
35 Achleitner, *Plotteggs*, p. 9.

forms, that imposing universalist idiom composed of such "classical," mythic-sacred vocabulary items as the cube, the spiral, the crescent, the veil, the portal, and the labyrinth.

If, however, the aesthetics of the minimalist avant-garde take more than a bit of a good-natured drubbing in *Die Plotteggs kommen*, Achleitner also parodies the panic unleashed in "formalist" defenders of the traditional media by the minimalists' works and theories. In *Die Plotteggs kommen*, these formalists are not sophisticated art critics such as Clement Greenberg and Michael Fried, however, but petty-bourgeois urbanites looking to unwind from their white-collar labors in pristine, picture-book landscapes. The narrator recounts his encounter with one such pastoral tourist, who is so enraged at the the Plotteggs' disturbance of the view that he has in mind —

> to invite a famous Viennese painter who supposedly would consider how these little monstrosities could be better integrated into the landscape. He imagined a nice bit of painting that could, of course, in a pretty way be abstract. I could not resist the remark that in this region already during the Second World War, thus in the Third Reich, they had had good experience of getting whole factories, transmission stations, or barracks to disappear through painting. The man didn't like this comparison.[36]

The narrator's suspicious interest in the Plotteggs and failure to appreciate the touristic landscape eventually culminates in the discovery of the manuscript of his "report" and a hairbrained hearing to investigate his activities in the region. His most dangerous "crime," which is expiated only through the confiscation and destruction of his manuscript and his expulsion from the hotel, is having failed to "have integrated myself in the days of my residence into the landscape."[37] Fortunately, our clever narrator had foreseen this danger and kept a copy of his manuscript. He hence is able to divulge to the world the portentous arrival of the Plotteggs despite the local authorities' attempt to censor him.

Achleitner further implies an association of the Plotteggs with avant-garde art with a reference to the most radical, anti-formal manifestation in Austrian art in the 1960s, the Vienna Actionist tendency associated with the artists Otto Mühl, Günter Brus, Hermann Nitsch, and Rudolf Schwarzkogler. Achleitner's literary cabaret works, often performed in collaboration with other members of the original Wiener Gruppe, are seen as an important inspiration for the work of the Actionists, and the Wiener Gruppe writers themeselves occasionally participated in Actionist events. Now, twenty years after the last "actions" of Brus and Mühl in Vienna, Achleitner's narrator finds himself relaxing in the countryside, watching a tractor haul a half-formed, "embryonic" Plottegg to another site. He considers "whether overall this whole agrarian actionism has more to do with this landscape than my Biedermeierish need for views and quiet, which was really only prepared to perceive its reproductive aspect."[38] From the touristic, Biedermeierish point-of-view, such rural actionism seems as shocking, negative, and destructive as Vienna Actionism might once have appeared to the average middle-class consumer of middle-high culture:

---

[36]   Achleitner, p. 29.
[37]   Achleitner, p. 39.
[38]   Achleitner, p. 13.

> Tourism researchers recognize in [the spread of the Plotteggs] a system of landscape extermination, so that men with certain habits of perception — perhaps those of Biedermeier painters — can no longer consume them in an aesthetic way. Only those who possess the so-called Plottegg-ly code have the capacity either to separate the two perceptual systems critically or to experience them as a new and indeed very exciting aesthetic system.[39]

Achleitner thus not only brings the Actionist's aesthetic provocations in resonance with the shocking effect of the Plotteggs on generic landscape perception, he also cleverly puts in question the relations of city and countryside that assumes that the avant-garde is a strictly metropolitan, "international" and cosmopolitan phenomenon. On the contrary, he seems to imply, the contestatory energies of the avant-garde can arise from highly local conditions. The Plotteggs are a regional, agrarian, rural avant-garde manifestation, yet perhaps ultimately even more baneful to a postcard-fed bourgeoisie than the long-since canonized performances of the Vienna Actionists. In its very existence and presence, the Plotteggian avant-garde expresses its natural contempt for the view-hungry, urban middlebrow, and neither in the universal language of modern science nor in Actionist intensities of bodily shock, but in a round Styrian agro-industrial dialect, rooted in the "forms of life" of a particular regional locale.

Achleitner ends his report with two postscripts, which offer an ambiguous final comment on the fate of the Plotteggs' dialectal avant-garde. In the first of the two postscripts, the narrator reports having seen a few Plotteggs in front of the Künstlerhaus in Graz. He recounts having heard from a friend that the Plotteggs had appeared in the city and were being used to point out directions or carry advertisements for exhibitions. However, they had provoked the emotions of passersby, who had rolled them into the streets, cut them up, and even set them on fire. He reports:

> Although, as one can see from the very objective police reports, the Plotteggs acted completely passively, they unleashed the greatest aggression. Indeed, precisely their balled-up passivity, their mute presence, provoked the actions of the residents of Graz.[40]

The Plotteggs, having entered into the Styrian capital city of Graz and confronted the urban cultural space of the exhibition hall, now provoke an "actionism" that resembles in its anarchic effects the urban avant-garde provocations of earlier years. Yet the final postscript is more ambiguous, situating the Plotteggs' avant-gardism, hence by implication the space of dialect as well, between two social poles, that of actionism and advertising. Here the Plotteggs come to be associated with the Humanic shoe store chain, which many years before Beneton's notorious ad campaign of the 1990s, made its mark in Austria with a series of advertisements successfully employing avant-garde visual and textual means. This epilogue is, one might say, a self-reflexive moment for Achleitner about the possibilities and limitations of an oppositional avant-garde in Austria, from the secessionists and expressionists, to the Wiener Gruppe and the Actionists, to the younger generation of media artists today:

---

[39]   Achleitner, p. 17.
[40]   Achleitner, p. 45.

On a further visit in the Styrian provincial capital (on Friday, 13 November 1992) I found in the surroundings of the Künstlerhaus a few Plotteggs. They were in part torn apart, their skins pulled off, or blocking the paths through the park. The less wounded showed the inscription HUMANIC. Naturally I can no longer at this level continue the story and I consider it to be definitely closed.[41]

---

[41] Achleitner, p. 47.

Michel Delville

How Not to Die in Venice: The Art of Arakawa and Madeline Gins

Building upon the Kantian insight that reality largely amounts to our awareness of it, Gins and Arakawa have created an art that combines linguistic and visual (including iconic) stimuli as well as various forms of concrete and near-concrete poetry to explore the implications of the modern awareness that personal experiences and concepts of reality are biased due not only to the relative position of the observer but also to the mental processing of our sensations. My purpose here is to review Arakawa and Gins's artistic development and assess the relevance of their collaborative architectural and conceptual works to the development of modern poetics.

> *Forgetting mind, its complications,*
> *My hand is free; The All appears.*
> *I use devices, simultaneously.*
> *Look — a halo penetrates the Void.*
> Zen Masters
> (quoted in Madeline Gins's
> *Helen Keller or Arakawa*)

> *An image as vague as this is self-sufficient ...*
> *my imaginary trophy, which bursts only*
> *with that exquisite absence of self.*
> Stéphane Mallarmé

Arakawa's "Blank" and the Poetics of the Negative Mystic

In June 1997, *Reversible Destiny*, the first major US exhibition of the collaborative art of Arakawa and Madeline Gins opened at the Guggenheim Museum SoHo. It featured two ongoing projects, *The Mechanism of Meaning* — a cycle of paintings, diagrams and words-in-painting begun in 1963 — and a separate section devoted to their more recent experimental architectural sites. These two works-in-progress can be seen to represent the two main "phases" of Arakawa and Gins's career up to the present day. Whereas the visual puzzles and language games of *The Mechanism of Meaning* concentrate on the themes of representation, perception and cognition and can therefore be seen as a continuation of Arakawa's conceptual drawings and collages from the early 1960s, the *Reversible Destiny* sites address the question of how art can enact what Samira Kawash recently described as an attempt to "multipl[y] and complexif[y] the ways in which the body engages with architectural surround."[1]

---

[1]   Samira Kawash, 'Bodies at Risk: The Architecture of Reversible Destiny', *Performing Arts Journal*, 20/2 (1998), 17.

What these projects have in common is a rejection of the notion that art should be the vehicle of self-expression and an emphasis on works that stimulate the beholder's participation in the creation of meaning through various forms of interactive experiments. Building upon the Kantian insight that reality largely amounts to our awareness of it, the mixed media panels of *The Mechanism of Meaning* create an art that combines linguistic and visual (including iconic) stimuli as well as various forms of concrete and near-concrete poetry to explore the implications of the modern awareness that personal experiences and concepts of reality are biased due not only to the relative position of the observer but also to the mental processing of our sensations. Central to this project is what Arakawa has termed "blank." On the surface, Arakawa's notion of "blank" is reflected in his use of isolated words and fragmented narratives interrupted by gaps, silences and empty spaces, which testifies to a Beckettian desire to build an art of emptiness and "lessness." But the more specific relevance of Arakawa's "blank" to contemporary aesthetics and poetics is best examined in the context of an early painting, entitled "Landscape" (1968).[2] "Landscape" is one of Arakawa's early "minimalist" paintings. It comprises a number of dots labeled by means of arrows and familiar objects as well as two empty boxes, signaling the presence of empty signifiers that nonetheless seem to designate an unnamed object. Those two boxes point to the existence of a pre-verbal state that precedes the creation of meaningful, fixed relationships between words and objects, self and world.[3] In the context of Arakawa's "Landscape," "blank" thus would not seem to denote emptiness per se but, rather, "an event preceding language," a pre-linguistic, pre-signifying state which potentially coordinates our experience.[4] According to the critic Dagmar Buchwald blank "denotes by approximation that which precedes and underlies all thought, action and perception and cannot be directly thought, acted, or perceived."[5] Gins and Arakawa themselves have described "blank" as a "neutral positing — in the sense of holding it open; it is what is there but undifferentiated, so it is not nothing … It is what fills emptiness."[6] In Arakawa's 1982 painting, "Blank Dots," such a pre-forming, pre-configuring space is described primarily as an image-forming process, a "FORMING BLANK … OUT OF WHICH UNRECOGNIZABLE PLACES JUMP, SHAPING VOLUMES INTO IMAGES."[7]

There are a number of connecting lines between Arakawa's notion of the blank as a inchoate state of (pre-)consciousness that is neither meaningless nor meaningful, neither nothing nor something, and Rosmarie Waldrop's definition of the "negative mystic." Waldrop has used the term "negative mystic" to refer to modern and contemporary poets "whose terminology and whose efforts towards a transcendence put them in a mystical tradition," a tradition in which "the meaningful joins the meaningless, and the scientist the mystic." Meister Eckhart's famous insight, "Gott ist Nichts," provides the conceptual ground of such

---

[2]   Arakawa and Gins, *Reversible Destiny* (New York: Guggenheim Museum Publications, 1997), p. 34.
[3]   "Dots can stand for things" (Madeline Gins, *Helen Keller or Arakawa* [New York: Burning Books/East-West Cultural Studies, 1994], p. 128).
[4]   Arakawa and Gins, *Reversible*, p. 134.
[5]   Arakawa and Gins, p. 26.
[6]   Arakawa and Gins, p. 36.
[7]   Arakawa and Gins, p. 27.

negative aesthetics, which is based on the recognition that "the absolute is also the void."[8] Yet most of the poets she has in mind "are not mystics in the normal sense of the word; they are at best 'negative,' or perhaps abstract mystics, since the transcendence they try to explore is not God, but the void" itself.[9] Among modern poets, Waldrop reminds us, Stéphane Mallarmé, who claimed to have created his work "only by elimination … all acquired truth being born only from the loss of an impression," was one of the first artists to conceive of the poem as an approximation to the void of silence (the "poème tu, aux blancs") and an expression of the "Nothing which is the truth":

> Language, even when it denies all earthly objects, still stands in front of the nothing. Even the word "nothing" is still a word, and therefore still something. But since the silent poem is not possible, Mallarmé has to make do with approximations: such as to negate every object as soon as it is named and, more important, to dislocate French syntax. This has two functions: it obscures meaning which, too, hides the void which is the truth. And it gives an impression of disjunction and fragmentation which Mallarmé welcomes. For fragments approach the Nothing and are therefore "preuves nuptiales de l'Idée."[10]

Mallarmé's conception of the blank space of the page as what Waldrop terms "a kind of abstract void, a void of pure spirit," his exploration of silence as "an empty transcendence," enabled him to create paradoxical objects, which are denied as soon as they are named (one is reminded here of his "absent tombeau," "aboli bibelot," and "vols qui n'ont pas fui").[11] Similarly, Arakawa's "Landscape" prompts a heightened, reenergized attentiveness and inventiveness on the part of the reader/viewer, who is required to make sense of a paradoxical diagram that signifies both the physical absence and the nominal presence of the "object" described.

Architectural Body: Reversible Destiny Sites and the Poetic Subject

What remains essentially a thought experiment in *The Mechanism of Meaning*, becomes, in the *Reversible Destiny* projects, an entire philosophy of life as it has reached the stage where Arakawa and Gins's multidiscursive approach has given way to a truly multidimensional "thinking/feeling field." *The Site of Reversible Destiny*, completed in Yoro, Japan, in 1995, comprises artificial terrains, labyrinths, gardens, walls, paths, as well as a series of strangely-shaped, gravity-defying buildings that seem meant as a challenge to the predictable flat areas and vertical walls of our everyday reality. The result is a kind of multilevel, three-dimensional Cubist labyrinth that attempts to disorient walkers and challenge their most basic conceptions of perception and space. Such sites sometimes require visitors to execute conflicting instructions (such as following, at the same time, two or three arrows that move in opposite directions) and urge them to keep their bodies "in a state of imbal-

---

[8] Rosmarie Waldrop, *Against Language? "Dissatisfaction with Language" as Theme and Impulse towards Experiments in Twentieth Century Poetry* (The Hague: Mouton, 1971), p. 17.

[9] Waldrop, p. 17.

[10] Waldrop, p. 18.

[11] Waldrop, p. 21.

ance for as long as possible," making simple actions like standing or walking unbalanced by the indeterminacy and unpredictability of the artificial landscape.[12]

One of the most important considerations in dealing with architecture on this level is determining the boundaries of self and world: "to what degree the world that envelops a person's body belongs to that body and is in some way integral to its functioning has not yet been determined [...] Where does person leave off and world begin, or, indeed, does this happen?"[13] In order to investigate those issues, Arakawa and Gins often require the viewer to touch, operate and even, in the case of the Reversible Destiny site, inhabit the work of art — like Diderot and D'Alembert before them (see their entries on "The Blind" and "The Apparent Distance of Objects" in the *Encyclopaedia*), Gins and Arakawa believe in the necessary interaction of the senses of sight and touch in the apprehension of external objects, especially as regards the perception of distance and depth or relief. By literally drawing us into the work of art, the sites of reversible destiny place particular emphasis on the trajectories of self and body in the hope of revealing alternative ways of understanding and acting in the world.

Arakawa and Gins's reversible destiny sites take as their central premise the idea that architecture assumes an unavoidable responsibility in the structuring of the self. Acting as it does as an outer skin dictating our behavior, beliefs, perceptions as well as our ways of living our lives, architecture influences everybody physically and mentally in regard to how we can deal with reality at large. Instead of "consuming" architecture, Arakawa and Gins argue, we should be "involved [...] in a process of self-invention."[14] As I have suggested, such an attitude presupposes a willingness to relinquish normative modes of apprehending space and time. Arising in Arakawa and Gins's theoretical writings about reversible destiny sites is the question of how our potential for perceiving the world can be augmented or maximalized. By multiplying the perceptive vectors by which we organize our experience, reversible destiny sites seek to account for the fact that "the fabric of the world equals all a person presently perceives plus all she believes she perceives or believes herself to have ever perceived plus all she might perceive."[15] In their description of one of their experimental houses — of which more will be said later — Arakawa and Gins write that the building "accommodates the body's endless desire to draw close to and be in rapport with virtually everything."[16] Reversible destiny sites urge us to reach beyond the bounds of ordinary perception (which involves the selection of details, the primacy of the visual, the separation of body and mind, the privileging of a particular point of view, and the imposition of a linear continuity on the real) in order to embrace a multiplicity of "landing sites" (a "landing site" refers to the place where the body interacts with the object perceived).

[12]   Arakawa and Gins, *Reversible*, p. 209.
[13]   Arakawa and Gins, 'Person as Site with Respect to a Tentative Constructed Plan', in *Anywhere*, Vol. 2, ed. Cynthia Davidson (New York: Rizzoli, 1992), p. 58.
[14]   Arakawa and Gins, *Reversible*, p. 2. There is also a moral and political concern underlying Gins and Arakawa's reversible destiny sites, one which is linked with the artists' conviction that "those who cease being passive in relation to architecture are less likely to be cruel and murderous" (*Reversible*, p. 246).
[15]   Arakawa and Gins, *Reversible*, p. 146.
[16]   Nick Piombino, 'Sites and In-Sites of reversible Destiny', in *POTEPOETTEXT*, no 4. (Elmwood, Conn.: Potes and Poets Press, 1997), n. p.

Clearly, Arakawa and Gins's blank — the prime moving principle behind all of the sites of reversible destiny — does not result so much from "a process of elimination" (Mallarmé's favorite method) as from what Charles Bernstein describes as "a confounding by multiplication."[17] Such a process enacts a radical transformation of the self achieved through a new coordination of the senses. Ideally, Arakawa and Gins's reversible destiny sites should enable the visitors to the sites to "[become] increasingly able to field an ever greater number of possibilities" in a way that would eventually teach us "how to live as a maximally invigorated sensorium."[18] In this respect, Arakawa and Gins's ideal reader/viewer resembles the protagonist of Borges' short story, "Funes, the Memorious" (1942), who in falling from a horse has acquired a capacity for total recall. Ireneo Funes perceives and remembers everything, not just the particulars of the world around him, but literally everything he has thought of, experienced or imagined:

> A circumference on a blackboard, a rectangular triangle, a rhomb, are forms which we can fully intuit; the same held true with Ireneo for the tempestuous mane of a stallion, a herd of cattle in a pass, the ever-changing flame of the innumerable ash, the many faces of a dead man during the course of a protracted wake. He could perceive I do not know how many stars in the sky.[19]

However, the state of total awareness that characterizes Funes' consciousness paradoxically entails a number of psychological and intellectual limitations. Funes is indeed "almost incapable of general, platonic ideas." It is not only difficult for him "to understand that the generic term dog embrace[s] so many unlike specimens of differing sizes and different forms"; he is even "disturbed by the fact that a dog at three-fourteen (seen in profile) should have the same name as the dog at three-fifteen (seen from the front)." Finally, he finds it very difficult to fall asleep because "to sleep is to be abstracted from the world"! Towards the end of the story, Borges' narrator issues a warning: "the truth is that we all live by leaving behind," which is to say that a certain degree of selection, generalization and abstraction is necessary to the psychological survival of the individual. Funes, who lives in a world in which "there [are] nothing but details, almost contiguous details," is a helpless individual whose refusal of categorization and naive commitment to an anti-Platonic form of realism leaves him intensely vulnerable and incapable of coping with the endless detail and variety of the physical world.[20]

But Gins and Arakawa would probably reject such commonsensical objections and reply that reversible destiny sites are first and foremost about the suggestion, recognition, definition and reconfiguration of more possibilities within a constructed space. Indeed, the multiplication of perceptual landing sites is first and foremost a means to an end, a necessary step towards an understanding of "how it is possible to be a body, or a sensorium, and what goes into forming a person."[21] As we will see, reversible destiny does not amount to a rejection of abstraction but, rather, strives towards the attainment of a "stretchable" abstrac-

---

[17]   Charles Bernstein, *Content's Dream: Essays 1975-1984* (Los Angeles: Sun & Moon Press, 1986), p. 192.

[18]   Arakawa and Gins, *Reversible*, pp. 11; 241.

[19]   Jorge Luis Borges, *Ficciones*, ed. by A. Kerrigan (New York: Grove Press, 1962), p. 112.

[20]   Borges, p. 115.

[21]   Arakawa and Gins, *Reversible*, p. 241.

tion liable to effect the physical and spiritual transformation of the individual and thereby "engage questions of existence more intensely."[22] Lastly, reversible destiny also has to do with what is probably one of the most extraordinary proposals ever put forward in the history of Western aesthetics, one which is meant to conduct nothing less than a "frontal attack on mortality itself."[23]

Reversible Destiny

> *We do not die because we must, we die because it is a habit,*
> *to which one day, not so long ago, our thoughts became bound.*
> Raoul Vaneigem

> WE HAVE DECIDED NOT TO DIE.
> Arakawa and Madeline Gins

In order to fully appreciate the nature of Arakawa and Gins's project "to construct sensoria that will elude mortality," it is helpful first to consider the following examples of experimental houses designed by Arakawa and Gins to expand the limits of the human mind and body by reversing the parameters ruling our experience of time and space.[24] In "Rotation House," one of the experimental houses devised in the context of the Reversible Destiny project, the five different rotations of the rooms make the rooms appear to be different in size and in form even though their size and form are identical — the rooms, Gins and Arakawa conclude, "act as spatial anagrams" of each other. As the residents move from one room into another, the actions performed and repeated in the "living space" within the building inevitably become estranged from themselves. They are "struck by how the same features appear different or remain to some degree the same from one rotated version of the room to another."[25] Another example of such anagrammatic reversibility is the doubling of rooms in the "Twin House," a construction in which next to every room is "a twin [room] with identical layout but oppositely pitched terrain."[26] Because the two halves of the building consist of identical walls and enclosures juxtaposed at different angles of perspective, the residents know "that an action performed in one part of the house might equally well have been performed in another," which, by dislocating the notion of the uniqueness of our actions and individuality, "makes the course of events seem less inevitable and surely less weighty." The doubling of walls and rooms effected by the "Twin House" eventually results in the doubling of the self, altering our sense of being in a way that enables us to transfer our lives and actions into those of phantom doppelgangers occupying the other half of the house.

---

[22]   Gins, *Keller*, p. 261; Arakawa and Gins, *Reversible*, p. 241.
[23]   Arakawa and Gins, p. 313.
[24]   Gins, *Keller*, p. 238.
[25]   Arakawa and Gins, *Reversible*, p. 283.
[26]   Arakawa and Gins, pp. 304; 270.

One necessary condition for this "doubling" of the self is a readiness to "neutralize" one's subjectivity.[27] "No longer needing to have a personality," Arakawa and Gins write, the residents of their experimental houses "adopt a wait-and-see policy toward themselves."[28] But the dissolution (or suspension) of personality required by reversible destiny houses does not imply the death of the subject, nor does it have to lead to a dissociation from outer reality. On the contrary, it calls for a heightened attention towards one's surroundings while simultaneously reaffirming the importance of the notion of proprioception, the body's knowledge of its own depth, texture and placement, an awareness that in Charles Olson's writings determines "how to use oneself and on what." In the symmetrical environment of the 70-foot long cylindrical "Architectural Body" entitled "Ubiquitous Site" (1992-1994), now an essential part of the Nagi Museum of Contemporary Art in Japan, the central notion, once again, is the possibility for the proprioceptive self to "supplant identity" as the visitor who enters the symmetrically organized cylindrical building — having lost its balance and traditional bearings — is invited to "cast the little that remains of its identity as a person, outside itself," thereby coordinating with an "architectural body" that seems to exist both within and outside the bounds of subjectivity (since for Arakawa and Gins the body of a visitor cannot be separated from the space occupied by it).[29] Such a notion becomes directed towards the blurring of boundaries between traditional divisions between past, present and future, as well as between self and community ("'Beginning,' 'past,' 'future,' 'I,' 'me,' and 'you,'" the artists write, "are all words that have no place in this process. They are superfluous") and, ultimately, life and death as the avowed desire of the artists is to "escape the mortal condition."[30] At this stage, it has become obvious that Arakawa and Gins's projects have more affinities with philosophy and cognitive psychology than with any modern tradition of art and architecture. As Samira Kawash has remarked, both *The Mechanism of Meaning* and *Reversible Destiny Architecture* are conceived as experimental apparatuses or interactive technologies rather than as formal or aesthetic expressions."[31] "Medium and form," she concludes, "are secondary to a process of inquiry that is engaged in and carried out through the reader/viewer/participants/inhabitant's interactions with the painting, page, or spatial surround."[32]

Arakawa and Gins's attempts to abolish the basic categories and dualities that guide the subject's awareness of itself can be usefully compared with Baudrillard's *Symbolic Exchange and Death*, in which he lays the ground for a redefinition of contemporary social theory based on an analysis of symbolic exchange and its effects on the rituals of death. In

---

[27] In *Helen Keller or Arakawa* (1994), Madeline Gins quotes a "practical mystic" (p. 257), the Zen master Dogen, for whom the rational mind of scholars "fail[s] to understand the flowers of emptiness, because of their ignorance of emptiness" (p. 269). For the Zen Buddhist, the awareness of emptiness is facilitated by a capacity to cancel one's subjectivity in order to open oneself to new ways of contemplating our environment. Such a conception links up with what *The Mechanism of Meaning* describes as the "neutralization of subjectivity" (Arakawa and Gins, *Reversible*, p. 55), a process by which the subject divests itself from the most central beliefs conditioning our subjective modes of interpretation.

[28] Arakawa and Gins, p. 55.

[29] Arakawa and Gins, *Architectural Body* (Tuscaloosa: University of Alabama Press, 2002), p. 189.

[30] Arakawa and Gins, p. 189; interview with Charles Bernstein, *LineBreak* no. 13.

[31] Kawash, 'Bodies', p. 20.

[32] Kawash, pp. 20-21.

his chapter on "Political Economy and Death," Baudrillard argues that life and death and the way we relate to death largely depend on a "disjunctive code" that prevents us from thinking otherwise than by subscribing to such dichotomies as "mind and body, man and nature, the real and the non-real, birth and death."[33] In certain "primitive" societies, in which, according to Baudrillard, such a disjunction does not exist death is conceived of as part of the community's symbolic circulation, whereas in our contemporary Western societies the dead are no longer "beings with a full role to play, worthy partners in exchange." "Death," Baudrillard concludes, has become "a delinquency, and an incurable deviancy":

> There is an irreversible evolution from savage societies to our own: little by little, the dead cease to exist. They are thrown out of the group's symbolic circulation. [...] In the domestic intimacy of the cemetery, the first grouping remains in the heart of the village or town, becoming the first ghetto, prefiguring every future ghetto, but are thrown further and further from the center towards the periphery, finally having nowhere to go at all, as in the new town or the contemporary metropolis, where there are no longer any provisions for the dead, either in mental or in physical space.[34]

Baudrillard then proceeds to examine Robert Jaulin's anthropological study of ancestral initiation rites and Marcel Mauss' writings on the potlach (a Native American ceremonial festival involving the exchanging or destruction of gifts and counter-gifts) and concludes that those rites establish "a reciprocal relationship between the ancestors and the living."[35] In the "primitive" order described in Jaulin's *La Mort Sara*, for example, the group has to "swallow" the young initiation candidates, who "die 'symbolically' in order to be reborn":

> It is clear that the initiation consists in an exchange being established where there had been only a brute fact: they pass from natural, aleatory and irreversible death to a death that is given and received, and that is therefore reversible in the social exchange [...] At the same time the opposition between birth and death disappears: they can also be exchanged under the form of symbolic reversibility.[36]

It is not, Baudrillard writes, a matter of "staging a second birth to eclipse death." What is at stake in these initiation rites is the possibility for "the splitting of life and death" to be "conjured away" by the power of the "revolutionary" symbolic, which is defined as "neither a concept, an agency, nor a 'structure,' but an act of exchange and a social relation which puts an end to the real, which resolves the real, and, at the same time, puts an end to the opposition between the real and the imaginary," thereby suggesting "a possible reversibility of death in exchange" — a possibility confirmed by the exchange of gifts and countergifts in Mauss' analysis of potlach.[37] Baudrillard's reading of Sara initiation rites also interprets initiation as "the social nexus, the darkroom where birth and death stop being the terms of life and twist into one another again; not towards some mythical fusion, but [...] to turn the

---

[33]   Jean Baudrillard, *Symbolic Exchange and Death*, trans. by Iain Hamilton Grant (London: Sage Publications, 1993), p. 205.
[34]   Baudrillard, p. 126.
[35]   Baudrillard, p. 131.
[36]   Baudrillard, pp. 131; 132.
[37]   Baudrillard, pp. 132; 133; 147,

initiate into a real social being."[38] In *Helen Keller or Arakawa*, Madeline Gins also criticizes the Western world on account of its privileging of individualism over communality in a society encouraging what Baudrillard defines as the "extradition of the dead and the rupturing of a symbolic exchange with them."[39] She insists on the centrality of the "communal nature of self-consciousness" which is lacking in the non-East, "except among American Indians."[40] For Gins, as for Baudrillard, one way of counteracting the effects of the ghettoization of the dead is to search for a communal basis for conscious life established through a new social and architectural space. Gins and Arakawa's project for a "City without Graveyards" is one such space. Their more recent project for an *Isle of Reversible Destiny* which they hope to build on La Certosa, in Venice, stands as a labyrinth of manifold tentativeness "compris[ing] 365 gardens in which to observe one's actions and study how not to die."[41] The site will contain numerous "passageways and trenches" whose fluid structures, reversed repetitions and complicated symmetries contrast not only with the cemetery of San Michele but also, in the larger context of Venetian architecture, with the Palladian ideal of the building as an autonomous, socio-economic unit, closed unto its own circular and horizontal supremacy of being, and informed by the classical values and proportions of the Vitruvian canon.[42]

Poetic Reversibility

In the closing chapter of *Symbolic Exchange and Death*, Baudrillard designates the poetic as the supreme example of the principle of symbolic reversibility. Baudrillard's definition of the poetic is inspired by Saussure's "law of the coupling" according to which the principle of symmetry and repetition at work in Saturnian poetry results in the mutual annihilation of phonemes consumed by the "cycle of redoubling" which allows each vowel to be abolished by its "anagrammatic double."[43] Starting from the recognition that there is some analogy between the exchange of gifts and counter-gifts in ancestral cultures and the principle of the vowel and the counter-vowel in Saussure's study of Saturnian poetics, "or, in more general terms, between any given signifier and the anagrammatic double that cancels

---

38 Baudrillard, p. 132.

39 Gins, *Keller*, p. 127.

40 Ibid., p. 176.

41 Arakawa and Gins, *Reversible*, p. 257.

42 *Firmitas, commoditas* and *venustas*, suggesting firmness or permanence, comfort, and beauty (as an attribute of harmony and proportion), respectively.

43 Jean Starobinski, *Les Mots sous les mots* (Paris: Gallimard, 1971), pp. 195; 236. Saussure's "law of the coupling" posits that "a vowel has no right to figure within the Saturnine unless it has its counter-vowel in some other place in the verse [...] The result of this is that if the verse has an even number of syllables, the vowels couple up exactly, and must always have a remainder of zero, with an even total for each type of vowel." "The law of consonants," Saussure writes, "is identical, and no less strict: there is always an even number of any consonants whatever." Finally, the "Law of the Theme Word" states that "entire verses [are] anagrams of other preceding verses, however far off, in the text" so that "polyphonies visually reproduce, when the occasion arises, the syllables of an important word or name, whether they figure in the text or present themselves naturally to the mind through the context" (Starobinski, *Mots*, pp. 21; 28; 33).

it," Baudrillard develops a theory according to which that the poetic is a paroxistic form of symbolic exchange in which, to quote Julia Kristeva on "Poetry and Negativity," "logical laws of speech have been weakened, the subject dissolves and, in place of the sign, the clash of signifiers eliminating each other is instituted."[44]

For Baudrillard, this principle of poetic reversibility is applicable not only to Saussure's Saturnian verses but to modern poetry as a whole. Like Kristeva before him, he posits "the ambivalence of the poetic signified (and not its mere ambiguity)" as follows:

> it is concrete and general at the same time, it includes both (logical) affirmation and negation, it announces the simultaneity of the possible and the impossible; far from postulating the "concrete versus the general," it explodes this conceptual break: bivalent logic (0/1) is abolished by ambivalent logic ... The negativity of the poetic is a radical negativity bearing on the logic of judgment itself. Something "is" and is not what it is: a utopia (in the literal sense) of the signified. The thing's self-equivalence is volatilized. Thus the poetic signified is the space where "Non-Being intertwines with Being in a thoroughly disconcerting manner."[45]

But the antithetical sense Baudrillard and Kristeva regard as one of the central properties of poetry is by no means exclusively associated with poetic language — rather, poetry only foregrounds and systematizes an element of reversible ambivalence which is inherent in language itself. According to 19th century philologist Karl Abel, early Indo-European and Semitic languages have many words that mean one thing and also its opposite. The Ancient Egyptian word for strong ("ken"), for example, was also the word for "weak," and it was only by means of an additional sign or a gesture that one could distinguish the two sides of the antithesis. Abel's theories were later rediscovered by Freud, who, in his review of Abel's essay, "The Antithetical Sense of Primal Words," argues that "man has not been able to acquire even his oldest and simplest conceptions otherwise than in contrast with their opposites" and that it was only gradually that he "learnt to separate the two sides of the antithesis and think of the one without conscious comparison with the other."[46] Freud cites further examples of antithetical meanings, including the Latin word "altus" (meaning both "high" and "deep") and the German "Boden" (meaning both "attic" and "ground floor"), and eventually concludes with Abel's discovery that many words from the Aryan and Semitic languages originally could "reverse their sound as well as their sense" (the examples he cites include the pairs "Topf" [German for pot] and "pot"; "hurry" and "Ruhe" [German for rest]; "care" and its archaic near-synonym "reck."[47]

This principle of sonic and semantic, phonemic and morphemic, reversibility has some affinities with the inverted and modified symmetries of Gins and Arakawa's anagrammatic houses. More specifically, the reversible bipolarities that characterize *Twin House* and *Ubiquitous Site* appears as a three-dimensional conceptual extension of Arakawa's own concept of "cleaving" (itself an "antithetical" word, since it signifies both "to part or di-

---

[44]   Ibid., p. 236. Julia Kristeva, *Séméiotiké: Recherches pour une sémanalyse* (Paris: Seuil, 1969), p. 340.

[45]   Baudrillard, *Symbolic*, p. 219.

[46]   Sigmund Freud, 'The Antithetical Sense of Primal Words', trans. by Joan Riviere, *Collected Papers*, Vol. IV (London: Hogarth Press, 1957), p. 187.

[47]   Freud, p. 190. Here, I am indebted to Ben Watson's book, *Art, Class, and Cleavage*, which first drew my attention to Karl Abel's theories.

vide" and "to adhere closely"), a notion systematically and specifically explored in "Splitting of Meaning," the seventh section of *The Mechanism of Meaning*. In the panel entitled "This Is About to Split," a series of dots and pinheads point to basic "body-schemas" such as head, neck, thorax, arm, pelvis, forearm, hand, thigh, leg and foot (which George Lakoff has defined as elemental, apparently universal structures we automatically and unconsciously use to structure a mental image of a thing or scene perceived) are associated with words like "sky," "sun," "mountain" or "ship," thereby building unusual pairs of signifiers whose combination opens up new possibilities of meaning.[48] If the semantic junction between the printed and the handwritten words often remains "unnatural" (the main exception, of course, being the combinations created by "LEG/leg" and "shoes/FOOT"), a hierarchical pattern is reestablished by the corollary likeliness of body and landscape (the sky whose superior position in the landscape is associated with the HEAD, the NECK with the sun, etc.). Lastly, the juxtaposition of printed/stenciled and handwritten words is indicative of the uneasy interaction between the gestural and the mechanical in the act of naming and reproducing the real. The final reference to "moving property" is ambiguous. Does it serve as an additional reminder that the act of naming may result in the (mis-)appropriation of "moving" objects through language? Is it supposed to warn us against the danger of the reification and commodification of the painting or of the unnamed and unseen individual (the viewer?) that is doing the "talking" and the "walking" and may well eventually become a "moving property"? Or are the implications of this final punchline more positive in prefiguring the transformed self that emerges from the process of the "splitting of meaning"?

Other exercises in the cleaving of meaning include a panel instructing the viewer to "SAY one" and "THINK two" and the following post-Magrittean illustration of the reversibility of visual and verbal signs/bidirectional arrows — one is, once again, reminded of Mallarmé's paradoxical objects ("absent tombeau," "aboli bibelot") as well as Rosmarie Waldrop's more recent suggestion that poetry should strive for an "excluded middle" located between right and wrong (left and right, back and front, …), inscribed in the double aspect of the sign even as it attempts to deconstruct it.[49] The aim of such visual and verbal paradoxes is to encourage us to put the ambivalence of the (poetic) sign to direct use and extend it to how we can combat the irreversibility of our perception of space-time and our use of language by neutralizing the deadening effects of habit and repetition.

In the light of the architectural experiments described above, one can easily see that Arakawa and Gins's claim that their sites enact the "possibility of a nonmortal human life" is not to be taken in a metaphorical sense only.[50] The implications of this project, however, are left deliberately ambiguous by the artists themselves. Are reversible destiny sites providing "infinite quantities of spacetime necessary for living" liable to multiply their visi-

[48] Arakawa and Gins, *Reversible*, 77. George Lakoff, "Testing the Limits of Brain Plasticity. Or, Why Is There a Wall Down the Middle of the Tub?" In Arakawa and Gins, *Reversible Destiny*, p. 118.

[49] Arakawa and Gins, *Reversible*, pp. 77; 93. For a summary of Waldrop's conception of poetic language and its interaction with language of Western rationality, see her appendix to *The Lawn of Excluded Middle* (Providence: Tender Buttons, 1993).

[50] Arakawa and Gins, *Reversible*, p. 313.

tors' horizons and permit them to exist on different levels at once?[51] Is it a continuation of the modernist faith in the possibility of nonlinear time and, by extension, of a consciousness unfettered by the need to frame experience along a linear narrative line?[52] Are Gins and Arakawa merely positioning themselves against the deadening of the senses when they argue that "learning how not to die starts with learning how to live as a maximally invigorated sensorium"?[53] Should the suggestion that we should "[take] a stance against death" be metaphorically associated with the idea of "growing young" as a result of our "becoming increasingly able to field an ever greater number of possibilities"?[54] Or are architectural surrounds supposed to express the body's changing relationship with its environment/the universe in a way that would prolong itself beyond the death of a human being?

The answers to these questions matter less than the implication that our most fundamental and deeply-rooted notions of self as well as our understanding of how the world can be perceived and understood ought to be revised according to the recognition that "changing the conditions of perception changes perception itself, and changes what it means to be a person perceiving."[55] Looking at Arakawa and Gins's visual/verbal paradoxes and poetico-architectural sites one begins to understand how the mind and body can be fruitfully disoriented into producing an alternative/poetic subject that rejects the notion that we are completely bounded by the mechanisms that traditionally construct us. Only in such a way can their "postutopian" sites act as a motivating force for developing "less dying" subjects who refuse to take their linguistic and concrete environment for granted and would welcome an opportunity to systematically allow themselves to restructure their lives and aspirations. In the same way as some of the most interesting poets of this century have tended to reject traditional conceptions of poetry as a sentimentalized utterance, dedicated to providing lyrical comfort and aesthetic delight, Arakawa and Gins's reversible destiny rejects the notion that architecture should be designed to (merely) provide convenience, safety and stability. They argue, instead, for a radical redefinition of what constitutes the self and its experience of time and space, one which is grounded in the necessity to theorize the subject as body, rather than just as a model of interiority.

---

[51] Ibid., p. 302. Commenting on the "doubling of horizons" which results from such projects as the "Twin House" and the "Ubiquitous Site House," Arakawa has declared that "by creating a second horizon, or better yet many more, we can be released from the out-of-date moral values or obsolete structures of common sense that accumulate on the ground-surface we normally exist on. We'd be truly free to develop potentially more fruitful and expansive moral values." Insisting on the necessity for his "landing sites" to transcend the methods and conditions of the philosophical, poetic and the aesthetic and account more completely for the transformations that occur in the apprehension and configuration of volumes, colors, weights and spaces, he adds: "Poets and philosophers have said much about the possibility of such a world. But theirs is a world of words and ideas without shape or color or weight. Theirs is a fiction, no matter how wonderful. Painting turns out to be only such a fictional world, too" (*Reversible*, pp. 32-33). See also Gins and Arakawa's response to Jean-François Lyotard in *Reversible Destiny* and their definition of "growing young" as "becoming increasingly able to field an ever greater number of possibilities" (p. 11).

[52] See Jean-François Lyotard's suggestion that Reversible Architecture might neutralize "the distribution of time between beginning and end" (Arakawa and Gins, *Reversible*, p. 11).

[53] Arakawa and Gins, p. 241.

[54] Arakawa and Gins, pp. 299; 11.

[55] Kawash, 'Bodies', p. 23.

In his essay entitled "Every Which Way but Loose," Charles Bernstein writes that "the idea that genres, if not the aesthetic itself, is a barrier to perceptual transformation connects the projects of Arakawa and Gins and Blake to a range of practitioners from Mallarmé and Williams to Duchamp and Cage, all of whose antifoundational investigations have a visual and verbal component." "In retrospect," he adds, "we might say that these artists do not so much abolish the aesthetic as extend and transform it, partly because the boundaries of the aesthetic, our willingness or ability to see something as a work of art are surprisingly mobile. [...] But if aesthetic is not a static category, then it may be possible for the 'same' object to be viewed, alternately, as aesthetic and not aesthetic. In the case of Reversible Destiny, the goal is neither to aestheticize the nonaesthetic or to deaestheticize the aesthetic but rather to create a zone that is no longer subject to this oscillation." As we know, this pendulum movement between the aesthetic and the nonaesthetic has been a recurrent concern in the history of the contemporary avant-garde. The happenings, ready-mades and spectaculars of the revolutionary avant-garde merged art into life even as they proclaimed the destruction of art as art in an act of joyful self-destruction. Postmodern art, after abolishing traditional separations between high and low and positing the relativity and constructedness of the real, rejected art in favor of the glamorous surfaces of commodity culture or of the use of concepts as material. Instead of prolonging the movement of the pendulum that swings between such polarities as art and life, self and world, Gins and Arakawa's main concern is with developing an aesthetic that would encompass different systems, use-values and activities that continue to be kept separate by most avant-garde artists. At a time when Arakawa and Gins's conceptual works and thought experiments are beginning to extend into the domain of city planning (several reversible destiny sites have already been developed in Japan), reversible destiny suggests that 21st century poetics will probably have to embrace much more than just prosody, genres, and forms, or even literary criticism per se, and encompass the consideration of not just form and content but also of cognitive psychology, art, experimental psychology, linguistics, architecture, and the mechanisms of the perceiving body. Only by enlarging the notion of "poetics" to accommodate for this larger compendium of methods can we truly hope to come to terms with works that support the process of this aesthetic revolution. Such an as yet unformed field of study may soon prove to be one of the forming blanks out of which 21st century aesthetics and poetics will emerge.

Steve McCaffery

Parapoetics and the Architectural Leap

This paper is divided into three uneven sections. The opening two are short, the first offers a "soft" manifesto-like exposition of parapoetics; the second discusses a related matter: the paralogicality of the frame. The final section comprises a *part mapping of* and a few *suggestions toward* areas of potential parapoetic investigation. Judged on the normative criteria for academic papers it is premature, partial at best and thoroughly inconclusive. Seen as attempting to realize a parapoetics intervention it will be judged to be an utterly abortive attempt — and quite correctly so. However, as the speculative and tentative tenor of the first part indicates, the third part is a probe into uncertainties and unnowns. A notable absence is any lengthy discussion of the important architectural contributions of the Situationists. That discussion is planned for a subsequent article.

I. Parapoetics

Foucault reminds us that epistemic rupture, in radical breaks within power-knowledge machines precipitate "endings." By contrast, the Deleuzian dynamic of "becoming" offers a kinetic, projective model. Becomings inflect trajectories and the geographic, offering "orientations, directions, entries and exits. [...] [with] no terminus from which you set out, none which you arrive at. Nor are there two terms, which are exchanged. [...] Becomings are not phenomena of imitation or assimilation, but of a double capture, of non-parallel evolution [...]."[1] We are all heirs to this intimate inheritance of becoming — hardly an abyss and hardly the space of some grandiose Icarus effect — but a precise and fecund topological dynamic nonetheless. Unlike endings, becomings temporarily occupy an interstice; they are always realized in the between, in an uncertain transitivity and a transient inscription that for some might register an angst, for others the interstitial sublime.

The death God, the end of Man, the end of theory, the death of poetry, the death of the subject, the death of art, courtesy of Hegel, the death of man courtesy of Foucault, the death of Marxism courtesy of North American Departments of English, the end of narrative courtesy my friend with a smile like those horses in Picasso's Guernica. Having survived a tedious catena of such mortifications and eschatologies I'll not add to the list the death of poetics. Crisis is a notion frequently complicit with endings and I sense no crisis in poetics but do note complacency in matters of potentiality and scale. Accordingly I urge a shift into a purposefully fuzzy and still virtual discipline I call parapoetics. Similar to David Carroll's notion of the paraesthetic, the term denotes a critical responsibility to approach poetry through its relation to extra-poetic domains. To borrow Carroll's own description, it's figured as "something like [a poetics] turned against itself [...] a faulty, irregular, disordered, improper [poetics] — one not content to remain within the area defined by the [poetic]."[2] Celan believed that naming occurs in the depth of Language and yet to accord to naming a definitional power is to end a being as becoming. Dr. Johnson warns that to "circumscribe

---

[1]   Gilles Deleuze and Félix Guattari, *What is Philosophy?*, trans. by Hugh Tomlinson and Graham Burchell (New York: Columbia University Press, 1994), p. 2.

[2]   David Carroll, *Paraesthetics: Foucault, Lyotard, Derrida* (New York: Methuen, 1987), p. xiv.

poetry by definition will only show the narrowness of the definer," a sentiment endorsed by Schlegel in his oxymoronic definition of romantic poetry as poetry that can't be defined.[3] Similarly, I want to avoid a specific predetermination of what constitutes parapoetics and leave it suspended as a non-determined concept and thereby allow critical desire to put mastery at risk. Abandoning the pursuit of theoretical dogmatism it will require that a negative capability be applied within the pernicious doublet Foucault concatenates as power — knowledge.

The *Concise Oxford Dictionary* offers numerous meanings for the prefix *para*: 1. beside. 2. beyond. 3. a modification. 4. a diametrically opposite relation. 5. a form of protection or warding off. The larger OED adds further variations to these seemingly contradictory senses that strike me as particularly attractive to poetic practice:

> In composition it has the same senses, with such cognate adverbial ones as "to one side, aside, amiss, faulty, irregular, disordered, improper, wrong": also expressing subsidiary relation, alteration, perversion, simulation, etc.

What's appealing in "para" is its evasion of the janiformity of a *post-* whose consequences, Derrida adverts, involve "a surrender to the historicist urge."[4] Among other things, *para* provokes a shift from temporal to spatial conceptualization and positioning. Moreover the lateral adjacency of "beside" offers a multiplicity of satellitic invocations: the friend, neighbor, relative, lover, guide, witness and judge. *Beside* also is between, interstitial and intervalic, as well as extra, outside. Accordingly I'll be speaking more about the place of parapoetics than its ontology, on where it is and can be, than on what it is. Purposefully left undefined, the important step is to inscribe and activate its forces. Redirecting Derrida's call to architecture I write, "Let us never forget there is a poetics of poetics" and that poetics is beside poetics.[5] Heuristic rather than foundational, parapoetic desire does not seek to adumbrate upon the specificity of a discipline but rather to probe the fungibility and centrifugality always latent within the ontologically or intellectually discrete. As such it takes its place within the anti-Kantian lineage that denies the specificity of art and also offers a counter-move within the current new "anxiety" of specialization rather than influence. Operating as a probe into uncertainties and as a force of disruption among stability, it aims to transform a total unity into multiplicity. Foucault and Blanchot encourage the "thinking of the outside" as a critical practice of transgression, one that refuses the stability of alterity while at the same time avoiding the incorporating move to totality. Parapoetics demands that singular disciplines or practices remove themselves in order to achieve a self-

---

3   Samuel Johnson, 'Preface to Pope', in *Prefaces, Biographical and Critical to the Works of the English Poets*, Vol. 7 (London: C. Bathurst, J. Buckland, W. Strahan et al, 1781), p. 331.

4   "The *post-s* and *posters* which proliferate today (poststructuralism, postmodernism, etc.) still surrender to the historicist urge. Everything marks an era, even the decentering of the subject: post humanism. It is as if one again wished to put a linear succession in order, to periodize, to distinguish before and after, to limit the risks of reversibility or repetition, transformation or permutation: an ideology of progress" (Jacques Derrida, 'Pont de Folie – Maintenant L'Architecture', in *Rethinking Architecture: A Reader in Cultural Theory*, ed. by Neil Leach [London and New York: Routledge, 1997], p. 324).

5   Cf. Derrida, 326.

comprehension in a manner that avoids a transcendental installation of the theoretical attitude, and submit to a voluntary disability. Assuming the burden of this kind of thinking, parapoetics works against the promulgation of any discursive formation as a complete and closed system and relatedly seeks to go beyond the discretion of Deleuze's "fabulation of a discipline to come."

Free from a fixed definition it's also emancipated from a predetermined destination, and able to install itself within the dialectical tensions and determinants of any number of target fields. Rather than serving as the critical mode of poetics, a species of self-policing and of external probing, parapoetics signals a shift in critical desire away from the poem as such toward other disciplines and discourses. Working between the seams and cracks consequent to the inevitable play between discourses, upon and without the hyphenated space of power-knowledge, parapoetics adopts more a contaminatory than a combative stance, marbling the smooth and certain propositional plane of discourse and ideas. Parapoetics does not support disciplinary cross-dressing and is not to be deposited in other disciplines as some governing metatheory. Deracinated and detached from poetics proper, and maintaining its distance from any discourse that seeks to master or explain, it can be likened to a hesitation within a caesura. For these reasons parapoetics will always be both a lot more and a little less than poetics.

II. The Frame-Up

> *All movements have direction. But why just one direction and not several? Movements can produce breakouts and new connections.*[6]

Ronald Aronson encourages us to think of theory as a tool not a framework and much of Derrida's *The Truth in Paining* explores the philosophical intricacies of working and engaging the frame.[7] Frames both individuate and recontextualize and their ultimate power is cartographic. We see the acute stakes of framing in our current geopolitical and sexual climates. On one hand the melting of national boundaries and proactive deframings under the pressure of economic ideologies in Europe and North America (NAFTA and the EEC), and on the other a Balkanization of Europe and Africa from political and ethnic pressures to maximize territorial coding. The struggle toward legal ratification of same-sex marriages is a debate fought out in a judicial theatre and hinges on the right to set up a frame within an existing frame.

Framing, of course, is the prime culprit in transforming *objects as such* into objects *of* theory, thereby guaranteeing a pacification of the chosen object field and the impossibility of the latter modifying the theoretic domain. For this reason theoretical endeavor is antipathetic to empiricism whose method runs counter to such framing. Despite theory-frames being designed to ensure a unilateral flow of power sufficient to preserve the integrity of its method, the logic of the frame moves against settled internal preservation. French architect

---

[6]   Yago Conde, *Architecture of the Indeterminacy*, trans. by Paul Hammond (Barcelona: Actar, 2000), p. 251.

[7]   Ronald Aronson, *After Marxism* (New York: The Guildford Press, 1995), p. 227.

Bernard Cache suggests that "the structure of the modern frame offers a certain amount of play. [...] The rigid parts of the frame still retain a certain geometry, but their articulation is mobile and their equilibrium results from the play of tensions that run through the system as a whole."[8] Frames are caught up in a contradictory logic in so much as the boundaries they set out to demarcate are constantly threatened by external elements and forces. Rather than preservers of integrity frames are conduits facilitating a promiscuous transit of forces from inside out and from outside in; they organize a contradictory yet mutual relation of an exterior to an interior that, like Foucauldian thresholds, construct an untenable divide between incompatible forces struggling for dominance. Derrida only pragmatizes this observation in his suggestion to "work the frame" as both boundary and conduit. Deleuze and Guattari emphasize the omniprobability of the frame reversing its function and serving to deframe in a process by which what is preserved internally finds a relationship to something external in a way that opens it up to the outside.[9]

The paralogicality of the frame bears comparison to the nature of dissipative structures, defined and investigated in the field of nonlinear thermodynamics by Ilya Prigogine and Isabelle Stengers. Dissipative structures are "forms of supermolecular organization requiring the continuous dissipation of energy and matter) through the increase of small random fluctuations."[10] The theory of dissipative structures is emerging as a formative notion in numerous disciplines, provoking Fernández-Galiano to consider it "the new scientific paradigm of the age."[11] Both buildings and the city can be conceived as open thermodynamic systems dependent for their existence on nutritional elements and energy flows. As Prigogine and Stengers observe in a cell or a city alike, we find "that these systems are not only open but live on their openness, nourishing themselves with the flows of matter and energy reaching them from the outside world [...]. [T]he city and the cell quickly die when separated from their mediums, for they are part of the worlds that nourish them and constitute a sort of local and unique incarnation of the flows that never cease to transform."[12] Likewise, both cell and city require the constant dissipation of energy, be it in the form of waste produce or the movement of populous, in a constant spreading beyond frames and boundaries. In sharp contrast to the practice of comparative poetics outlined by Earl Miner, parapoetics does not work to constitute and defend the discrete frame of the poem, but rather explore how the frame can be challenged to open up a poetics without borders.

---

[8]   Bernard Cache, *Earth Moves*, trans. by Anne Boyman and Michael Speaks (Cambridge: The MIT Press, 1995), pp. 108-9.

[9]   Cf. Deleuze and Guattari, *What*, p. 187.

[10]   Luis Fernández-Galiano, *Fire and Memory: On Architecture and Energy*, trans. by Gina Cariño (Cambridge: The MIT Pres, 2000), p. 114.

[11]   Fernández-Galiano, p. 114.

[12]   Fernández-Galiano, p. 79.

III. The Architectural Leap

> *The language revising its own architectures is the cloud*
> *palace and drift of your desire.*
> Robert Duncan

Stein's call to "act as if there was no use in a center" is cannily prophetic of contemporary cultural desires, and in current poetics the ideas of rupture and multiplicity seem more attractive than the one of continuity. Derrida leaves "what is writing" an open question and the same is required of poetics. Feeling that contemporary poetics has reached an impasse in *exclusively* poetic territories, I wish to propose a leap or "becoming" toward both urban texture and architectural theory as initial parapoetic domains. An exclusive focus on the poem-as-such severely curtails the potential critical range of poetics, and for the latter to maintain a vital critical function then a radical readjustment of its trajectories seems required; a move Arakawa and Madeline Gins refer to as the "poetic leap." The purpose of this leap isn't simply to obtain knowledge or display it in a different discipline, nor to plunder a terrain for concepts and ideas useful to one's own practice. The architectural jump involves *the knowledge of how and when to delay knowing*; how to be active in a state of suspended certainty. As Koestler puts it "The act of creation is forgetting, at the proper moment, what we know." Via the poetic leap one is no longer beside but elsewhere. In the spirit of Bataille's oxymoronic formulation (that to love poetry one must hate poetry) the initial poetic leap will be a turn against its traditional object field and detach poetics from poematics. With explorations beyond affinities and analogies, parapoetics will situate interstitially, the way punctuation falls *between* meaning. Circumscribed within the broad thematics of disciplines and movings, parapoetics will focus on the interval where contamination, paralogicality, uncertainty, and misprision precipitate discovery, unforeseen collaboration and contestation. As regards specific dynamics, in parapoetic logic, an entrance is the continuation of an exit by other means. And who knows, perhaps poetics after the postmodern might well be a parapoetics inside it.

Disciplines, like structures and language, are simultaneously closed and open, containing heterogeneity within a frame of the homogenous. To insist on the specificity of both the poetic and the architectural is to seriously limit both research and the critico-creative enterprise inside, between, and across the two. "[W]hy should "literature" [*or* architecture] still designate that which already breaks away from literature — away from what has always been conceived and signified under that name — or that which, not merely escaping literature, [*or* architecture,] implacably destroys it?"[13] To repeat a well-known claim of Derrida's: "A writing that refers back only to itself carries us at the same time, indefinitely and systematically, to some other writing."[14] Beyond a critical engagement with this heterogeneity within the so-called homogenous is an urgent need to shift not the mode but the target of poetics' transitivity.

---

[13] Jacques Derrida, *Dissemination*, trans. by Barbara Johnson (Chicago: University Press, 1981), p. 3.
[14] Derrida, p. 202.

Aaron Betsky has emerged as the popular theorist of that decentralization condition and dissolution known as sprawl. Sprawl shatters the tense logic of the frame. Not only is it an architectural and urban condition, sprawl is the condition of modernity. Pollution is sprawl, contemporary knowledge is sprawl. Sprawl is the authentic landscape of the contemporary but enters painting as early as Turner. Sprawl is the given condition not the cursed share of architecture. Betsky insists that "The issue is not how to stop sprawl but how to use its composition, its nodes and its leaky spaces to create a kind of architecture."[15] As a blotting or formless spreading out from strategic nodes — malls, airports, etc. — sprawl constitutes both the dematerialization of physical structures and modernity's urban given. It registers the contemporary city's inclination to heterology and centrifuge whose resonant inclination is to deframe. Betsky's name for this formless dystopia is exurbia "where human forms meld into the remains of nature and where order becomes so thin that we recognize its most basic components." For Betsky urban sprawl may even provide a redemptive dimension that takes us "away from the high-rise tendencies of the city [and puts] us back on earth where we confront the realities of ground and weather." While declining the temptation to dangle such redemptive carrots I would insist however, that in maintaining parapoetics as a deliberately non-determined concept, we advocate a certain conceptual and creative sprawl.

Why the leap into architecture? From "stanza" to the "prison-house of language" architecture is a dominant figure within the very formulation of the linguistic. Architectural metaphors haunt writing to a degree sufficient to cause us to question a merely benign metaphoric presence. One of Heidegger's lasting insight is into how both language and architecture ground us in the world. In architecture, as in language, man dwells (poetically or not) whether in open mobility or confinement. "We appear to ourselves only through an experience of spacing which is already marked by architecture."[16] Heidegger and Derrida alike suggest that prior to becoming social subjects we are all architectural bodies.[17] However, to Derrida's grammatological conception of architecture as "a writing of space, a mode of spacing which makes a place for events" the qualification needs to be annexed that architecture too is the materialized conception of dwelling and that dwelling is fundamentally a relation of ontology to spaces.[18] In that sense it serves to return being to its problems by way of *oikos* rather than *poeisis*. And if Bachelard is correct when claiming that all inhabited space bears the essence of the notion of home, then the link between reading and dwelling appears to be far from a strained analogy.

The myth of Babel implicates the two distinct phenomena of architecture and human speech, from which has developed an enduring complicity. The metaphoric saturation of architectural terms in other discourses (including both philosophy and literature) is well known: the Prison House of Language, deconstruction, the poem's fabric, foundation, etc. Derrida claims the architectural metaphor of ground to be the core of philosophy.[19] But beyond a metaphoric presence, architecture has consistently offered writing a constructive

[15] Aaron Betsky, *Architecture Must Burn* (Corte Madera, CA: Gingko Press, 2000), n. p.

[16] Derrida, 'Point', p. 324.

[17] Cf. Arakawa and Gins, *Architectural Body* (Tuscaloosa: U. of Alabama Press, 2002).

[18] Arakawa and Gins.

[19] Peter Eisenman and Jacques Derrida, *Chora L Works*, ed. by Jeffrey Kipnis and Thomas Leeser (New York: The Monacelli Press, 1997), p. 105.

model and, though hardly sister arts, architecture's intimate relation to the literary is historically tangible, even down to its grammatological contours.[20] Architecture provides the formal model for Saint Teresa's *Interior Castle*, Jeremy Taylor's *Rules and Exercises for Holy Dying* (figured in the Preface as a tour through the rooms of a charnel-house), George Herbert's *The Temple* and Christopher Harvey's *The Synagogue*. The arguments of Donne's magnificent sermon "Death's Duel" are built around the three prime architectural supports of foundation, buttress and contignation. "The foundations suffer them not to sink, the buttresses suffer them not to swerve, and the contignations and knitting suffers them not to cleave."[21] In his 1850 Advertisement to *The Prelude* Wordsworth recalls his conception in 1814 of the relation of his two earlier poems, *The Excursion* and *The Recluse*, in architectural terms that recall Herbert. "[T]he two works have that relation to each other [...] as the Antechapel has to the body of a Gothic Church." Even his minor pieces when collected and "properly arranged, will be found by the attentive reader to have such connection with the main work as may give them claim to be likened to the little cells, oratories and sepulchral recesses, ordinarily included in those edifices." More recently, Ronald Johnson's long poem *ARK* adopts as its formal model "a kind of *naif* architecture on the lines of the Facteur Cheval's Ideal Palace, Simon Rodia's Watts Towers, or Ramond Isidore's mosaic house in the shade of Chartres" with Johnson's earlier poem, *Radi os*, a selected textual deletion of *Paradise Lost*, envisaged as the final and one hundredth book of *ARK* and "conceived as a kind of Dymaxion Dome over the whole."[22] (Mark Scroggins elaborates on *ARK*'s architectonic features: "[Johnson] calls his poem a 'model for a monument.' And its three major divisions reflect this spatial metaphor: 33 sections of 'Foundations,' 3 of 'Spires,' and 33 of 'Ramparts.' *ARK*, in turn, was to have been a 'dome' over the whole, a crowning and covering shell like that over Monticello, the U.S. Capitol, or the Roman Pantheon. The poem, then, is conceived of as in some sense a literal object, a literal architecture."[23] Dante, in *De vulgari eloquentia* II. 9 offers a distinction between stanza (literally "room") and canzone that illustrates the presidential status of architectural thinking:

> And here one must know that this term (*stanza*) has been chosen for technical reasons exclusively, so that what contains the entire art of the canzone should be called *stanza*, that is a capacious dwelling or receptacle

[20] B. L. Ullman draws attention to a canny congruity between Gothic architecture and its corresponding scripts. Developing out of the earlier Carolingian form and embracing especially the "picket fence" effect of Merovingian, the main features of Gothic script are angularity and broken lines (*fraktura*); the replacement of circular stress by a polygrammic one; extreme condensation and letter-fusions (called *textura*); standard heavy shading becomes; a marked increase in abbreviations and embellishments increase e. g. hooks, hair lines and marginal pen flourishes (B. L. Ullman, *Ancient Writing and its Influences* [Cambridge: The MIT Press, 1969], pp. 118-25).

[21] John Donne, *Devotions upon Emergent Occasions together with Death's Duel* (Ann Arbor: University of Michigan Press, 1959), p. 165.

[22] Ronald Johnson, *ARK* (Alberquerque, N. M.: Living Batch, 1996), pp. 56; 50; 56.

[23] Mark Scroggins, *Louis Zukofsky and the Poetry of Knowledge* (Tuscaloosa: University of Alabama Press, 1998), p. 295.

for the entire craft. For just as the canzone is the container (literally lap or womb) of the entire thought, so the stanza enfolds its entire technique.[24]

The interrogative crux structuring the entirety of Augustine's *Confessions* (a book that frequently addresses the infinite as a locus) is a *temporal* problem articulated as an architectural issue of impossible housing. I call on you, Lord, to you the Infinite to come and inhabit me, I who am but finite. Mark Z. Danielewski takes up this same impossibility in his recent novel *House of Leaves* where the house on Ash Tree Lane is bigger on the inside than it is on the outside.

For its part, the materiality of language has provided an abundance of architectural possibilities. The dramatic and decorative possibilities of the letter shape as an interior space functions as the basic premise of the Medieval "inhabited" initial, but Johann David Steingruber brings about a more complex fusion of function and the fantastic in his *Architectural Alphabet* of 1773. The thirty-three plates reveal formidable achievement and show patently feasible functional designs. Steingruber's quintessentially Baroque wit is retained as a trace element in Steven Holl's investigation into the intimate congruence of certain letterforms and architectural design in relation to context and urban syntax.[25]

Offering an attractive alternative to Bloom's anxiety of influence, Viktor Shklovsky argues for a deflection of influence. Put simply, the theory advances that artistic or disciplinary influence is transmitted not in an immediate and direct line within the same discipline, but in an entirely different domain. The transmission of artistic and cultural influence travels like the knight's move in chess, not from fathers to sons but from uncles and aunts to nieces and nephews.[26] A recent example is Language Writing's influence on musicology seen in Brian Ferneyhough's embrace of disjunction in his New Complexionism. Rather than literary continuity via canon and hierarchy why not a deflectional move to geography, or architecture? (It's the trail of the transmission out of its current site that is important). So in the virtual interrelations between poetics and architecture along a Shklovskian model, we might adopt an architectural configuration and rethink the concept of a poetic movement, and poetic practice in general, as the construction of a project in relation to a chosen program, itself relating to an actual preexisting site. Additionally, the programmatic ideology of architecture facilitates rethinking that socio-ontological problematic complex named "community" through the architectural notion of "site." Site as locus and topos has a fecund, aristocratic history stretching far back beyond

---

[24]   Quoted in Giorgio Agamben, *Stanzas: Word and Phantasm in Western Culture*, trans. by Ronald L. Martinez (Minneapolis: University of Minnesota Press, 1993), p. vii.

[25]   See Steven Holl, *The Alphabet City. Pamphlet Architecture # 5* (Princeton: Princeton University Press, 1980); Holl who provides several examples of "E, H, O, B, L, U, T, X" and "H" shaped buldings and grid blocks. Of particularly note are Albert Kahn's 1921. General Motors Building, Detroit, designed as three interlocking and partly superimposed "H" types, and Benjamin Marshall's "X" shaped Edgewater Beach Apartments in Chicago. Exploration into the analogical possibilities of letter-forms and their composition out of a multitude of different beings and objects has a lengthy historical precedent. See for instance the rich gatherings contained in Hugues Demeude, *The Animated Alphabet*, trans. by Ruth Sharman (London: Thames and Hudson, 1996), and Massin, *Letter and Image*, trans. by Caroline Hillier and Vivienne Menkes (New York: Van Nostrand Reinhold, 1970).

[26]   Conde, *Architecture*, p. 195.

Olson through the *genius locus* to Aristotle's claim that "place is something, but it also has a certain power."[27] Bernard Cache's Deleuzean-informed architecture lets poetics abandon the otiose binary of form and content and take up the triplet of frame, vector and inflection. Cache's complex theorizing on the status of the image warrants careful scrutiny and perhaps, additionally, a bold application in *poesis*. Similarly, it might be asked: how would catachresis find an architectural realization, or equally, an axonometric method in poetry?

Perhaps then we can learn more about the discourse of the poem by examining it from architecture's alterior position, and through a purposeful displacement of poetics into architecture. The dialogue between these two practices occurs as much within, as between, each other, and the integrity of both practices should be risked. Parapoetic strategy seeks out not what is confluential but also conflictual in these two practices, as well as what each is displacing and becoming. Contemporary architecture shows a cartographic caution around establishing boundaries and domains. Indeed, it is coming to understand that discrete disciplinary issues can't all be raised in architecture itself, (involving, among other things, the broader philosophic issues of ontology, presence, history, topos, memory and mimesis); there are additionally the wider socio-political issues of urbanism, the city, and context, and perhaps most paramount, a relation to human bodies, as well as the broader matters of co-ordination, material, and scale, and the relation of interiority and exteriority.

Bernard Tschumi is not alone in stressing the conceptual nature of architecture as its paramount purpose. Tschumi compares it to Lacanian psychoanalysis whose goal is not curative and the patient's recovery occurring as a felicitous indirect effect: "To make buildings that work and make people happy is not [the] goal of architecture but, of course, a welcome side effect."[28] I currently concur, however, with Robin Evans in seeing architecture as the construction of the preconditions that govern the way bodies occupy and negotiate space — a credo not far removed from Yago Conde's claim that "The habitual exclusion of the body and its experiences of any discourse on the logic of form would be instances of the lack of any intertextual impulse."[29] Architecture is a form of action centering on users and the key question of architectural form is a question of architecture's relation to the scale and matter of human freedom.

However, having said that I have to admit that the question of what "is" architecture has become much more difficult to answer in recent times. Traditionally, architects are subject to the same constraints as a Poet Laureate. Forced into a species contextual bricolage as a compromise formation, their profitable work is commissioned construction within predetermined spaces and for the most part within fixed, urban, and spatial exigencies. Owing to the governing economy of commission the vast majority of architectural projects remain conceptual. With the rise of paper and information architecture in the 1960s and subsequently virtual architecture, the practice was suddenly liberated from the binding functionalist mandates and found itself free to investigate numerous theoretical issues. As a conse-

---

[27] *Physics* 4.1.2086, quoted in Georges Didi-Huberman, *Fran Angelico: Disemblance and Figuration*, trans. by Jane Marie Todd (Chicago: University of Chicago Press, 1995), p. 18.

[28] Berard Tschumi, *Architecture and Disjuncture* (MIT Press: Cambridge MA., 1998), p. 267.

[29] Conde, *Architecture*, p. 197. See 'Towards Anarchitecture', in *Translations from Drawing to Building and Other Essays*, ed. by Robert Evans (Cambridge: The MIT Press, 1997), pp. 11-33.

quence, contemporary architectural theorizing emerges not as a self-certain or consensual discourse but as a vibrant metamorphic terrain of dispute. In Solà-Morales's estimate "At the present time, [architectural] criticism resembles hand-to-hand combat: a contest between information seeking public recognition and the power of collective sanction vested in those supposedly able to bestow it."[30] The impact of philosophy on recent architectural thinking has been consequential, precipitating both attempts at application and actual collaborations.[31] As early as 1970 Robin Evans envisioned an *anarchitecture* conceived to function as the tectonic of non-control and in 1973 architectural historian Manfredo Tafuri proclaimed "from now on form is not sought outside of chaos; it is sought within it."[32] Much contemporary architecture, like performance, seems to challenge its seemingly inescapable parousial condition by attempts to destabilize presence and orientation. Solà-Morales contrasts effectively the traditional locus of stability, durability and memory with the contemporary locus of event:

---

[30]   Ignasi de Solà-Morales, *Differences: Topographies of Contemporary Architecture*, trans. by Graham Thompson and ed. by Sarah Whiting (Cambridge: MIT Press, 1997), p. 138.

[31]   Derrida's perdurable challenge to architectural practice is to have introduced the impossible into architectural practice via an insinuant philosopheme: the Platonic *Chora*. His architectural collaboration with Peter Eisenman on the Parc la Villette starts with a lengthy reflection by Derrida on *chora*, an intractable concept found in Plato's *Timaeus*. Although *chora* "figures the place of inscription of *all that is marked on the world*," it is a pre-originary "place without space, before space and time" (Eisenmann, *Chora*, pp. 22, 91). The whole direction of the project moves far beyond the paradoxical origins that Harbison senses in Louis Kahn's Unitarian Church in Rochester, where the architecture gives the sense of "reaching back to early forms which precede anything known to us" (Robert Harbison, *Thirteen Ways: Theoretical Investigations in Architecture* [Cambridge: The MIT Pres, 1997], p. 11). Working to problematize the clear distinction between sensible and intelligible *chora* is a situational space beyond all normative notions of place, and responsible for situating the variant logics of exclusion and inclusion, while remaining beyond the laws its situates. Despite "giving place" *chora* (being neither a donor-subject nor a support or origin) does not give place in the manner of an *es gibt*. Derrida calls *chora* a paralogical and metalogical super-oscillation (Eisenman, *Chora*, p. 15) operating between and above the oscillations of a double exclusion (neither-nor) and of the participational (both this and that). With the sum of its negative features (non-ontological, neither a void nor an interval, nor a determined place, a something which is not a thing, a reference without a referent, without a self-identity, and incapable of representation other than negatively), it is not surprising that *chora* does not provide the security of architectural ground or a base. It is not that *chora* is absence or the presence of absence, as Eisenman at one point seems to believe, but rather that *chora* remains conceptually intractable and unsayable. Despite Derrida's avowal "that non-representable space could [give] the receiver, the visitor, the possibility of thinking about architecture" (Eisenmann, *Chora*, p. 35), one is still prompted to ask what factor or factors rendered the Parc de la Villette a collaborative failure? The inability to translate deconstruction into architectural thinking and practice? An initially ill-conceived philosophemic contribution on Derrida's part? The patent failure of his collaboration with Eisenman on this project, a project characterized by Derrida's reticence and Eisenman's consistent misprisions, misapplications and refusals to allow the philosopher's contribution to affect the architect's designs, stands as both a warning and a challenge to paracritical thinking. The entire collaboration can be found in Eisenman. Both Cache and Solà-Morales demonstrate the impact of Deleuze's thinking on architecture.

[32]   Robin Evans, *Translations from Drawing to Building and Other Essays* (Cambridge: The MIT Press, 1997), pp. 11-33; Manfredo Tafuri, *Architecture and Utopia: Design and Capitalist Development*, trans. Barbara Luigia La Penta (Cambridge: The MIT Press, 1976), p. 96. Inflecting a related sentiment architect Nigel Coates refers to the "richly stimulating chaos" brought on by the emergent forms of techno-media and communications (Johnathan Glancey, *Nigel Coates: Body Buildings and City Scapes* (New York: Watson Gupthill, 1999), p. 16.

The places of present-day architecture cannot repeat the permanences produced by the force of the Vitruvian *firmitas*. The effects of duration, stability, and defiance of time's passing are now irrelevant. The idea of place as the cultivation and maintenance of the essential and the profound, of a genius loci, is no longer credible [...]. From a thousand different sites the production of place continues to be possible. Not as the revelation of something existing in permanence, but as the production of an event[33]

Sentiments echoed in Cache's tenet that "if the expression 'genius loci' [*sic*] has a meaning, it lies in the capacity of this 'genius' to be smart enough to allow for the transformation or transit from one identity to another."[34] The works and proposals of Peter Eisenman, Koop Himmelblau, Nigel Coates, and Bernard Tschumi appear extremely provocative in this area. Architecture's traditional investment in functionality include, as its central desiderata, safety, stability, permanence, control, anesthesia, consumption, and comfort. All are called into question as requisite elements by the diverse works of Archigram, Daniel Libeskin, the late John Hejduk, and Zaha Hadid.[35] Indeed, early in 2001, the radical procedural architects Gins and Arakawa abandoned architecture for their newly formed practice of *Bioscleave-configurature*. As well as a common belief that there can be a positive quality to disequilib-rium and contradictions, what unites these architectural thinkers is the trenchant, uncom-promising repudiation of architectural modernism's functional ethic and its attendant em-phasis on problem solving over problem production.

Even though German Romanticism is known to have avoided the linguistic in the simple complicity sought between architecture and music, and despite Victor Hugo's famous warn-ing that "the book will kill the edifice" — (a prediction at the heart of this problematic rela-tion between poetics and architectural theory) — current architectural thinking, via Der-rida's impetus, is being redirected to the architectonic possibilities of language, textuality and writing.[36] Preeminent is Peter Eisenman's advocacy of discursive rather than figurative architecture, opening up to the mirrored possibility of how writing can be inscribed in ar-chitecture and equally architecture in writing.[37] One aspect in his work readily lending itself

---

[33] Solà-Morales, *Differences*, pp. 103-4.
[34] Cache, *Earth*, p. 15.
[35] *Archigram* chronicles the work of this late 1960s British collective as told by its members. A cross section of Libeskind's theoretical writings and architectural projects, including the Berlin Museum Extension with the Jewish Museum, can be found in his monograph *Countersign* (London: Academy Editions, 1991). Hejduk's ephemeral, traveling architecture (termed "vagabond" by Antony Vidler) is briefly discussed in Vidler's *The Architectural Uncanny. Essays in the Modern Unhomely* [Cambridge: The MIT Press, 1992], pp. 207-14). The trilogy, *Mask of Medusa*, *Vladivostok*, and *Soundings* offer a chrestomathy of his architectural projects and theories. Hadid's work is readily available in *The Complete Work* (New York: Rizzoli, 1998). Her important architectural statement "Another Beginning" appears in Peter Noever's *The End of Architecture? Documents and Manifestos* (Munich: Prestel Verlag, 1992).
[36] "As well as his famous proclamation that "architecture is in general frozen music," Schelling also cites the architecturally relevant myth of Amphion whose music causes stones to inhere and formulate the walls around Thebes (Friedrich Schelling, *The Philosophy of Art*, trans. by Douglas W. Scott [Minneapolis: University of Minnesota Press, 1989], p. 177). This confluence of musical and the architectural is echoed in Goethe's later description of architecture as "petrified music" (a description he later modified to "silent music" *verstummte Tonkunst*). See Vidler, *Architectural*, p. 231.
[37] The most cogent critique of Eisenman's approach is Robin Evans, 'Not to be Used for Wrapping Purposes: A Review of the Exhibition of Peter Eisenman's Fin d'Ou T Hou S' in Evans, *Translations*, pp. 119-51.

to a parapoetic scrutiny is the virtuality of a diagrammatic model for writing. Eisenman himself believes (perhaps over ambitiously) that such a writing-as-diagram is possible and will provide "a means of potentially overreaching the question of origin (speech) as well as the metaphysics of presence."[38] Eisenman stresses the diagram's deconstructive potential as the following vertiginous and typical sentence suggests: "The diagram helps to displace presence by inserting a not-presence as a written trace — a sign of the not-presence of the column — into the physical column. This trace is something that cannot be explained either through function or meaning."[39] However, the axonometric nature of the diagrams offers a more parapoetic potential. The chief feature of axonometric diagrams is parallel projection which effectively collapses the governing dualism of vertical and horizontal planes, freeing up the possibility of thrusting the observer into decentralized disequilibrium.[40] Axonometric presentation maximizes presentational possibilities, showing more sides than it is ever possible to view. For Eisenman "The diagram is a tactic within a critical strategy — it attempts to situate a theoretical object within a physical object [and is capable of producing] spatial characteristics that both blur iconic forms and produce interstitial spatial possibilities."[41] There are clear intimations that poetics is already exploring at least the effects of axonometry. The disjunctive poetics that emerged in the late 1970s produced texts by Bruce Andrews and Susan Howe whose immediate effects are decenteredness and readerly disequilibrium. Ron Silliman's New Sentence (due to its paratactic emphasis and rule of non-integrationing sentences,) constructs precisely those interstitial spatial possibilities that Eisenman speaks of.[42] The white hiatus between letters, words, and sentences, what Silliman calls the twenty-seventh letter of the alphabet and marking the virtual space of non-integration, makes reader intervention possible on the level of semantic construction and connotative tracking. A similar quality of axonometric distortion occurs in much of Clark Coolidge's poetry and in the systematic-chance- generated texts of Jackson MacLow. In his recent book *Alien Tatters*, which retains the sentence as its minimal unit of composition, grammar and syntax in a superficially normative way:

> Monkey come down from that roof with my mother's
> dowery. These baleful scenes can be made to explain. It was
> just that dare of a day. Expediency Beranger they called for.
> A collided ice to the vitamin point.

---

[38]   Peter Eisenman, *Diagram Diaries* (NY: Universe, 1999), p. 213.

[39]   Eisenman, p. 213.

[40]   "An axonometric drawing consists of a plan which is set up truly but turned to a convenient angle. The verticals are then drawn on this and to scale. By these means, all the horizontal and all the vertical elements of the building are represented correctly and so to the same scale. *Anything which is neither truly vertical nor horizontal becomes distorted*; but an axonometric drawing, once one has learnt to disregard the distortions, can teach a very great deal about structure" (Peter Murray, *The Architecture of the Italian Renaissance* [London: Thames and Hudson, 1986], p. 237, emphases added). Axonometric effects, of course, are not novel; they are central to the logic of the paragram and to analytic cubism. Like axonometry, the latter applies a structural logic chiasmatically across the normative rules of figuration and design. Within early-20th century literature the most effective axonometric poetry is Gertrude Stein's *Tender Buttons*. Parapoetics, of course, would investigate the benefits of including distortion within a study of the structural elements.

[41]   Eisenman, *Diagram*, pp. 206; 202.

[42]   See Ron Silliman, 'The New Sentence', in *The New Sentence* (New York: Roof Books, 1987), pp. 63-93.

Mondo Pianissimo of the bulky Colorado. This is not as
silly as might be turned to in times of expectancy, clearing
right out. Pencil-thin silhouette just down the barrel from
all aim. The cow made smaller by the light.[43]

Although the two most characteristic features of the new-sentence — parataxis and non-integration — stylistically dominate in the passage, catachresis and grammatical transgressions help attain an intense quality of disequilibrium. Considered axonometrically, not as a text but an architectonic, we can say that the grammar and syntax function as the vertical and horizontal elements in an "angled" axonometric structure through which "diagonal" elements (in the form of catachresis and undecidability) provide informational and semiological distortions.[44]

Eisenman too, is attracted to text and trace as ways of denying architecture both originality and expression. He seeks a radical incorporation of alterity in which a work is defined in terms of another author, a process involving "a search for the signs of absence within the necessary presence of architecture."[45] This incorporation of otherness in sameness is precisely the method of Tom Phillips in *A Humument*, Ronald Johnson's *Radi os*, and John Cage's various "writings through." All three employ a practice of treating a source text, using methods of written readings through which a latent text is exhumed and the source texts partly deleted. Johnson's source is *Paradise Lost*, Cage's include *Finnegans Wake*, *Walden*, and Thoreau's *Notebooks*. To give one example: in *A Humument*, a text, excavated from W.H. Mallock's forgotten 1892 novel *A Human Document*, Phillips paints over vast areas of the pages, creating efficacious rivulets of text that open up a latent content. Each page of Mallock's novel offers Phillips a reservoir of paragrammatic possibilities and a tactical opportunity for local improvisations within constraint. The exhumed text releases a difference in sameness, the result being a stunning intermedia work: part text, part pictorial transformation in pen, ink and acrylic gouache. But beyond its visual impact *A Humument* raises the proprietary question as to whose words are these? The Victorian Mallock's certainly, and reproduced in the exact same place on each line as he planned. Yet they serve to deliver, a new text, a text out of a text, Phillips' text as the text by Mallock that Mallock never wrote.

Parapoetics might also address how applicable to poetics are the three deconstructive questions that Eisenman sees evoked by the diagrammatic:

1) Can the metaphysics of presence be opened up or displaced? Is there another way to think presence other than through fullness? 2) Is there a way to rethink the relationship between the sign and the signified as other

---

43   Clark Coolidge, *Alien Tatters* (San Francisco: Atelos, 2000), p. 41.

44   The above interpretative analysis merely laminates a theory onto texts whose disjunctive qualities suggest an analogy to axonometric diagramming. The question of how axonometry can be *consciously* employed as a creative method find a ready answer in the realm of computer-constructed texts and visual poems, where on-screen deployment and display promises most effective results. The poetic possibilities of axonometric syntax, display and semantics are not addressed in an otherwise excellent collection of articles investigating the format and political possibilities of computers and the Internet gathered by Darren Wershler-Henry, "Cyberpoetics" issue of *Open Letter*, 10th Series no. 6, special edition (fall) 2000.

45   Eisenman, *Chora*, p. 132.

than a motivated relationship? 3) Is there a way to rethink the subject as other than a subject motivated by a desire to have architecture communicate a sense of place and ground?[46]

Let me digress briefly on a parallel but variant history of reception, specifically the deconstructive and the folding turn in architecture and literature. Mark Wigley claims that architecture (circa the mid-80s) was "the last discourse to invoke the name of Derrida."[47] Without doubt the strategic introduction of instability into stable structures and relations remains Deconstruction's theoretical contribution to architecture. The architectural demands of deconstruction are clearly stated by Jeffrey Kipnis: "The architect must find methods to simultaneously embody more complex organizations of multiple and contradictory meanings while at the same time meeting the responsibility to shelter, function and stand."[48] By 1993 however the interest in deconstructive architecture had significantly waned with interest shifting to the architectural implications of Deleuze's concept of the fold. Greg Lynn suggests that folding offers an alternative and preferable fluid and connective logic to the deconstructionist impasse of conflict and contradiction. Where deconstruction inspired architecture of brutal diagonals, plication encouraged curvilinear, folded, heterogeneous forms. "If there is a single effect" Lynn notes, "produced in architecture by folding, it will be the ability to integrate unrelated elements within a new continuous mixture."[49] Deleuzean curvilinear logic facilitates dissipative structures with porous movements of external forces into interior domains, and the concomitant inclusion of non-colliding discontinuities. This proclivity to generative theory is generally absent in the literary field where deconstruction and plication, (despite Rodolphe Gasché's warning that general textuality is irreducible to the properties of specific literary texts,) have largely fostered a critical apparatus to be laminated over texts for interpretative purposes and has had a comparatively weak impact on the production of primary texts. This linked but un-even development is not to be lamented but rather noted for opening the possibility of cross-disciplinary intercourse.

Shifting focus from predominantly theoretical matters, I want now to suggest that the most fruitful target for parapoetic attention is the city. Wittgenstein, a practicing architecture himself, compares language to "an ancient city: a maze of little streets and squares, of old and new houses," while Sherwood Anderson writes of a post-melancholic, neglected city of words rebuilt and recast by Gertrude Stein:

There is a city of English and American words and it has been a neglected city. Strong broad shouldered words, that should be marching across open fields under the blue sky, are clerking in little dusty dry goods stores, young virgin words are being allowed to consort with whores, learned words have been put to the digger's trade. Only yesterday I saw a word that once called a whole nation to arms serving in the mean capacity of advertising laundry soap.

[46]   Eisenman, *Diagram*, p. 212.
[47]   Mark Wigley, 'The Translation of Architecture: The Producr of Babel', in *Deconstruction III* (London: Architectural Design. Academy Editions, 1994), p. 6.
[48]   Eisenman, *Chora*, p. 138.
[49]   Greg Lynn, 'Architectural Curvilinearity: the Fold, the Pliant and the Supple', in *Architectural Design* (London 1993), p. 8.

For me the work of Gertrude Stein consists in a rebuilding, an entire new recasting of life, in the city of words[50]

Architectural theories and debate, however, provide more complex notions of the city than Wittgenstein's and Anderson's simple metaphoric rendition, civic theories that might modify literary encounters with the city. Architecture tells us how it frames light in space, and is committed to creating photic and thermal, as well as human circulation, and that the interior of its products marks its living history. In this way architecture emerges as a form of action. Buildings and their complex articulations onto, and relations to, towns and cities, are characterized like language by defeasibility and lability; they assume and evolve through numerous functions independent of both architectural form and original purpose. This feature specifies the paragrammatic force of dwelling; the occupied house or building as a dissipative structure.

This specification, however, does not eliminate a certain perdurability of form. Reflecting on the Palazzo della Ragione in Padua, Aldo Rossi notes how "one is struck by the multiplicity of functions that a building of this type can contain over time and how these functions are entirely independent of the form. At the same time, it is precisely the form that impresses us, we live it and experience it, and in turn it structures the city."[51] Rossi's pragmatic observation allows us to return to Wittgenstein's description of language in a non-metaphorical way. There is no city just as there is no language only linguistic utterances, and architectural usage and events. The growing displacement of structural and general linguistics by pragmatics is symptomatic of a shift in interest from form to usage and to a sense of language as both a changing dwelling and a lived experience. In the light of this shift, Barthes' highly competent semiological readings of the city appear less relevant to living than to obey Lebbeus Woods' call to "build our buildings and then discover how to live and work in them."[52]

British architect Nigel Coates, founder of NATO (Narrative Architecture Today, a.k.a "Nigel and the Others") emerged out of the Thatcherian design-boom of the 1980s with an ebullient theory of the architecture of the city that combines filmic handling of space with collage and surprise. There is something flaneuristic about Coates' methodological approach to city architecture: "It's about getting under the skin of the city, about going with the flow, seeing where it takes you, and then responding in appropriate ways. A healthy city, or a city you want to be in, is always changing; it's an organism, not a machine running on fixed lines. This sense of a city being alive informs both our response to the city as architects, and the individual buildings we design."[53] Notwithstanding this laudable declaration of commitment, Coates' projects so far (apart from the proposed redesign of the sleazy

---

[50] Ludwig Wittgenstein, *Philosophical Investigations*, trans. by G. E. M. Anscombe (London: Macmillan, 1953), p. 8(e); Sherwood Anderson, 'The Work of Gertrude Stein', Introduction to Gertrude Stein's, *Geography and Plays* (New York: Something Else Press, 1968), pp. 7-8.

[51] Rossi, *Architecture*, p. 29.

[52] Lebbeus Woods, *The New City* (New York: Simon and Schuster, 1992), p. 80. See, for example, 'Semiology and the Urban' in Leach, *Rethinking*, pp. 166-72, first presented as a lecture in May 1967, under the sponsorship of the *Institut Français*, and the Institute of the History of Architecture at the University of Naples.

[53] Glancey, *Coates*, p. 14.

environs of King's Cross) do not reflect a particularly positive response to the prevalent social predicament of poverty, the need for shelter, low-income domiciles, etc.. According to Glancey, Coates approaches the city "as a vibrant organism rather than a grid of geometric lines. It's about living, about meeting people, about accidental encounters, changes, risk-taking, sex."[54] Such sentiments would not be out of place in any number of Situationist texts on unitary urbanism.[55] However, notably absent in Coates' notion of the organic, vital city and his neo-liberal soft planning is a critical awareness of ideological or economic governing forces so apparent to Constant and Jorn. The myopic range of Coates' vision becomes apparent when measured against the ominous backdrop of co-optation and global economic controls outlined succinctly by Richard Rogers:

> Despite all our new wealth — material and intellectual — most of the world's inhabitants are denied the opportunity to lead decent lives. The swollen stomachs and shriveled faces of Third World children, the cold and squalor that our pensioners have to endure, the increasing number of people who live lives in boxes and doorways stand as an indictment of a society which has the capacity to eradicate poverty but prefers to turn its back. And beyond the exploitation and injustice which is so central a feature of our civilization looms the prospect of ecological disaster [...]. The predicament in which we find ourselves has a direct bearing on our appreciation of architecture. For in architecture, as in other areas, an exciting surge of creativity, discovery and invention has been frustrated by the same selfish interests that now sustain global poverty and threaten the environment [...]. The despoliation of our built environment is only a small part of a broader pattern — a pattern in which new advances in ideas and technology are harnessed not to public values but to private interests.[56]

We must remain alert to architecture's ominous expansion in the hyperrealism of the neo-liberal dream, alert to the colonizing force in which architecture is mobilized by a compound telos of planning-for-profit. It is an alarming fact that this link of architecture and building to property, ownership and profit is not a recent discovery. In early medieval times we find Hildebert of Lavardin placing architecture in the category of "*ultra privatum pecuniae modum fortunae*" i. e. "mercenary" things and financial gain.[57]

"Cities are in reality great camps of the living and the dead where many elements remain like signals, symbols, cautions. When the holiday is over, what remains of the architecture is scarred, and the sand consumes the street again."[58] Rossi's meditation on temporality and decay here, marked as they are by the philosopher's distance, and transmitted from the transcendental position of the theoretical attitude, seem most akin to Gibbon's musing in the ruins of the Capitol Rome that sparked in him the idea to write the *Decline*

---

[54]   Glancey, p. 14.

[55]   As well as Knabb's excellent collection of Situationist texts and reports of specifically architectural interest are Mark Wigley, *Constant's New Babylon; The Hyper-Architecture of Desire* (Rotterdam: 010 Publishers, 1998); and Simon Sadler, *The Sitiationist City* (Cambridge: The MIT Press, 1998).

[56]   Richard Rogers, *Architecture: A Modern View* (London: Thames & Hudson, 1990), pp. 7-9.

[57]   Quotes in Liane Lefaivre, *Leon Battista Alberti's Hypnerotomachia Poliphili* (Cambridge: The MIT Pres, 1997), p. 200.

[58]   Aldo Rossi, *The Architecture of the City*, trans. by Diane Ghirardo and Joan Ockman (Cambridge: The MIT Press, 1984), p. 10.

and Fall.[59] Yet elsewhere, Rossi realizes that cities are first and foremost a composite of artifacts, and to ignore (as urban studies do) "those aspects of reality that are most individual, particular, irregular, and also most interesting" leads to useless, artificial theories.[60] Juvenal emerged as the critical conscience of Rome, starting a legacy of poetic scrutinization of the city as the dysfunctional hospice of incurables. Gay, Johnson, the Shelley of *Peter Bell the Third*, Baudelaire, Aragon, and Eliot: all fascinated and repelled by the inoperability of the metropolis. From Dioce to Wagadu the dream of civic construction haunts Pound's *Cantos* as a thematic counter stress to the lure of fragments and floating signifiers.[61]

Despite the digital information highway and the extended community brought about by electronic communication, Georg Simmel's 1903 reflections on the metropolis and mental life seem more pertinent than ever. What distinguishes the metropolitan inhabitant is a blasé attitude to life brought on by the collision of constant extra-sensory bombardment with internal stimuli. Part product of, part defense against, metropolitan overload, the blasé subject struggles for an autonomy and circulation homologous to the flow of currency and commodities.[62] The fascinating power of the city can be specified in an economic, ideological irony: that the people who use the city are simultaneously and for the most part unconsciously used by it. Tafuri isolates and elaborates the Capitalist nature of the western city: "Objectively, structured like a machine for the extraction of surplus value, in its own conditioning mechanisms the city reproduces the reality" of the modes of production.[63] The soft city, transparent city, the wired city, the digital city. Whichever you choose, cities still need to be experienced as used and as the sites of consumption and production. Yet to resuscitate Le Corbusier's vision of architecture as the supreme mediator between realism and utopia seems as arrogant as it is ill advised.

In conclusion let me suggest that you receive these rambling thoughts as a caveat against the fruit of that marriage of practical reason and the Kantian faculties we baptized some time ago as specialization. The current ideology governing graduate studies does not encourage attacks on thetic dogmatism. Rather it supports the trenchant ideology of the frame. Doubtless an argument can be made that specialization safeguards the heterogeneity

---

[59] "It was at Rome, on the fifteenth of October, 1764, as I sat musing midst the ruins of the Capitol while the barefooted fryars were singing Vespers in the Temple of Jupiter, that the idea of writing the decline and fall of the City first started to my mind" (p. 305).

[60] Rossi, p. 21.

[61] Pound's own view of the fragment might be deduced from his own Confucian beliefs that structure the relation of parts to whole. "The metaphysic of the Confucian *Chung Yung* or *Unwobbling Pivot*" comments Peter Makin, "is that things are not heaps of contingent dust-drift, but have essential principles, which are durable; which are part of an overarching tendency or Principle in the universe and which, being a shaping and therefore good principle operative in man as in other things, a man may come to understand. This metaphysic is all about the relation between wholes and fragments. The mosaic is not its little glass and gold-leafed fragments; the Virgin shines down from the apse at Torcello when, or if, half of the fragments that make her have fallen …" (Peter Makin, *Pound's Cantos* [Baltimore: Johns Hopkins University Press, 1985], pp. 235-36). The architectural pertinence of Makin's observations is obvious.

[62] See George Simmel, 'The Metropolis and Mental Life', in *Rethinking Architecture: A Reader in Cultural Theory*, ed. by Neil Leach (London and New York: Routledge, 1997), pp. 69-79.

[63] Tafuri, *Architecture*, p. 81.

of discourses from domination by a single master narrative. However, the adverse consequences of the frame and the frame's governing contradictory logic have already been outlined. Aaron Betsky calls for an anchoring inside the amorphous vertigo of sprawl by means of slow space. Decelerate the speed of today and make the world stand still.[64] Against this moot tactic of survival I would suggest a *becoming* through agencies of difference: and so towards a spiral poetics, a clinamen architecture, a poetics of folding so as to construct free spaces that can only function as ephemeral interstices.

Hölderlin insists that the highest poetry is that in which the non-poetic element also becomes poetic.[65] I wonder if the call in this claim to added negativity is pertinent to research. Let's attempt to problematize our specialist knowledge by placing it in a broader cartography; map antithetical and intersecting zones as a preliminary to nomadic practices; deframe and rethink research along spatial not chronological lines akin to Jed Rasula's notion of accidental research in which conceptual agility replaces a focussed detailism. Experience at least the "internal drifts" of disciplines and even contemplate the possibility of random access research. According to Marcos Novak, "our understanding of territory is undergoing rapid and fundamental changes: with the scope of pragmatic experience both space and community are rapidly becoming non-local."[66] Random Access is emerging as the most powerful virtual tool in epistemological capital. Novak believes it's becoming "a way of life characterized by precise and instantaneous affiliation," and "disembodied proximity implies the extension of random access to progressively larger parts of our experience."[67] I would extend the applicability of Novak's claim to the disciplines of knowledge. Novak further suggests that "The virtual and cyber worlds form a continuum [...] There is something of what we call cyberspace in virtuality and something of what we call virtual reality in cyberspace. [...] Cyberspace is always the 'exterior' of virtual reality, because it always reserves the additional space of possibility, in contrast to actuality. Possibility is the fundamental characteristic of everything that is 'other,' since possibility always contains the unknown."[68] Derrida's essay on Tschumi's *Point de Folie* introduces the term *maintenant*. Now. A temporal indicator marking the time, the only time, when both endings and beginnings occur in the protracted space of a becoming.

That said as I'm ending.... Now. But perhaps as a poet, as the poet in me, I should add a coda: *The poem may well be dead, but as the architect said one is never finished with the poem.*

---

[64] It may please Betsky to know of support for his theoretical position is growing. The Italian *Città Lente* or "Slow Cities" Movement, inaugurated by Paolo Saturnini, was implemented in 2000 in small towns and cities. An offshoot of Carlo Patrini's Slow Food movement, founded a decade ago to counter the proliferation of homogenous fast food outlets, *Città Lente* is committed to a preservationist policy of traditional architecture and gastronomy. As reporter Megan Williams explains Saturnini, the Mayor of Greve-in-Chianti, "is carefully constructing barricades to keep at bay the tide of homogeneity that globalization has washed into similar-sized communities around the world. From fast-food chains to cell-phone antennas to car alarms. The Small [sic] Cities people have said 'No thanks' to many of the trappings of modernity."

[65] 'Reflection,' in *Sämtliche Werke* 4:1, p. 234-35.

[66] Marcos Novak, *Trans Terra Form: Liquid Architecture and the Loss of Inscription* [www.t0.or.at/~krcf/nlonline/nonMarcos.html].

[67] Novak.

[68] Novak.

Karen Mac Cormack

MUTUAL LABYRINTH: a proposal of exchange[1]

This paper is a variation on one originally presented at the "Transgressing Boundaries and Strategies of Renewal in American Poetry" conference at the Universidad de Salamanca in May 2000, concerning the productive and enduring influence of visual art (and its techniques) on poetry, and the potentially vital exchange between poetry and innovative architectural practice, particularly the work of Gins & Arakawa as it served as my introduction to innovative architectural potential.

> A number of artistic practices have had to redefine their territory and their course of action, due to the classifica-
> tions which situated them, the institutions which sheltered them, no longer being valid.[2]

> Consider 'I' an architectural assertion and work out the details of how so.
> The task of coordinating the parts falls to the critical artist, the coordinator
> of events, the conductor of assertions.[3]

The techniques of collage, erasure, and overlay, when applied to *writing* often produce a more severe discomfort or dislocation in the *reader* than such examples do in viewers of film and/or video works. Yet changes in the English language (or versions of the English language to be precise) continue their impact on a near-daily basis. Language isn't static, yet frequently readers appear to take false comfort in the illusion that it provides a *terra firma* of both grammar and meaning. So when readers unaccustomed to innovation encounter poems by Susan Howe, or Diane Ward, or Lise Downe, their responses might be hostile, at least initially. Indeed, to read innovative writing is a marginalized activity, even if the writing of poetry (innovative or otherwise) seems on the rise, at least in North America. The phenomenon of a book of poetry becoming a bestseller belongs more to the beginning

---

[1] The following is a slight variation on a paper originally presented at the *Transgressing Boundaries and Strategies of Renewal in American Poetry* conference at the Universidad de Salamanca in May 2000, concerning the productive and enduring influence of visual art (and its techniques) on poetry, and the potentially vital exchange between poetry and innovative architectural practice. I briefly discuss this influence of visual art on contemporary North American writing by women poets, especially those (such as Diane Ward and Lise Downe) who also work, or have worked, in visual artistic production. (In this different context mention also should be made of those British poets engaging in visual art practice, such as Allen Fisher, Alan Halsey, Maggie O'Sullivan, and Tom Raworth.) While my current research concerns the architectural projects of Bernard Cache and Marcos Novak it was the work of Gins & Arakawa that served as my introduction to innovative architectural potential).

[2] Yago Conde, *Architecture of the Indeterminacy* (Barcelona: Actar, 2000), p. 81.

[3] Arakawa and Gins, 'The Tentative Constructed Plan as Intervening Device for a Reversible Destiny', *A + U* (Tokyo), no. 255 (December 1991), 131.

of the last century or earlier still. That is not to say that poetry (of any provenance) is no less *valid* today, but its validity in cultural terms obviously means something different in 2000 than it did in 1900. To dismiss poetry as an outdated form of creativity is to overlook the comparative marginalization of the contemporary art film, for example, or the seemingly perennial perception that Gertrude Stein and James Joyce's writing is "experimental."

As antecedents to contemporary poets/visual artists, the works of such modernist writers as Stein (though herself not a visual artist), Mina Loy, and Djuna Barnes all bear evidence of an informed visual practice. While it would be facile to catalogue a collection of 'painterly' poems this in itself wouldn't go far in terms of exploring strategies of innovation in North American poetry. A similar 'list' of poets whose work is obviously affected by visual art would be equally unproductive. Even the notion of an inherited tradition of such influence implies nothing beyond the obvious. If anything, as an example of resistance, the *lack* of interaction between disciplines (even between different genres of *writing*) is even more prevalent.

If these techniques of collage, erasure, and overlay are painterly and/or sculptorly, and if montage is customarily applied to film and/or video sequencing, then just as these visual arts have evolved in the past one hundred years, what is the contemporary productive exchange between poetry and visual art or an expansion thereof? It seems to me that the architectural projects of Arakawa and Gins is one probable answer to this question. In one of her poems Ward writes "The form of sculptures is earthquakes," a statement echoed in Radovan Ivsic and Annie LeBrun's comment on Gins & Arakawa's *Reversible Destiny — Yoro* (Japan), "In effect, many different levels and changes of terrain await us, ready to surprise us, throw us off balance, transport us outside ourselves."[4]

I've chosen as examples of the writing of Downe and Ward poems that contain numerous explorations and references to glass (mirrors and windows). In Lise Downe's first collection *A Velvet Increase of Curiosity* is a poem, quoted here in part, entitled "Vehicle":

> a riot of broken surrounded by adhesive
> becomes clear
>   opening to window
> night raining the morning of Thursday
> showers of amber glow internal
> incandescence
>   essence of cloud walking upon the earth
>
> by walking
> the statement "all chairs have legs"
> distributes the term "chair"
> the letter couched in burgundy
> vowels flaming delivery to define obsidian
> as glass
>
> writing becoming
>   passing
> and becoming again
>   as delta[5]

---

4   Arakawa and Gins, *Reversible Destiny* (NY: Guggenheim, 1977), p. 195.
5   Lise Downe, *A Velvet Increase of Curiosity* (Toronto: ECW Press, 1993), p. 64.

I wish to draw special attention to "the statement 'all chairs have legs'/distributes the term 'chair'/the letter couched in burgundy/vowels flaming delivery to define obsidian/as glass/writing becoming/passing." Here language and grammar are set next to and then combine with imagery in a deliberate juxtaposition. This is not an overtly "painterly" poem, though I will suggest that its influence is more painterly than architectural.

Diane Ward's collection *Relation* contains a section of what she refers to as "concept lyrics" in which the poem "Glass" appears. Here writing isn't "becoming/or/passing," rather "Us and we-s tell our ones: [...] through shattered glass that held our display." The poem in full reads:

Behind things you need, all
recede, white line, heels reflect

In the mind, deciding for the dark,
is the panel behind the panel

Us and we-s tell our ones:
distinguish between, to follow

And another and you and me
and us and another and them

Grown white-hot, we're apart as if
through shattered glass that held our display

like glass, breaking up, but like
bone — first the callous grows

11/2 parts felspar, 3 parts sodium
sulphate and carbon, 41/2 parts limestone,

15 parts dolomite, 17 parts
soda, 50 parts quartz sand
These ingredients together intimately
mixed — it would mean so much to me.[6]

Though they are both visual artists as well as poets, Ward's and Downe's experience differs considerably. Ward is the youngest of the 'first generation' language writers and her publishing history began in the 1970s. Downe, though writing for many years, didn't begin publishing until the 1990s and her early magazine appearances were often in the U. S. instead of Canada. To my knowledge Ward is no longer a visual arts practitioner and Downe is.

If a trajectory is traced in terms of the impact of *visual art* on innovative North American writing by women, from Stein through Loy and Barnes through Barbara Guest and Susan Howe to Diane Ward and Lise Downe (to name but a few) then one eventually

[6]   Diane Ward, *Relation* (New York: Roof, 1989), p. 50.

arrives (via film-maker/poet Abigail Child) to the project, architectural in its scope, that is the focus of this paper, Gins & Arakawa's *Reversible Destiny*.[7]

Arakawa's "cessation of painting" occurred at the end of the 1980s and as stated by Charles Haxthausen, his "focus on architecture in the 1990s should be understood not merely as a change of medium [...] It constitutes a *radicalization of aims*."[8] Certainly the simultaneous growth (and shift) in their more than thirty-year collaborative practice is major (Gins began as a writer and Arakawa as a visual artist, and both have subsequently engaged with architecture, additionally.)

The *Reversible Destiny* project is evidence of Arakawa and Gins' belief that "Architecture is a tool that can be used as writing has been, except that it can have a far more extensive range of application."[9] For them, "The task of architecture is to mete out the world in such a way that it might be reflected on body-wide. And what does thinking — global body-wide thinking — need? Thinking surely needs perseverance in the matter at hand, the continual pursuing of that which perplexes, a coming at it and to it from all sides."[10] To enact this, as the architect Johannes Knesl describes it, "When it comes to placing a 'house' on the terrain, [they] crumple the classical floor plan that founds, generates, supports, and clarifies the meaning of the building and turn it into a labyrinth of horizontal and vertical repetitions of resembling miniconfigurations of pieces of wall that are inversions of a classical wall."[11] This project involves the creation of experimental dwelling and work places, gardens, communities, even whole cities to be based on notions that go beyond the customary ones of conventional architecture, indeed that call for an ethical revolution involving "an intervening role for architecture within the perceiving process."[12] At its most extreme the project calls for "the primary purpose of life in our time should be 'to not to die'."[13] Responses to this vary considerably, but *whatever* one's response it shouldn't interfere with an appreciation of the multiple aspects of their strategies. I concur with Ivsic and LeBrun's

---

[7] A brief mention should be made of the artist Robert Smithson's influence on upper case-equal sign language poets, women and men. Also, of Norwegian-French poet Caroline Bergvall's *Éclat*. (From personal correspondence with Bergvall: "it was, yes a commission for something called Writing Live, a London Arts Board funded commission series which was managed by the Institution of Rot, North London, an artist-run house in which the 4 pieces by writers took place in Spring 1996. I developed *Éclat* in direct response to the site. The artist who manages the Institution (and his home), Richard Crow, has an aesthetic very inspired by Artaud and gothic-industrial music aesthetics. (Might imagine) I found that not so conducive to my own work: black walls, cold closed run-down environment. [...] So I wrote the texts through this dilemma, not wanting to be disappeared but wanting to express that threat (and plausibility) of cultural disappearance of me in such place. *Éclat* became a guided walkman tour, as a reflexion and an apposition to, rather than an erasure of or being erased by, the ideologies of the space. One would see and be in, and feel the chill of, the space while also being caught in what the text was saying and my guiding the visit through it...I was completely thrilled to hear from a friend when she came back to the kitchen (starting-point, lowest point in many English houses) that she had got lost!!").

[8] Arakawa and Gins, *Reversible*, p. 29.

[9] Arakawa and Gins, p. 12.

[10] Arakawa and Gins, *Architectural Body* (Tuscaloosa: University of Alabama Press, 2002), p. 10.

[11] Arakawa and Gins, *Reversible*, p. 217. He continues by stating that "in classical architecture, the wall is what creates the harmoniously proportioned room, founding unit of classical space."

[12] Arakawa and Gins, 'Tentative', p. 132.

[13] Arakawa and Gins, *Reversible*, p. 215.

statement that "The term reversible destiny neither implies nor announces the possibility that time might be reversible. What interests them [Arakawa and Gins] is that one can reverse one's course, one can turn the page, one can [...] More than anything else they want to make us see, or rather, to put it in our power to experience, the strange liberty of palindromes: for example, the strange freedom to go either way when reading a phrase, equally well right to left and from left to right [...]".[14] My own interest in their projects does not extend as far as "to not to die." (Prior to *Reversible Destiny* [and subsequently incorporated in it] came *The Mechanism of Meaning*, which will also enter into this discussion). As a poet I find that many of their *Reversible Destiny* projects could be meaningfully applied to the writing and reading of innovative poetry.

For Gins and Arakawa the pronoun "I" is already an "architectural assertion" because it creates spatial relations, establishing what they call "fiction of place" in opposition to "factual distances."[15] The architect Ed Keller puts it most aptly — "As they theorize the body and the subject, Arakawa and Gins project a human who does not submit to a dialectical subdivision. The inchoate no longer means 'outside of language' or 'unformed.' An inchoateness of the body becomes a cessation of habit — becomes a processible and developmental state."[16] They assert that the world is composed of three types of landing sites: perceptual, imaging, and "architectural" or "dimensionalizing."[17] (To this I would add the emotional landing site, as evidenced in love relationships and friendships).[18] For them, "If the basic unit of concern is the body, not an abstract body considered apart from impulses and movement, but the body in action, then will not the concepts most central to the living of a life be those formed — no matter how fleetingly — through architectural encounters?"[19]

A parallel to this would be the model or productive reader (living) in "language," in the act of reading an innovative poem, the poem being actualized through the writer and reader's textual activation or encounter. Surely a component in "the basic unit of concern (being) the body" is that even "the body in action" lives with and within language, spoken or written. So the forming of architectural encounters is done so in conjunction with language. (Does this make language itself an architectural encounter, too?)

To Gins and Arakawa's "fiction of place" I would complicate the binary regarding its opposite of "factual distances" by proposing a poetry of <<is>> with <<is>> as a constantly shifting 'particular,' differing from "the fiction of place as detail."[20] I'm still considering the relation of the constantly shifting 'particular' to a dimension and am inclining towards it

---

[14]   Arakawa and Gins, p. 198.

[15]   Arakawa and Gins, 'Tentative', p. 32.

[16]   Arakawa and Gins, *Reversible*, p. 217.

[17]   Arakawa and Gins, *Architecture: Sites of Reversible Destiny* (London: Academy Editions, 1994), p. 19; Arakawa and Gins, *Architecural Body*, pp. 20-32.

[18]   In *Architectural Body* Arakawa and Gins discuss "The mapping of 'events and locatings'" so as to "be able to reflect all manner of experience"; they propose a landing-site "molecule" formed of "two landing-site 'atoms' [named perceptual and imaging]." I propose that an emotional landing site occurs as a(n) (special/particular?) instance of a clinamen of these atoms, so also an event marker in and of experience.

[19]   Arakawa and Gins, *Reversible*, p. 12.

[20]   "the perceiving,/brings about the perceived image [of] fiction of place as detail"; Arakawa and Gins, *To Not To Die*, p. 108.

being potentially everywhere at once, but activated locally. (So poetry represents a meaningful particular architecting of and through language by perplexing it?)

The innovative poetry now referred to under the blanket term of "language writing" (beginning in the 1970s and having produced at least three "generations" up to the present day) facilitated, among other things, an appreciation of and ability to perceive *language* in and of itself beyond a transit theory of meaning. Language writing provided us with the means to negotiate grammatical disjunction and slippage of meaning (in addition to semiotics and Umberto Eco's open text and model or productive reader), and cyberspace is providing us with new ways to read beyond the intransigence of paper. (Within this it's crucial to bear in mind that the act of reading has itself changed and evolved. Unfortunately I've no time here to consider the medieval approach, as discussed by Mary Carruthers, whereby one "chooses" one's way through a text and "authority and author [are] conceived of entirely in textual terms."[21] Gins and Arakawa's concurrent practice included *The Mechanism of Meaning* (1963–1973, and 1996), a "series of interactive exercises and thought experiments [...] through each exercise, viewers actively participate in the formation of meaning from a particular and specified perspective. They observe a slippage from meaning (or nearmeaning) to nonsense, and sift through and recombine elements and events in the process of construing meaning.[22] (I've deliberately quoted this description written by Michael Govan for its similarity to much of the critical writing on language writing and the proximity to Umberto Eco's open text and model or productive reader.)

For those of us, writers *and* readers, who have come to "embrace the notion that no system of meaning can be closed or stable and that the truth of any one way of taking the world cannot be canonically established" (as F. L. Rush wrote of Arakawa and Gins) then their ongoing work provides multiple innovative strategies, beyond writing and reading to the various acts comprising the practice of "everyday life" and our accompanying perceptions of it.[23] In considering poetry as part of this everyday life, and aware that poetry's meaning and practice in contemporary terms will not remain "fixed," it is surely the poet's responsibility to encourage *evolving* ways of poetic activity and perception.

Gins and Arakawa's architectural sites rework negotiating "architectural surrounds," while emphasizing, encouraging, and indeed provoking an awareness of the process of perception. "Each instance of perception lands as a site."[24] A favourite example of mine is their *Rotation House*, in which "rooms act as spatial anagrams":

> Five rotations of a room become a house. Overall size and form hold constant, except for changes in features due to the different room-types [...] residents find themselves repeatedly being struck by where within [...] this version of the room-module, various nooks, crannies, curves, and angular surfaces are to be found [...].This continual series of assessments and comparisons [...] brings about [...] a greater degree of alertness and a far sharper than ordinary sense of the architectural surround.[25]

---

21   Mary Carruthers, *The Book of Memory* (Cambridge: Cambridge University Press, 1990), p. 190.
22   Arakawa and Gins, *Reversible*, p. 9.
23   Arakawa and Gins, p. 45.
24   Arakawa and Gins, 'Landing Sites' (unpublished ms., 1990), p. 146.
25   Arakawa and Gins, *Reversible*, p. 283.

How a poetic encounter might be produced in an architectural surround such as the *Rotation House* is not yet known. Just as writing benefitted productively from the techniques of collage and cut-up imported from visual art early in the twentieth century then how the writing and reading of poetry can be extended and developed by such a radical approach to architecture and to perception is what concerns me presently.

What would be the poetic equivalent of Gins and Arakawa's *bioscleave house*?

> how this house has been pieced together is a centrally important feature of it. Assembled to form the whole of it are merely two wall-configurations (soon to be described), with repeated use made of each of the two, and a huge pressed-earth propeller-shaped terrain that lies flat on the floor as the floor. Step inside and you find what appears to be a campground in the midst of a rolling meadow — a propeller shaped meadow, or as we shall from now on refer to it, a prop meadow. The ceiling too, too, has a terrain–: prop meadow once again. The prop meadow also sits atop the house as its roof, the interior landscape brought outside and raised up to be closer to the sky. To recap: one, two, three meadows: floor, ceiling, roof [...]. The house describes it own formation, it might be said.[26]

In thinking about language as the primary environment (this thanks to Steve McCaffery whose observation/insight I'm indebted to) and the way language interacts, intersects, defines, absorbs, modifies as "architecture" is informing my own writerly production. What Arakawa and Gins provide us with is an architecture as open-ended as it is processual. The *Rotation House* is not a "work already completed, the house continues to be at work."[27] "Constructed to exist in the tense of *what if*, architecture that 'hypothesizes' presents itself as intentionally provisional."[28] I suggest that a sensing of this insight that language and its components comprise the primary environment is apparent especially in Gins and Arakawa's proposal for the "Antimortality Fractal Zipper City," wherein "all contours [...] have their basis in twin L-shaped labyrinths that abut."[29]

So I'm now considering "poetry" as almost a particular assemblage of perceptual angles, degrees, and vectors even, in what is the process of creative ideas being constructed through and in and in relation to language. The proposal of exchange between poetry and the intentionally provisional architecture of Arakawa and Gins is that a poetry of <<is>>, with the <<is>> a constantly shifting 'particular' might produce (in relation of language-as-primary-environment to architectural surrounds) sets of landing sites that would afford "insightful" mobility and negotiation in these mutually indeterminate and productive acts termed innovative poetry, and an "architecture that hypothesizes." (To introduce an innovative poetic into the practice of architecting? To 'activate' architecture poetically?)

Gins and Arakawa have written that "By compelling the body to move in two or more contradictory ways at once, the multilevel labyrinth systematically impedes the formation

---

[26] Arakawa and Gins, *Architectural Body*, p. 103. A comparable text would be Ron Silliman's *Ketjak*, in terms of "how this house has been pieced together [being] a centrally important feature of it."

[27] Arakawa and Gins, *Reversible*, p. 146.

[28] Arakawa and Gins, *Architectural Body*, p. 38.

[29] Arakawa and Gins, *Reversible*, pp. 252-253.

of the single, seemingly unified trajectory [...]"[30] Hopefully this is what will continue to develop similarly to the writer and reader of innovative poetry.[31]

---

[30] Arakawa and Gins, *Architectural Body*, pp. 94-95.

[31] The architectural projects of Arakawa and Gins aren't without precedents. Some of these would include: Constant's "labyrinth houses" [...] "consisting of a large number of rooms of irregular form, stairs at angles, lost corners, open spaces, culs-de-sac [...] provide places of adventure" et al. (Anthony Vidler, *The Architectural Uncanny* [Cambridge: MIT, 1992], p. 213; hereafter referred to as *AU*); "Matta Echaurren's "intrauterine" design for an apartment dedicated to the senses, published in *Minotaure* 11 (1938), was a deliberate attack on the commonplaces of the bourgeois home. The perspective view shows materials and forms that merge nature and the inorganic, the mathematical and the tactile. it was, Matta noted, "a space that will bring into consciousness human verticality." A true vertigo machine, composed of "different levels, a stair without a handrail to overcome the void," it was also a space of psychological interaction. its columns were "psychological Ionic"; its furnishings "supple, pneumatic." Matta specified inflatable rubber, cork, paper, and plaster for the soft areas, all for better contrast, framed in an "armature of rational architecture." Matta Echaurren, 'Mathématique sensible — Architecture du temps' (adaptation by Georges Hugnet), *Minotaure*, 11 (1938), p. 43; (also Vidler, *AU*, 153); Reyner Banham and François Dallegret's 'The Environment Bubble', *Art in America*, no. 53 (April 1965) (also Simon Sadler, *The Situationist City* [Cambridge: MIT], p. 39); Michael Webb's "Cuschicle" (for Archigram) 1966-1967, a "complete nomadic unit" (Sadler, *SC*, p. 136); a helicoidal house noted by Guy-Ernest Debord in 'Théorie de la dérive', *Les lèvres nues*, no. 9 (Brussels, 156), who admired its flexibility, was "presumably based in turn on Bruce Goff's extraordinary Bavinger House, Norman, Oklahoma, 1950-1955. The building combined the baroque, Frank Lloyd Wright-ish form beloved by the situationists with a daring suspended structural system of the type adopted by New Babylon's Hanging Sector, amplifying aspects of the work of Buckminster Fuller, such as his Dymaxion House, 1927." (Sadler, *SC*, fn. 103, p. 193) "Constant embraced the idea, envisaging a system of movable partitions within a fixed framework." (Sadler, *SC*, p. 132). Cf. Gins & Arakawa's Ponge-inspired snail house in *AB*, p. 33-46.

Jeff Derksen

"The Obvious Analogy Is With [Architecture]": Megastructural *My Life*

Taking the theoretical perspectives constructed by Fredric Jameson, Hal Foster, and Bernard Tschumi, this asks whether texts can be read architecturally, and what the spatialization of the text might mean. Specifically, the chapter puts the long poetic postmodernist sequence in dialogue with the late modernist megastructures of the 1960s. Reading Lyn Hejinian's *My Life* against the structures of architects such as Corbusier, this chapter proposes one answer to those questions and reminds us of the social and economic preconditions of both the questions raised and the answers suggested by form.

I.

"The appetite for architecture today," Fredric Jameson proposes in his reading of architecture in the postmodern, "must be in reality an appetite for something else."[1] This something else, it turns out, is text. Following what Hal Foster has designated "the textual turn" where a "new model of art as text" emerged from the influence of poststructuralism on postmodernism, it became relatively easy, even inviting, to read cultures, nations, history, the body, landscape, and architecture as texts.[2] Built space offers itself up to Jameson's reading in which rooms are words, corridors and hallways are articulating verbs and adverbs, and architectural details are adjectives which modify the space. These "sentences" of built space are then read from a grammatical and syntactical position by a reader/dweller and the entire built space (or text/architecture) is located within the larger text of the urban.[3] But this grammar of architecture as narrative (building on Todorov's structuralist gem, *The Grammar of Narrative*) ultimately deflects a reading of architecture itself, as architecture must be textualized — rendered into *something else* — in order to be read. Once textualized, it cannot be text and architecture in the same moment. And once its constituent parts are reduced to a grammar with programmatic uses, architecture takes on, once again, a static or even monumental appearance. Textualization, following the textual turn, does not necessarily escape the crisis within literary studies.

Bernard Tschumi, in shifting from the structural to the performative, establishes a parallel between architecture and literariness though a shared event horizon: "The unfolding of events in a literary context inevitably suggested parallels to the unfolding of events in architecture."[4] Along with addressing temporality as well as spatiality, the advantage in Tschumi's formulation is that architecture is not made static by establishing grammatical functions for spaces, but rather built space will be determined by its uses and not by its syntactical positioning. But a counter material narrative in which architecture can

---

[1] Fredric Jameson, *Postmodernism, or, The Cultural Logic of Late Capitalism* (Durham: Duke UP, 1991), p. 98.
[2] Hal Foster, *The Return of the Real: The Avant-garde at the End of the Century* (Cambridge, Mass.: MIT Press, 1996), p. 71.
[3] Jameson, *Postmodernism*, p. 105.
[4] Berard Tschumi, *Architecture and Disjuncture* (MIT Press: Cambridge MA., 1998), p. 146.

simultaneously be architecture and text and still remain open to rearticulations of its spatial and social meanings also exists. This narrative is a modernist moment rather than Jameson's postmodern paradigm. The Ministry of Education and Health building (MES) in Rio de Janeiro is a defining site of architectural modernism's alteration by local conditions, materials, political economy, construction practices, patterns of development and structures of feeling. As Valerie Fraser points out in her *Building the New World: Studies in the Modern Architecture of Latin America 1930-1960*, the internationalist style was translated quickly into a national style and vernacular in Brazil. But this national style, arising out of European modernism, was not merely or narrowly national; it embodied a forward-looking transnationalism as well, as nations dug out a place for themselves in the world system and the project of modernization. The MES building, begun from an original plan by Le Corbusier in 1936 and altered by a team of Brazilian architects which included Oscar Niemeyer and landscape architect Roberto Burle Marx, stands as an example of the complexities of a modernization project materialized architecturally.

The textual key lies in a detail. An original idea from Le Corbusier — and an element already existing in Latin architecture — was a system of fixed brise-soleil to counter the South American sun. Le Courbusier's design was improved upon by the Brazilians so the sunbreaks could be adjusted to best block the sun according to the time of day and season. Not only did the mobile sunbreaks give the façade a kind of animation via *tropos* (reminiscent of Charles Olson's process of topos, tropos and typos in poetics), but this rearticulation of the façade was able to add a textual and social element to the building. As Fraser describes it: "Over the years, the Cariocans have exploited this façade as a sort of giant billboard, with the louvres arranged to spell out simple slogans."[5] The MES building is, in this instance, both textual and architectural, as well as modern and vernacular. Facing the major avenues of the city, these "slogans" could alter the social syntax of the city rather than the building merely being subsumed into it. In this moment, the building is simultaneously text and architecture, narrative and event, social and spatial.

Following these narratives, the correlative question developing from the textualization of architecture is, Can texts be read architecturally? What would be the impulse to spatialize texts? Is this linked to "the spatial turn" that Edward Soja identifies as "a turn to new ways of thinking in which space occupies a central position as a form of analysis, critical inquiry, practice, theory-building, politics"?[6] Certainly there is a trail of parallels and intersections with architecture and poetry in the twentieth century that lends a reciprocal reading. Adolf Loos' famous 1908 article "Ornamentation and Crime" coincides roughly with the Imagist Manifesto from 1913; William Carlos Williams' statement "the poem is a machine made of words" parallels Le Corbusier's notion of a building as a "dwelling machine"; New Brutalism's relationship to the "honesty" of materials is also found in avant-gardist poetic positions from the Russian Formalists onward. More recent parallels include the strikingly similar relationship of transgresssion, stability, excess and ideological formations in Steve McCaffery's essays on poetics in *North of Intention* and

---

[5]   Valerie Fraser, *Building the New World: Studies in the Modern Architecture of Latin America 1930-1960* (London: Verso, 2000), p. 160.
[6]   Edward Soja, 'Lessons in Spatial Justice', *Hunch*, 1 (1999), p. 99.

Tschumi's *Architecture and Disjunction*; the use of software to generate architectural shape by Greg Lynn's Form architectural office is similar to poets who use software to generate poetic form, such as Jackson MacLow and Brian Stefans, and with web-based poetry using Flash software. Only the Dutch sociological approaches to cities, such as MVRDV's datascapes (shown in their 1999 *Metacity Datatown*) lacks a clear poetic correlative, for sociological impulses in poetry have been around issues of class and place (as Olson's *Maximus Poems* indicates, and as Reznikoff's *Testimony* exemplifies), while it appears this project in architecture is a methodology to categorize "use" of buildings and space, but with no means to differentiate class usages.

The parallel I want to investigate — read? — here is between the long poem and an architectural impulse that is set both in (and in some ways) between modernism and postmodernism — the Megastructure. Beginning with the formal similarities of Lyn Hejinian's on-going long poem, *My Life*, and the model of architectural Megastructures from the late fifties through the late sixties, I will move towards the relationship of the production of meaning — textual, spatial and social — and the position of an imagined reader/dweller in built and textual space. This intersection of the relationship of the productive reader and the "user" of architectural space leads to a larger — and antagonistic — problematic of the relationship of how social meaning is made spatial, and how space is central to the production of social meaning.

While it is possible to draw parallels between the structure of text and the structure of built space, a more vital and ultimately more socially thick relationship is in how the spatial/architectural meets the textual/poetic in the social space of meaning production. The mechanics of meaning production — and the construction of a productive reader/dweller — runs through the binaries of determinism (architectural/textual) and agency and the structural and subjective. For the Language poets in the early 1980s, an avant-gardist North American formation, this struggle begins with the rejection of the closed text and leads to the theorization of the productive reader who is given agency through the specific devices of the open text. In architectural theory, the binary struggle leads to the rejection of the instrumentalism of built space and a turn toward a more active dweller whose "flexible" lifestyle will determine the space through use. Yet, in both cases, the "primacy of form" is conquered to be replaced by the primacy of another form: open replaces closed text, instrumental spaces are replaced by flexible or adaptable spaces. At stake, or under a speculative project, is the constitution of a model of a reader/dweller in relation to the social.

II.

The Megastructure is situated perhaps at the end of a modernist instrumentalist gesture of social and spatial planning which sought to extend into the totality of life, and at the beginning of a postmodernist project of collage, historical references, and vernacular uses of architecture that opened toward the current emphasis on flexibility.

The relationship of the structural and the subjective in built space, a key aspect of the Megastructure, is illustrated in a well-known moment of Megastructure history — Le Coubusier's Algiers plan from 1931 and its Fort l'Empereur. Reyner Banham describes Le Corbusier's drawing as depicting, "in curving and accelerated perspective, the massive substructure of an elevated super-highway, built like a giant bookcase of reinforced concrete on the shelves of which the inhabitants have built two-story houses to suit their own tastes, not necessarily in *le style Corbu*."[7] Banham goes on to note that Le Corbusier provides a prototype for the megastructures of the sixties in two elements that are carried forward: "[O]n the one hand, a massive, even monumental, supporting frame; on the other, various arrangements of habitable containers beyond the control of the architect."[8] Le Corbusier's "bookshelf" allows for insertion of indvidually designed housing units into the supporting structural frame. This insertion that is bound by rules of height and width, but not of style and is therefore understood as being beyond the control of the architect who designed the Megastructure. Famously, the drawing depicts a 'Moorish' house near the centre of the structure, highlighting the range of architectural styles that could be shelved in the frame. Rather than just seeing this as a design variation, it is an attempt, central to the definition of Megastructures, to account for space for the subjective within the determining framework of the structural. Variation in a Megastructure moves in two ways: beyond the singular architect (or heroic architect) whose finished project is a *Gesamtkunstwerk* with no input from the dweller, there is also a movement beyond the built space as the dominant organizing principle of the dweller. Megastructures establishe the tension of the structural and the subjective as a productive constraint that is to be resolved spatially. What is spectacular in Megastuctures is, of course, the scale at which this tension is staged.

Banham's own description of the Fort l'Empereur leans toward a textualization. Curiously, the image of a bookshelf semantically connects to a recurring and morphing sentence found in *My Life* (which recurs as a structural element) in Hejinian's text: "I wrote my name in every one of his books." The assertion of the subjective (or even "personal") into the structural is key, whether it is a megastructural frame or the (gendered) structure of an existing library. Banham's excellent history traces a convincing importance of the Megastructure from existing structures to speculative projects. The existing architectural models begin with Italian hillside towns, the Cliff Palace pueblo in Mesa Verde, Colorado, the Ponte Vecchio, Florence, through the academic complexes (Scarborough College, Toronto; Simon Fraser University, Vancouver) to the realization of many megastructures in Montreal at Expo 67 year (also Canada's centenary), which included Buckminster Fuller's U. S. pavilion dome, and the theme pavilion "Man the Producer" with its "zones of possibilities" that coincided with Constant Nieuwenhuis' Situationalist impulses in his Neo-Babylone model. Also featured at Expo 67 was the Megastructure housing project, Habitat, by Safdie with pre-fab concrete housing capsules stacked and plugged into a supporting substructure.

---

[7]   Reyner Banham, *Megastructure: Urban Futures of the Recent Past* (London: Thames and Hudson, 1976), p. 8.
[8]   Banham, p. 8.

The history of unrealized speculative megastructural projects is spectacular and futuristic, freed of course from the usual constraints of building and the negotiations of materials, governments and clients. Speculative projects and models are the discursive site of possibilities within architecture and can point to an imagined future to counter hegemonic views on the forms of dwelling and of social organization. The speculative moves through the discursive and links to the social. This movement is enacted by the Japanese Metabolists in their massive speculative projects through the late fifties into the early sixties. Using the new technological possibilities for materials and a monumental use of concrete to address Tokyo's rapid growth, the Metabolists laid a groundwork for Megastructures to come. Kiyonoru Kikutake's Ocean City project (1962), which was to float on concrete islands, combined permanent and temporary elements: the cylindrical concrete towers would hold plugged-in dwelling units that could (theoretically) drop off and be replaced, metabolically, like leaves on a tree, according to the needs of the city. Kenzo Tange's massive visionary Tokyo Bay project (1960) extended the city 18 kilometres on the water via a linked structure (which doubled as a highway) across the bay and sent out A-frame housing structures which were terraced with stacked living units across the other half of the bay. These extendable projects that reacted to an expanding urbanism tried to establish a homology between the organic growth and development of the city (and, on a smaller scale, the body) with the Megastructure. Nowhere is the relationship of the structural and the subjective more tenuously and dynamically worked out than in the permanent aspect of the Megaprojects in contrast with the metabolic growth, alterations and shedding of the temporary housing units.

The speculative project that had the most impact visually and conceptually was Archigram's Plug-In City (1963-64). Sharing the detailing, that, like Tange's Boston Harbour project of 1959, materializes the speculative, this drawing of the futuristic megacity represents an adaptable and open-ended urbanity featuring plug-in units that could be rearranged via cranes. Yet true to earlier megastructural projects, the city used the A-frame structures (derived from Walter Gropius) and towers reminiscent of Metabolist projects, as well as following Tange's "proposal for a mass-human scale form which includes a megaform and discrete, rapidly changeable functional units which fit within the larger framework."[9] Again the permanent and temporary aspects of the megastructure are evident. The seemingly oppositional functions of massive scale yet quick, adaptable and flexible elements give the Megastructure its metabolic character, an openness in which the structural adapts to the subjective, in a rewriting of architectural detemvinism, rather than overriding potential uses with a program that inhibits adaptability. Banham foregrounds this openness and adaptability in Archigram's "open" city, elements that "are the essentials of Archigram's vision from Plug-in City onwards, striving for a city structure that would yield to individual desires more pliantly than previous forms of cities, and would derive its aesthetic from a demonstration of that compliance. Everything about the two drawings suggested permissive change and variability."[10] The "permissive" aspect of Plug-In City is

---

[9] Fumihiko Maki, *Investigations in Collective Form* (St. Louis: Washington UP, 1964), p. 8.

[10] Banham, *Megastructure*, p. 96.

an extension of Le Corbusier's plan that allowed for style variation within the "giant bookcase" of Fort l'Empereur. But what Archigram has imagined is a city that is flexible to a much greater degree based on use rather than housing unit style.

By Plug-in City, in 1964 (designated "Megayear" by Banham) the ideas of the Metabolists had fused with "megadesign" of France and Italy to produce the formal characteristics of Megastructures. In *Megastructure Bibiography*, Ralph Wilcoxon defines the four key features of megastructures (which I quote from Banham):

1. constructed of modular units;
2. capable of great or even 'unlimited' extension;
3. a structural framework into which smaller structural units (for example, rooms, houses, or small buildings of other sorts) can be built — or even 'plugged-in or 'clipped-on' after having been prefabricated elsewhere;
4. a structural framework expected to have a useful life much longer than that of the smaller units which it might support.

These four elements delineate a Megastructure from simply any huge project, so that Megastructure is not, as Banham worries, "a concept [that] could absorb almost anything that could be stuffed into it — a grab-bag category containing anything that came to hand, so long as it was large."[11] But, despite this relatively precise description of defining elements, and despite the Megastructure's futuristic vision and its construction based on technological innovation (for instance, Safdie's Habitat in Montreal used mass-produced 70 ton concrete housing units fitted with modular fiberglas bathrooms), megastructural possibilities and enthusiasms faded in the late sixties. Aside from the obvious problem that the size of Megastructures made them difficult to finance and necessarily lengthy to build, two particular critiques dispersed support for Megastructures. First, despite their emphasis on being flexible or open toward the lifes of people who lived in them, Megastructures were so large, or were placed in such a way, that they would wipe out — or literally overshadow — existing patterns of urban life which had been established over time. Secondly, coming in the sixties, Megastructures were open to the critique that the "flexibility" that they tried to program in was in fact limited and offered no radical change in social relations. Despite its formation of a mega-urbanism and the potential collectivities, coalitions, or even radical democratic formations that could arise in such a built social space, and the imagined or built-in "permissiveness" of Megastructures that was to allow for a generative production of social space, Megaprojects were seen as overly deterministic. For instance, even with the mobility of plug-in units that could be shifted location and formations with cranes, and the inflatable balloons for weather protection, Plug-In City designed in a limited microstructural agency for the user/dweller.

The "Megastructure year" overlaps with what Marc Dessauce has dubbed "the inflatable moment" of pneumatic (or inflatable) architecture. Already Plug-In City had included inflatable elements, so the Megastructure and pneumatics did exist side by side despite their contrasts in scale, volume, weight and speed of construction. But, inflatables took the promise of a more open relationship to built space to another material, discursive, and

---

[11] Banham, p. 195.

ultimately, ontological level. Inflatables represented an architecture that was responsive, rather than deterministic, to the body and confronted a spatial and urban sense of alienation. The source of this alienation was understood to be the weight, volume, and history of urbanism and Paris, Vienna, and London became centers for inflatable projects. As Dessauce remarks, inflatables marked "a show of impatience" with the transformation of cities, but "beyond the fun and play, the inflatable ethos possessed a subversive constitution which recommended it to avant-garde practice, and the discourses of urban alieantation and ecology [...]."[12] It is the limited sense of agency that draws Archigram criticism from the more directly politicized Utopie Group — the group of Paris architects and intellectuals whose work with inflatable structures was tied to architecture as a socially transformative element.

In the catalogue for the project *The Inflatable Moment: Pneumatics and Protest in 68,* Utopie Group members, Jean Aubert and Jean-Paul Jungmann, toss ideological darts at Archigram as "stylists" with "real graphic talent."[13] While the Utopie Group sought to link ideology and architecture (particularly inflatable structures), they saw Archigram as operating on a separation of design and politics. As Jungmann caustically wrote in 1998: "The English Archigram was more pragmatic, and had no problem freely surfing for years on *the amazing, plug-in, living city, air hab, capsule-home,* etc. concepts. There was no ideological limit to their talent. Politics and design remained two different realms for them. But not for us."[14] This transition from hard to soft, from mega to inflatable, from concrete to transparent (and materialized in the transition from Expo 67 as the Megastructure finale and Expo 70 in Osaka as the inflatables showcase) is also, gravely located by Banham, as "the hinge of a crisis in architectural thinking that may also prove to have been the terminal crisis of 'Modern' architecture as we have known it."[15]

My Life likewise hinges on the categories of modernism and postmodernism, although not in a moment of crisis. Without rigidly defining modernism and postmodernism as stylistic and temporal categories, but rather opening them to uneven development and simultaneity, *My Life* brings the modernist gesture of a life-long poem into a set of problematics defined as postmodernist: the construction of subjectivity and gender, the position of the reader within meaning production, and (generally) the intersection of the subjective and the structural. The interface of the structural and the subjective in *My Life* can be read on a social level as an interface with Althusser's ideological state apparatuses — primarily the family, but also national ISAs — and a gendered subject. Even in the different scalar dynamics of text and architecture, the similarities between Megastructural properties and problematics of the subjective and the structural and Hejinian's *My Life* are immediately evident. *My Life* thematically enacts what Megastructures confronted structurally: the position of the subjective within the structural. But the confrontation in *My*

---

[12] Marc Dessauce, *The Inflatable Moment: Pneumatics and Protest in 68* (Princeton: Princeton Architecture Press, 1999), p. 14.

[13] Jean Aubert, 'Statement,' in *The Inflatable Moment: Pneumatics and Protest in 68*, ed. by Marc Dessauce (Princeton: Princeton Architecture Press, 1999).

[14] Aubert, p. 67.

[15] Banham, *Megastructure*, p. 9.

Life is on an ideological level and not, as the Utopie Group and others accused Archigram, on a design level. The foregrounding of the structural in *My Life*, through its formal transparency, lays bare not only this literary device but the determining effects of the social — via language — on subjectivity. This is the "old news" of the Language writers' project, yet one which "stays news" as ideas of social determinancy, instrumentalism, and the internalization of ideology give way to ideas of flexibility, individualization, and subjective assertion and consumption both in new poetry formations and in architectural discourse.

How does the structuring of *My Life* coincide or overlap with the four defining principles of Megastructures? Do the literary devices which structure *My Life* align with a construction modular units plugged-in, clipped-on into a structural framework capable of extension? The similarities between *My Life* and an architectural Megastructures are strengthened by looking at both the "structural framework" of her "autobiography" and by the structuring effects of its inter- and intratextuality.

My Life was first published by Burning Deck Press in 1980: that edition had thirty-seven sections of thirty-seven sentences. This ordering principle echoed the fact that when the book was first written, in 1978, Hejinian was thirty-seven years old. As well, each section represented a time in her life.[16] Correspondingly, Hejinian added eight new sections plus eight new sentences at various intervals within the existing sections when she revised the book in 1986.[17] Structurally, *My Life* is based on an unlimited expansion that is central to a megastructure. Its expansion happens on two levels: the structural framework can be infinitely added to as well as can the individual chapters or units. New units or *modular chapters* are plugged in or clipped-on to the existing framework, but the units are also added to from within. However, this expansion is based on maintaining the symmetrical relationship of the framework and the modular chapters, itself based on Hejinian's biological years at the time of writing. This symmetry complies to the gridded frame of many Megastructures and to the Metabolists' incorporation of natural change, of permanence and temporality.

The generative aspect of Megastructures and the Metabolist projects bears some resemblance to a procedural poetics. Marjorie Perloff has already noted the influence of procedural poetics on *My Life* with its 37 X 37 (and later, 45 X 45) grid or "square."[18] But, to return to the position that these formal similarities provide only a limited "reading" of architecture and text, it is the relationship of the structural to the subjective that provides an aesthetic and ideological tension. Perloff argues that "*constraint* or *procedurality* is not equivalent to the concept of *rule* in traditional metric," but that a procedural poetics "is primarily *generative*, the constraint determining, not what is already fixed as a property of the text, but *how* the writer will proceed with his composition."[19] This view of a productive constraint, or a productive determination aligns with two components of Megastructures.

---

16   See the biographic note in Lyn Hejinian, *The Cell*, Sun & Moon Classics 21 (Los Angeles: Sun & Moon, 1992).

17   See Marjorie Perloff, *Artifice of Absorption: Writing Poetry in the Age of Media* (Chicago: Chicago UP, 1991), p. 162.

18   Perloff, p. 164.

19   Perloff, p. 139.

First, Megastructures have (amongst others) the constraint of the structural frame, but this is shifted to a generative element through the adaptability of the housing units within the frame and by the altering of the frame itself through extension.

Intratextuality, that is achieved typographically and procedurally, further adds to the density of structure in *My Life*. Each section of *My Life* is contextualized or prefaced with an inset italicized epigraph: throughout the book these epigraphs are buried within other sections either verbatim or in a slightly altered form. As these sentences are not used intratextually until they have appeared as an epigraph, the earliest phrases ("A pause, a rose, something on paper," and "As for we who 'love to be astonished'") become the most repeated and run as structuring devices throughout the text. These regular, but unregulated, occurrences create the book's synchronic effect that Rosemarie Waldrop describes:

> The method puts in a nutshell the tension between the synchronic presentation and the essentially diachronic pattern of (auto)biography behind it. It also very beautifully embodies the nature of the subject of biography: the person is always both the same and changing with time and circumstance.[20]

However, to move away from the text as a temporal marker of a life (how *My Life* has generally been received), these repetitions build up a complex structure which can be perceived spatially as a frame rather than a representational model.

Likewise, the dense intertextual axis that accumulates through the numerous quotations from Hejinian's own texts both builds and extends the notion of a structural framework. These recontextualized fragments and sentences from other projects from Hejinian reoccur, recombine in hybrid forms, and comment on other texts and on the very method of intertextuality. This intertextuality not only links Hejinian's work structurally and semantically, it also extends the structural framework beyond *My Life*, paralleling the Megastructural principle of extension. Many intertextual references form this extended structure: the humourous appearance of a fragment about fleas in *The Guard, My Life, The Person* and *Redo*; the epigraphs "Altruism in poetry," "As for we who 'love to be astonished'" and "The obvious analogy is with music" from *My Life* that are reworked in *The Guard, Redo*, and *The Person*; and the recurrent images of weather, yellow and red, birds, dogs, cars, and water that run through these small books.

Banham took a textual turn in his description of Le Corbusier drawing the "obvious analogy" of a book on a giant bookshelf to illustrate the relationship of the structural to the subjective. Hejinian, in her description of the model of consciousness that the inter- and intratextual methodology proposes, takes a spatial turn. Hejinian describes this consciousness as "more closely resembl[ing] a stack or a pile, in which sentences or parts of sentences are the plates or potentially vast planes in a pile, banking frontally."[21] This spatial description inscribes an alternative model of subjectivity. This subjectivity does not appear as autonomous or natural, as somehow outside of the social relations that construct it,

---

[20] Rosemarie Waldrop, "'Chinese Windmills Turn Horizontally': On Lyn Hejinian", *Temblor*, 10 (1989), 220.
[21] Lyn Hejinian, 'Language & Paradise', *Line*, 6 (1985), 95.

instead it shows "the heterogeneity of the components leading to the production of subjectivity."[22]

Open City, Open Text and Contructing the Reader/Dweller

> *The devices of the production of subjectivity can be at the level of megapoli as well as at the level of the poet's play of language.*[23]

The tension of the structural and the subjective is not only worked out or negotiated thematically and formally, but is a central discursive problematic for both the spatial/architectural and the textual/poetic. The relationship of spatial and social determinism within instrumental architectural programs coincides with the move from a closed text and the construction of a productive reader within avant-gardist poetics. Hejinian's central essay "The Rejection of Closure" negotiates this binary between open and closed text, as well as establishing a homology between textual form and social formations:

> The "open text," by definition, is open to the world and particularly to the reader. It invites participation, rejects the authority of the writer over the reader, and thus, by analogy, the authority implicit in other (social, economic, cultural hierarchies [...]. The "open text" often emphasizes or foregrounds process, either the process of the original composition or of subsequent compositions by readers, and thus resists the cultural tendencies that seeks to identify and fix material, turns it into a product; that is it resists reduction.[24]

In the poetics of the language writers, the homology of language and social form privileges an effect for poetry based on a structural resemblance across the field of language: the homology possible after the "textual turn." is that society is structured as a language.[25] For the early theorizing of the language writers, this homology was binding, with the functions of capitalist society deeply embedded into all levels of language, even at the grammatical level: "Grammar as repressive mechanism, regulates free circulation of meaning (the repression of polysemeity into monosemeity and guided towards a sense of meaning as accumulated, as surplus value of signification)."[26] For the language writers this is a decidedly productive homology because it opens a range of speculation on the relationship between poetry and the social and between the micro-aesthetic and the macro-ideological.

Similarly, within architectural discourse, repressive social structures have been under-stood to be materialized in architecture, as Bataille argues, "In practice, only the ideal being

---

22   Félix Guattari, 'Language, Consciousness and Society', *Poetics Journal*, 9 (1991), p. 107.

23   Guattari, p. 115.

24   Lyn Hejinian, 'The Rejection of Closure', in *Writing/Talks*, ed. by Bob Perelman (Carbondale: Southern Illinois University, 1985), p. 272.

25   Foster, *Real*, p. 71-98.

26   Steve McCaffery, 'From the Notebooks', *The L=A=N=G=U=A==G=E Book*, ed. by Charles Bernstein and Bruce Andrews (Carbondale: Souther Illinios UP, 1984), p. 160.

of society, that which orders and prohibits with authority, expresses itself in what are architectural compositions in the strict sense of the term."[27] Bataille is not arguing distinctly for a closed text version of architecture — a model which would overly determine use, lifestyle, etc. — but is proceeding more homologically: that social power is expressed through architecture. This is still, however, a step removed from architecture as an ideological state apparatus, an apparatus that *inflicts* (rather than merely expresses) social regulation. Instead, determinism within architectural discourse has been understood, on one level, as a modernist social project. For Habermas that "[t]he spirit of modernism was to participate in the totality of social manifestations" overburdened the modernist architectural project.[28] A crisis or failure begins at this overburdened point because the utopian project of "preconceived forms of life" was "a hopeless underestimation of the diversity, complexity and variability of modern aspects of life, but also because modernized societies with their functional interdependencies go beyond the dimensions of living conditions, which could be gauged by the planner with his imagination."[29] Life always exceeds architecture, or within the new discourse of individualization, the subject always exceeds the structural: an abrupt flip of Althusser's formulation.

However, like the "moment" of inflatable architecture which sought to go beyond instrumentalizing a lifestyle and aimed toward the transformation of the social subject beginning with the relationship of architecture and urban space, the model of the open text and the rejection of closure do not aim at merely refiguring the text, but at transforming the reading subject. The opened text is the structural shift that allows the model of the productive reader to counter the alienating effect of commodified language. Essentially, the open text structurally enables the reader to construct meaning as a nonalienated producer in a similar (or homologous) position as the writer. Jed Rasula claims in his admirable book, *The American Poetry Wax Museum*, that: "Language poetry's most conspicuous contribution to a discussion of politics and poetic value has been an examination of the sublimated political asymmetries of the reader/writer relationship."[30] Yet, this denies the extension, that some language writers projected, into the social, not because Rasula views this as a contribution only within poetics, but because he structures it as refiguring the reader/writer relationship rather than the reader's relationship to ideology and therefore social relations. *The language writers seek the transformation of the reader rather than the transformation of uses of the cultural product.* This transformation of "use" and its extension into effects is cultural studies' imaging of a productive consumption and not the transformation of a social subject.

The program of Megastructures exists in this transformative tension as well. It sought to refigure the relations of urbanity, negotiate the rapid increase in city size, and to give the dweller a more active role in constructing social meaning — but all within a mega-heavy,

---

[27] Georges Bataille, 'Architecture', in *Rethinking Architecture: a reader in cultural theory*, ed. by Neil Leach (London and New York: Routledge, 1997), p. 21.

[28] Jürgen Habermas, 'Modern and Postmodern Architecture', in *Rethinking Architecture*, p. 230.

[29] Habermas, p. 232.

[30] Jed Rasula, *The American Poetry Wax Museum: Reality Efects 1940-1990* (Urbana, Ill.: National Council of Teachers of English, 1996), p. 406.

mega-monumental, and mega-architectural structure. In this active role, enabled at one level as variety in the design of housing units and at another level as rearrangable housing units, there is a transformation in the role of "the sublimated political asymetries" of the architect and the dweller. This asymetry had already been addressed poetically in Heidigger's proposition that, "Yet those buildings that are not dwelling places remain in turn determined by dwelling insofar as they serve man's dwelling."[31] And within the history of international conferences that had defined social roles for architecture, Banham notes: "The claims of urban 'spontaneity' had been canvassed as early as the 1951 meeting of the Congres internationaux d'architecture moderne (CIAM); subsequent movements of the fifties and sixties, notably the rise of Pop art, had emphasized the non-professional contribution to the visual urban fabric."[32] But beyond an equalization of the role of the architect and the imagined role of the dweller, the utopian moment of the inflatable was to imagine the transformation of a social subject through architecture and urban space. In this idelogical deployment of material, the inflatable moment corresponds to the transformative impulse of the language moment while the megastructural project was more (ironically) limited in its claims and scope.

The relationship of the open text and the closed text — one in which structural and authorial intentions (and by extension, social intention) are exceeded, appropriated or read in a manner that reveals the embedded ideology of the text (and thus transforms the reader into a social subject that can read ideology rather than misrecognizing and then internalizing it) — reside in the disjuncture between encoding and decoding. The productive reader is posed in an interstices of the subjective and the structural in a particularly ideological manner: the productive reader can bring a subjective, context-specific reading to a text, but this does not remain only on the subjective level (as it does in productive consumption) but it leads to a larger "decoding" of the ideological basis of the text and the recognition of the ideological structure and effects embedded in language itself. A utopian configuration for sure, but one based on ideology and effects and not only personal freedoms.

Similarly, in architectural discourse, a disjuncture between intention and determinism, and use and event opens up. For Tschumi, the research of the architect becomes the "exploration of the disjunction between expected form and expected use."[33] This disjuncture does not lead to a utopian formation of the user/social subject, but to a negotiation of the paired concepts of determinism and event, form and function. While the language poets' utopian moment imagined the text as the ideological vehicle to initiate a transformed social subject who could "read" ideology, the rejection of that sort of instrumentalism (even one so driven toward equitable relations in the production of meaning) in architecture leads to an architectural program that adapts to potential social uses by building in flexibility into structures and built space. When Rem Koolhaas gazed at the Berlin Wall during an early graduate-student days research project, he prophetically realized: "I would never again

---

[31]   Martin Heidegger, 'Building, Dwelling, Thinking', in *Rethinking Architecture*, p. 100.
[32]   Reyner Banham, *Megastructure: Urban Futures of the Recent Past* (London: Thames and Hudson, 1976), p. 9.
[33]   Tschumi, *Architecture*, p. 147.

believe in form as the primary vessel of meaning."[34] This primacy is replaced by the triumph of the subjective over the structural in which architecture's role is to enhance potential individualized uses while still retaining elements of functionalism.

A German critic, Andreas Ruby, reflects a predominant line in architectural discourse today and pronounces the end of utopian gestures in architecture: "In this age of post-critical research-based architecture, the architect turns his back once and for all on the idea of the creator as visionary of a utopian configuration to become a data manager of an increasingly complex reality."[35] Sadly, this impulse is at odds with other discourses, having already rejected a vision of a singular creator, which have taken a turn toward a reimagined utopianism. This return to a utopian imagination is a reaction to the truimphalist discourses of globalization which proclaim the neo-liberal global system as the inevitable shape of the world. There is the recognition that an ideological effect of the discourses of globalization (extending the classical effect of ideology) is to make globalism appear natural and not a process. In particular David Harvey has invoked a spatiotemporal utopiansim to counter this ideological effect. "Given the defects and difficulties of utopias of both spatial form and social process, the most obvious alternative (other than total abandonment of any pretense of utopianism whatsoever) is to build a utopianism that is explicitly spatiotemporal."[36] With the turn away from a larger more social imagination in architecture — one that goes beyond the management of complexities — architects will be left out of this refiguration of spatiotemporal relations.

My Life, and the utopian configuration of the productive reader in language writing, propose a social subject that negotiates the structural and the subjective. It is a formulation which recognizes the tensions and disjunctures as well as the overlaps and congruencies of social determinations (whether these are discursive or spatial) and agency at the level of the subject. While this concept has come under heavy questioning and even rejection by key member of the language writers' formation (notably Bob Perelman), if the dynamic that it textualizes and examines is moved into architectural discourse, the problematic then takes on a another level of social urgency. The rejection of instrumentalism, however heavily critiqued it may be, is never total — it is a continual program of a hegemonic formation. The world is always being shaped.

---

[34]   Rem Koolhaas and Bruce Mao, *S,M,X,XL: OMA* (Rotterdam: 010 Publishers: 1995), p. 227.
[35]   Andreas Ruby, 'The Specter of Research', in *Archilab 99* (Orleans: Archilab, 1999), p. 15.
[36]   David Harvey, *Spaces of Hope* (Berkeley: U of California P, 2000), p. 182.

Marjorie Perloff

John Cage's Dublin, Lyn Hejinian's Leningrad:
Poetic Cities as Cyberspaces

Beginning with the modernist city mapped so precisely by the Dublin of James Joyce's *Ulysses*, this chapter — a city both real and symbolic — this chapter examines the transformation of such places into the disembodied and rearticulated spaces of postmodernism. From John Cage's mesostic "writing through" of *Finnegans Wake* in his radio play *Roaratorio*, which both condenses Joyce's text with a distorting anamorphosis and also provides an aleatoric mapping of sonic space, to Lyn Hejinian's long poetic sequence *Oxota*, which transforms Pushkin's Petersberg into a late-modern Leningrad, the essay demonstrates how we can understand the results of such textual transformations in the terms of what Marcos Nowak has termed a "liquid architecture."

In Chapter 5 ("Lotus Eaters") of *Ulysses*, Leopold Bloom sets out from home to begin his circuitous voyage through Dublin. We read:

> By lorries along Sir John Rogerson's Quay Mr. Bloom walked soberly, past Windmill lane, Leask's the linseed crusher's, the postal telegraph office. Could have given that address too. And past the sailors' home. He turned from the morning noises of the quayside and walked through Lime street. By Brady's cottages a boy for the skins lolled, his bucket of offal linked, smoking a chewed fagbutt. A smaller girl with scars of eczema on her forehead eyed him, listessly holding her battered caskhoop. Tell him if he smokes he won't grow. O let him! His life isn't such a bed of roses! Waiting outside pubs to bring da home. Come home to ma, da, Slack hour: won't be many there. He crossed Townsend street, passed the frowning face of Bethel. El, yes: house of: Aleph, Beth. And past Nichols' the undertaker's. At eleven it is. Time enough. Daresay Corny Kelleher bagged that job at O'Neill's. Singing with his eyes shut. Corny. Met her once in the park. In the dark. What a lark. Police tout. Her name and address she then told with my tooraloom tooraloom tay. O, surely he begged it. Bury him cheap in a whatyoumaycall. With my tooraloom, tooraloom, tooraloom, tooraloom.[1]

Here is a classic Modernist treatment of the city. At one level, Joyce's fictional mode is one of scrupulous documentary realism: we know exactly *where* Bloom walks and what shops and buildings he passes; these are, moreover, *actual* sites, whose existence in 1904, the time of the novel, can be verified. Indeed, the map of Dublin provides Joyce with a basic geometric grid: the central area, approximately two square miles, is encircled by the canal and divided neatly into quarters. The river Liffey, running from west to east, bisects the city, and Sackville Street, running north and south, crosses the Liffey at O'Connell Bridge. "Lotus Eaters" is set in the southeast quadrant (from Westland Row and past Trinity College to the baths); the northeast quadrant contains the slum and dock areas ("Circe," "Eumaeus"); the southwest is the business district centering around the castle ("Wandering Rocks"), and the northwest features the Ormond Hotel ("Sirens") and Kiernan's pub ("Cyclops"). The center of town, from Nelson's Pillar down Sackville Street, across

---

[1]   James Joyce, *Ulysses* (New York: Random House, 1961), p. 70.

O'Connell Bridge, and through the shopping district, can be traced almost step by step in "Lestrygonians," when Bloom wanders the streets on the way to lunch. And in the "Hades" chapter, the funeral carriage makes its way from the southeast, through the city center, and on to the northern outskirts.[2]

It is well known that Joyce mapped out his characters' movements through the city with a slide rule and compass. At the same time, Dublin functions as symbolic locale: June 16 at 10 A.M., a hot sultry day in Dublin, is emblematic of the narcotic state of the Lotus Eaters, whose tale provides the mythic analogue for Joyce's chapter. At this "slack hour," the boy in front of Brady's cottages "lolls" and smokes a "chewed fagbutt." The "smaller girl" "eye[s] Bloom listlessly"; in the next paragraph, Bloom stops in front of the Oriental Tea Company, and daydreams about the exotic East. And further: Joyce has planted any number of metonymic images that prefigure what is to come: the "postal telegraph office" looks ahead to the Westland St. post office where Bloom picks up, under the pseudonym Henry Flower (again a lotus reference), the secret letter from his penpal Martha Clifford. The "sailors' home" points toward the garrulous old mariner of "Eumaeus"; "Lime street" is appropriately named for a chapter that centers on the longing for the Orient; "Bethel" points to Bloom's Jewish heritage; "Nichols' the undertaker" reminds him that at eleven, he is going to Paddy Dignam's funeral where the undertaker will be Corny Kelleher.

But Joyce — and this is again characteristic of Modernism — uses his Symbolist urban setting as a stimulus that prompts Bloom's very private stream of consciousness. "Tell him if he smokes he won't grow," he thinks watching the boy with his "chewed fagbutt," and then, being a non-judgmental, kindly type, he thinks better of this reprimand: "O let him! His life isn't such a bed of roses! Waiting outside pubs to bring da home. Come home to ma, da." And that thought, in turn, foreshadows the image of young Dingham's memory of his "da" in the Hades chapter. Toward the end of the paragraph, linguistic play begins to take over. "Met her once in the park. In the dark. What a lark." And then, thinking of Corny Kelleher, the undertaker, Bloom declares playfully: "Bury him cheap in a whatyoumaycall. With my tooraloom, tooraloom, tooraloom, tooraloom."

Joyce's Dublin, Eliot's London, Proust's Paris, Thomas Mann's Venice — these modernist cities are revealed to us through their architecture. Their materiality is palpable, the settings being startlingly real if not surreal (e. g. Eliot's "A crowd flowed over London Bridge, so many/I had not thought death had undone so many ..."), their value is complexly symbolic (Dublin as image of urban paralysis and loneliness, Proust's Paris as locus of class conflict and social climbing, Mann's Venice as the exotic Other); they elicit a new language which is polyglot, sophisticated, intricate — and determined to Make It New. In architectural terms, the Modernist city is the *metropolis*, as George Simmel characterized it in 1903:

---

[2]   See Richard M. Kain, *Fabulous Voyager: A Study of James Joyce's Ulysses*, rev. ed. (New York: Viking Press, 1958), pp. 37-39.

A man does not end with the boundaries of his body or the vicinity that he immediately fills with his activity, but only with the sum of effects that extend from him in time and space: so too a city consists first in the totality of its effects that extend beyond its immediacy.[3]

The city thus shapes human behavior: indeed, in *Ulysses*, the individual psyche becomes an extension of a very specific urban geography. It is, for example, when he crosses Townsend Street that Bloom comes face to face with the undertaker — a reminder of Dignam's funeral but also of his own mortality, his precarious existence.

The Modernist city, in short, is characterized by its density (both real and symbolic), its specificity and depth. Even in *Finnegans Wake*, where space and time become much more fluid and indeterminate, the *point de repère* is metropolitan Dublin, that "Irish capitol city [...] of two syllables and six letters, with a deltic origin and a nuinous end," which can boast of having "the most expansive peopling thoroughfare in the world," Dublin, with its "blightblack workingstacks at twelvepins a dozen and the noobibusses sleighding along Safetyfirst Street and the derryjellybies snooping around Tell-No-Tailors' Corner and the fumes and the hopes and the strupithump of his ville's indigenous romekeepers, homesweepers, domecreepers [...] and all the uproor from all the aufroofs."[4]

But what happens to this "uproor from all the aufroofs" in the elaborately condensed "writing through" of *Finnegans Wake* made by John Cage as a radio drama (*Hörspiel*) called *Roaratorio: An Irish Circus on Finnegans Wake*"? Is Dublin still felt as a presence in this postmodern performance piece or is the urban code displaced by a new emphasis on what has been called liquid architecture? These are the questions I wish to address here.

The title *Roaratorio*, as Cage tells Klaus Schöning who produced the radio piece for IRCAM in Paris in 1979, comes from the *Wake* itself, in a passage where the subjects of King Saint Finnerty the Festive prepare for "this longawaited Messiagh of roaratorios."[5] Cage calls it a "circus" because "there is not one center but [...] life itself is a plurality of centers."[6] *Roaratorio* is designed to be "free of melody and free of harmony and free of counterpoint: free of musical theory." Again, if an oratorio "is like a church-opera, in which the people don't act, they simply stand there and sing [...] a 'roaratorio' is [...] out in the world. It's not in the church."[7] And so "roaring" is par for the course.

But what kind of "roaring"? An entry into this curious homage to Joyce's Dublin may be found in a comment made by Schöning in the course of working with Cage:

A fugue is a more complicated genre; but it can be broken up by a single sound, say from a fire engine (from *Silence*)

Paraphrase: *Roaratorio* is a more complicated genre; it cannot be broken up by a single sound, say from a fire engine.[8]

---

[3]   Georg Simmel, 'Metropolis and Mental Life', in *The Conflict in Modern Culture and Other Essays*, trans. and ed. by K. Peter Etzkorn (NY: Teachers College Press, 1968), p. 12.

[4]   James Joyce, *Finnegans Wake* (1939; New York: Penguin Books, 1967), pp. 140, 6.

[5]   Joyce, p. 41.

[6]   John Cage/Klaus Schöning, 'Laughtears: Conversation on *Roaratorio*', in John Cage, *Roaratorio: An Irish Circus on Finnegans Wake*, ed. by Klaus Schöning (Köningstein: Athenäum, 1985), p. 107.

[7]   Cage/Schöning, p. 89.

[8]   Cage/Schöning, p. 19.

Another way of putting this is to say that Cage has *dematerialized* his chosen city and replaced it with what we now call *cyberspace*, "a parallel universe," in Michael Benedikt's words, "created and sustained by the world's computers and communication lines," whose "corridors form wherever electricity runs with intelligence."[9] In the realm of cyberspace, writes Marcos Novak:

> The notions of city, square, temple, institution, home, infrastructure are permanently extended. The city, traditionally the continuous city of physical proximity becomes the discontinuous city of cultural and intellectual community. Architecture, normally understood in the context of the first, conventional city, shifts to the structure of relationships, connections and associations that are webbed over and around the simple world of appearance and accommodations of commonplace functions.[10]

The "structure of relationships, connections and associations" of Cage's "discontinuous city" is characterized by its elaborate layering. The verbal text, to begin with, was produced, as I have shown more fully in *Radical Artifice: Writing Poetry in the Age of Media*, by submitting *Finnegans Wake* to a series of chance-generated operations (derived from the *I-Ching* but adapted for the computer on a program called *Mesolist*), that yielded a 41-page mesostic text, using the string "JAMES JOYCE."[11] As Cage explains it:

> A mesostic is like an acrostic; I used the name of JAMES JOYCE. And had I written acrostics the name would have gone don the margin, the left handside. But a mesostic is a road down the middle. So I would look for a word with *J* in it that didn't have an *A* because the *A* belongs on the second line for JAMES. And then a word with *A* that didn't have an *M*, and an *M* that didn't have an *E*, and an *E* that didn't have an *S* and in this way I made a path through the entire book.... [And further] I made the rule of not repeating a syllable that had already been used to express the *J* of James. So I kept an index, a card index ... [and reduced Joyce's 626-page text to] 41 pages.[12]

Thus, to take just one example, the first page of the *Wake* yields no more than the two short mesostics that open *Roaratorio*:

wroth with twoone nathandJoe
A
M
jhEm
Shen

pftJschute
sOlid man
that the hump tYhillhead of humself
is at the knoCk out
in thE park[13]

---

[9]   Michael Benedikt, 'Introduction', in *Cyberspace: First Steps*, ed. by Michael Benedikt (Cambridge and London: MIT Press, 1992).

[10] Marcos Novak, 'Liquid Architectures in Cyberspace', in Benedikt, *Cyberspace*, pp. 225-54; 249.

[11] See Marjorie Perloff, *Radical Artifice: Writing Poetry in the Age of Media* (Chicago and London: University of Chicago Press, 1992), pp. 150-61.

[12] Cage, *Roaratorio*, p. 75.

[13] Cage, p. 29.

The "knoCk out/in thE park" in those last two lines is a reference to Castle Knock, in the cemetery near the west gate of Phoenix Park in Dublin. But whereas in the *Wake*, Phoenix Park can be said to symbolize the Garden of Eden — the setting of H. C. Earwicker's innocent youth as well as his "fall" (he was caught peeping at or exhibiting himself to a couple of girls), in *Roaratorio*, such locales function neither realistically nor symbolically; rather Dublin becomes a kind of informational city, a dematerialized space that nevertheless — and this is the paradox — is always identifiable as a city that is not New York, not London, not Paris, not Istanbul or Delhi or Tokyo, but quite clearly Dublin.

Let me explain. When Cage was invited to provide "musical accompaniment" for his *Writing through Finnegans Wake*, he used the following procedure. The 41-page text became a ruler for the one-hour *Hörspiel*. Now, as Cage explains, "places mentioned in the *Wake* are identified in Louis Mink's book *A Finnegans Wake Gazetteer* [...] by page and line. And so a sound coming from Nagasaki, or from Canberra in Australia, or from a town in Ireland or a street in Dublin — could be identified by page and line and then put into this hour, where it belonged in relation to the page and line of *Finnegans Wake*."[14] The number of places mentioned (2462) was reduced by chance operations to 626, a number arbitrarily chosen so as to match the 626 pages of the *Wake* in the Viking edition.[15] About half of these were in Ireland and half of the Irish places in Dublin.

But how can "place" be represented in terms of sound on multitrack tape? Cage's method was to go to the places in question (or send friends and colleagues to those he could not reach himself) and then record the sounds actually heard on site. Here are his instructions to his fellow collectors:

> The recordings should be at least thirty seconds long and not longer than a few minutes. The sounds do not have to be chosen. Simply go to the place indicated ... and make a recording of whatever sound is there when you arrive.
> As I mentioned, I need a recording of ambient sound from your part of the world ... It will be used in a piece of music I'm making to be called *Roaratorio*, based on James Joyce's *Finnegans Wake*. It will be what could be called an *Irish Circus*. If you could send me a tape or cassette, preferably 1/4" tape, stereo recording (any length between 30 seconds and five or ten minutes) made in [...], I would be very grateful [...] You can simply accept the sounds which are in the place you go to when you make the recording. If there is some question about where you should go, you could answer it by some chance operation, such as dropping a coin on a map.[16]

It sounds, at first, like some sort of joke. What difference can it make, the reader may well ask, whether a baby's cry or church bell or the bark of a dog or running water is recorded in Dublin or in Kansas City? When Klaus Schöning recalls that "Trieste," mentioned in the *Wake*, enters the sound track in the course of a recording "seven thousand metres above Trieste and the Berlitz School of James Joyce," made "on the flight from Lyon to Belgrade," isn't he pulling our leg?[17] Obviously, whatever sound is recorded on such a flight can have nothing to do with Trieste. Again, when Cage explains to Schöning that

---

14 Cage, p. 89.
15 Cage, p. 95.
16 Cage, p. 119; the first two ellipses are Cage's.
17 Cage, p. 13.

collecting sounds in Ireland "meant getting up early in the morning and driving sometimes as late as ten o'clock in the evening [...] We would go say 200 miles and record a sound say in Skibbereen and it would be say just a dog barking or a chicken crowing, whatever happened to be there when we arrived," we may well wonder whether the one-minute recording made in Skibbereen was worth the effort.[18]

Let us suspend our disbelief for a moment and see how the sounds in question were placed on the "ruler." Not only does the hour-long performance contain 626 sounds based on the places mentioned in the *Wake*, but simultaneous programs were made from the actual sounds mentioned in Joyce's book as well as from "appropriate" music. First, a listing of the sounds cited in the *Wake* was made and again condensed by means of chance operations. These sounds were then classified into categories (such as thunderclaps, farts, musical instruments, bells, clocks, chimes, guns, animals and birds, water), and again transferred from their spatial position to a temporal one: for example, the reference to the "with what strong voice of false jiccup!" means that we hear a hiccup at the corresponding point in time (c. 1 minute) on the hour-long tape.[19] But note — and this is very important — that at the point where we hear the hiccup, the spoken mesostic text has reached the point of "and she allCasually/ansars hElpers," which has nothing to do with "Jiccup."[20] The information coming through the channel is thus multiform and layered: there is no dominant sound, no center.

And further: Cage has incorporated a variety of Irish musics into the piece. A friend told him that he should enlist the voice of Joe Heaney, "the king of Irish singers and one hundred per cent the real McCoy." Cage took a special trip to England where Heaney was performing, and the latter instructed him in the kinds of Irish music to include: "the flute, the fiddle, the bodhran [a sheepskin drum] ... and the Uillean pipes," as played by Seamus Ennis. Again, recordings of songs and melodies (in performances by soloists or composed variations of such solos) were superimposed on a multitrack tape to make a "circus of relevant musics."[21] The "score" includes familiar Irish songs like "Dark is the colour of my true love's hair" and "Little red fox," but also various hornpipes, reels, bodhran duets, and improvised pieces.

All these sounds were then superimposed on one another by a series of mathematical operations, the collection of sixteen multitrack tapes being combined into one. "The material," says Cage, "is then a plurality of forms"; it has "what Joyce called 'soundsense'."[22] But doesn't it matter, Schöning asks Cage, that the sound track often drowns out the reciter's voice so that the words cannot be understood? From Cage's perspective this is no problem, for "this is our experience in life every day. Wherever we are a larger amount of what we have to experience is being destroyed every instant. If for instance [...] you go to a museum where you would think that you have [...] peace and quiet as you are looking at the Mona Lisa someone passes in front of you or bumps into you from

---

[18]   Cage, p. 95.
[19]   Joyce, *Wake*, 4, ll. 10-11.
[20]   Cage, *Raratorio*, p. 29.
[21]   Cage, p. 175.
[22]   Cage, p. 103.

behind."[23] In keeping with the circus format, the sounds never coalesce or merge; they retain their individual identities. Nor can the sounds heard in any sense "accompany" the words or provide a musical setting. The separate strata remain separate.

To what extent is *Roaratorio* what Cage calls an "Irish Circus"? Does its locale continue to be Joyce's Dublin or is the new urban architecture amorphous? On the one hand, Cage wants to emphasize the work's internationalism: he tells Schöning that "Ciaran McMathoona, the chief in radio of the traditional music for the Irish folklore and a charming man" was "delighted that *Finnegans Wake* an Irish work — that a *hörspiel* on it should be commissioned by a German radio station [...] and that it should be made by an American with John Fullemann who is Swiss and his wife, who is Swedish."[24] Schöning adds that "it's a production of WDR Köln with KRO Hilversum and SDR Stuttgart"; and further, it was done in a French research studio. "The whole thing is international," Cage explains. "It's all the world."[25] On the other hand — and this is a characteristically Cagean paradox — there can be no doubt that the finished multitrack piece is designed to signify Irishness, even what we might call Dublinicity.

The sounds in question were recorded in such places as Ballyhooly (town in Co. Cork), Swords (N. Co. Dublin), Kish Lightship (E. of Dublin Bay), and Enniskerry (Co. Wicklow); sounds made in Ireland predominate (about three to one), but recordings were also made in places as far afield as Damascus, Prague, Baghdad, Madras, Sydney, and Lima. In the first few minutes of the "roaratorio" proper (3.10 to 4.10 on the tape), I distinguish the following sounds:

water poured into a bucket	laughter
fiddle music	gunshot
car braking	whistle
bird song	tram screeching to a halt
church bells	fire enging
baby crying	motor boat
cowbells	orchestra
automobile traffic	baby crying
rooster crowing	fire alarm
church choir	motorcycle
soprano singing	waterfall

And all the while, Cage is reading from his Joyce mesostics, the dominant sound being the repeated *J* of *James* Joyce.[26]

---

23   Cage, pp. 101-3.

24   Cage, p. 93.

25   Cage, p. 93.

26   The /j/ phoneme is foregrounded, not only by its repetition, but because /j/ is never a silent letter as are /y/ and /e/ and, when it appears in a compound like "neAtly," the /a/. The /j/ sound thus dominates: "pftJschute," "Jiccup," "Judges," "Jollybrool," "Jerrybuilding," "Jute," "Jubilee," "Japijap," etc.

The effect is to make us feel that we are in a particular space: Dublin, or at least Ireland, even as we can neither visualize that space nor make an architectural drawing of it, and even as the text is always opening up to the larger electronic world and admitting sounds from Buenos Aires or Canberra or Helsinki. In the same vein, Cage's is a text to be heard that must also be read, for in reading *Roaratorio*, one comes across many features that are obscured by the oral presentation, beginning with the *Wake*'s punctuation, which Cage has liberally spread around the page. Take the stanza:

> Juxta-
> explanatiOn was put in loo of
> eYes
> lokil Calour and lucal odour
> to havE

The oral performance hides the pun "loo"/"lieu," the phonetic spelling of "lokil Calour" ("local color"), with its play on the Norse God Loki and the Italian patriot Cavour, and the mesostic embedding of "Yes" in "eyes." Neither speech nor writing has priority in this nice exemplar of a Derridean system of differences.

It is a system of differences, one might add, that curiously anticipates the "informational city," as Manuel Castells has characterized it.[27] A recent *New York Times* architectural column by Herbert Muschamp describes the offices of the financial trading firm of D. E. Shaw in midtown Manhattan as tapping into the "international network of electronic communications that keeps the global economy humming. The 'streets' of this city have no potholes. They are paved not with asphalt but with telephone lines and radio waves that stretch between cities and leap across national borders." As for the offices themselves, they are open around the clock "though for much of that time the firm's windowless hexagonal trading room is unattended by human hands. Machines hold down the fort. Silently, with lights flickering, batteries of computers go about their programmed business [...] These machines are the traffic lights of the informational city."[28]

This description of the informational city helps us to make sense of Cage's project in his *Irish Circus on Finnegans Wake*. Although the language of *Roaratorio* is entirely Joyce's, that language, spliced, endowed with capitals where there should be none, and radically condensed by the process of lineation, is transformed into an electronic communications network, whose "streets" are telephone lines and radio waves that connect the many parts of the world where sounds have been collected: Joyce's text, condensed, minimalized, fractured, fades in and out in what is a floating abstract realm or space flow. At one level, Cage's seems to be the very model of the dematerialized city, "Dublin" as "realm of pure information [...] decontaminating the natural and urban landscapes, redeeming them, saving them from the chain-dragging bulldozers of the paper industry, from the diesel smoke of courier and post office trucks, from jet fuel fumes and clogged airports, from billboards [...]

---

[27]   Manuel Castells, *The Informational City: Information Technology, Economic Restructuring, and the Urban-Regional Process* (Oxford: Basil Blackwell, 1989), chap. 3, passim.

[28]   Herbert Muschamp, *The New York Times*, 8 July, 1992, Section 2, 1.

pollutions [...] and corruptions attendant to the process of moving information attached to *things*."[29]

But dispersal is only part of the story. In *The Global City*, Saskia Sassen has forcefully argued that "the territorial dispersal of economic activity at the national and world scale [paradoxically] creates a need for expanded central control and management": the city becomes the "command point in the organization of the world economy," the "key location and marketplace for leading industries." New York, London, Frankfurt, Paris, Hong Kong, São Paolo: in all these "maximum population and resource dispersal" has led to new systems of economic order and agglomeration, new systems of central control.[30] Just so, Cage's seemingly "open" and "decentered" *Circus* is governed, whether overtly or not, by the "command point" of the artist: Cage, after all, is always in control. If the sounds seem fortuitous, let us remember that they must be accommodated to precisely the hour format, that they come at points chosen and charted by Cage himself, who has planned every single detail. Indeed, if Joyce's geometric grid gives way to Cage's cyberspace, that cyberspace has its own super-programmer. The use of chance operations, we should note, does not mean that anything is left to chance.

Can the art work or poetic composition avoid this degree of control? The "liquid architecture" of *Roaratorio* may be dematerialized; it may well be an architecture that, in Marcos Novak's words, "is no longer satisfied with only space and form and light and all the aspects of the real world [...] an architecture of fluctuating relations between abstract elements," but this is not to say that dematerialization ushers in a new kind of freedom. Cage's Dublin may have "transcended" the boundaries of Joyce's four-square grid, but that transcendence is, after all, produced by the individual figure of the poet, controlling the multitrack tape performance from behind the scenes.[31]

I do not mean to imply that such artistic authority is a bad thing. Poetry is, after all, with rare exceptions like the Japanese *renga*, a form of individual production, and however much the author of the *Roaratorio* may have wanted to get rid of the ego, his stylistic signature remains highly individual, indeed uniquely Cagean. To take another, later example of this tension between the dematerialization of space and the specification of the poet's language, I want to look at a long poem published in 1991: Lyn Hejinian's 300-page *Oxota*, subtitled *A Short Russian Novel*.[32] This lyric novel is written in the fourteen-line rhyming stanza of Pushkin's *Evgeny Onegin* and its "story" consistently but very indirectly alludes to the love intrigues, social events, and nature descriptions of Pushkin's great poem. His Petersburg becomes her Leningrad, the Leningrad visited over a two or three-year period by a poet whose familiarity with the Russian language is only sketchy, and who is totally captivated by Russia even as she finds she cannot understand it.

---

[29] Benedikt, 'Introduction', p. 3.
[30] Saskia Sassen, *The Global City* (Princeton: Princeton UP, 1991), pp. 3-5.
[31] Novak, 'Liquid', p. 251.
[32] Lyn Hejinian, *Oxota: A Short Russian Novel* (Great Barrington: The Figures, 1991). For a fuller discussion of the poetics of *Oxota*, see my 'How Russian Is It: Lyn Hejinian's *Oxota*', *Parnassus: Poetry in Review* 17 (Spring 1993), pp. 186-209.

The title *Oxota* (Russian for "hunt"), refers, I think, to the poet's hunt for meaning. Whereas Pushkin's Tatyana is "hunted by love's anguish" (Book 3, xx), Hejinian's "describer-perceiver" hunts among words and sentences for clues and connections. But what Hejinian calls a "glass prose" (a transparency model, a window on reality) is no longer adequate. Narrative, in these circumstances, becomes a language game: as Hejinian put it in an essay called "The Rejection of Closure," "The very idea of reference is spatial: over here is word, over there is thing at which the word is shooting amiable love-arrows," and thus "the struggle between language and that which it claims to depict or express" is what determines the very shape narrative takes. "Language discovers what one might know, which in turn is always less than what language might say."[33]

From *Writing is an Aid to Memory* (1978) and *My Life* (1980), to her recent long metaphysical poem "The Person," Hejinian has refused all notions of the *self* as "some core reality at the heart of our sense of being," the still dominant myth of the "artist's 'own voice,' issuing from an inner, fundamental, sincere, essential, irreducible, consistent self, an identity which is unique and separable from all other human identities." Rather, "The person [...] is a mobile (or mobilized) reference point; or to put it another way, subjectivity is not an entity by a dynamic." "Certainly," Hejinian concedes, "I have an experience of being in position, at a time and place, and of being conscious of this, but this position is temporary, and beyond that, I have no experience of being except in position." Thus, "the experience of the self" is perceived "as a relationship rather than an existence."[34]

In this scheme of things, psychology means not self-revelation, as in a more traditional poetry, but, in Wallace Stevens's words, "description without place." Consider Chapter One, in which the narrator ("Lyn") arrives in Leningrad to stay (as we know from later poems) with the Russian poet Arkadii Dragomoschenko, whom she is translating.

> This time we are both
> The old thaw is inert, everything set again in snow
> At insomnia, at apathy
> We must learn to endure the insecurity as we read
> The felt need for a love intrigue
> There is no person — he or she was appeased and withdrawn
> There is relationship but it lacks simplicity
> People are very aggressive and every week more so
> The Soviet colonel appearing in such of our stories
> He is sentimental and duckfooted
> He is held fast, he is in his principles
> But here is a small piece of the truth — I am glad to greet you
> There, just with a few simple words it is possible to say the truth
> It is so because often men and women have their sense of honor.[35]

Where does this "scene" take place and what is its information channel? In good epic tradition, the poem opens *in medias res* with "This time," the implication being that "this

---

[33]   *Poetics Journal* 4 (May 1984), pp. 138-39.

[34]   "The Person and Description," Symposium on "The Poetics of Everyday Life," *Poetics Journal* 9: "The Person" Issue (1991), pp. 166-67.

[35]   Hejinian, *Oxota*, p. 11.

time" (arriving again in the Soviet Union) will be measured against another time which was somehow different. But "This time we are both" immediately displays Hejinian's deceptive flatness: the language seems totally ordinary, and yet it throws out any number of plot lines. Perhaps it means that "We are both here," but then who are "we"? And what is it we both are? Both poets, one American, one Russian, or one woman and one man? Both guests of the Soviet government? Both ready for a relationship? Or if "both" is construed, not as the predicate nominative but as the modifier of the predicative adjective(s), we might read it as "both tired and hungry, both frightened and elated," and so on.

Something, in any case, is about to happen "this time." The "thaw" of line 2 may well refer to the brief political respite of the Khrushchev years as well as the actual weather conditions; soon "everything [is] set again in snow." And just as Pushkin's dedicatory stanza describes his poem as the product "of carefree hours, of fun,/of sleeplessness, faint inspirations," Hejinian refers to "insomnia" and "apathy," warning her reader even as she warns herself that "We must learn to endure the insecurity as we read/The felt need for a love intrigue/There is no person — he or she was appeased and withdrawn." The "need for a love intrigue" refers, of course, to the Onegin-Tatyana romance which is Pushkin's "subject"; in our own fractured world, such "love intrigue" seems to have given way to the diminished romance of "relationship," and even then a relationship that "lacks simplicity." Indeed, all sorts of sexual and familial relationships, all more or less complicated, will be presented for our inspection, and part of the fun of reading *Oxota* will be to figure out who is drawn to whom, for how long, and what the sexual and/or political dynamics are.

In the meantime, the stage is set for the unfolding of events: "People are very aggressive and every week more so." The "duckfooted" colonel, who will appear and reappear throughout the narrative, an embodiment of "principles," and "sentimental" old truths, is introduced and then, like a stock character in a cheap thriller, mysteriously disappears again. And now the stanza ends on a turn of phrase that is brilliantly deployed throughout *Oxota,* especially in the early chapters, where the poet records how it feels to be a linguistic alien in a country one wants so badly to understand. "Here is a small piece of the truth — I am glad to greet you" is the poet's rendition of the way "polite" Russian hosts greet their American guests, the excessive formality of phrasing being a function of unfamiliarity rather than good manners.

Many of us have had the experience of meeting foreigners who seem extremely, if not excessively polite until we realize they are speaking a careful English based on the classroom model or grammar book. Translated into colloquial English, line 12 carries something like the locution, "Believe me, I am so glad to meet you." But in bringing "the truth" into speech twice, and in concluding that "It is so because often men and women have their sense of honor," we are immediately *in* a language world — and, in Wittgensteinian terms, the limits of my language are the limits of my world — that is largely alien to the American visitor. Accordingly, for the "we" who are "both," assimilation will depend, not on finding out what the words mean, but how they are used, how to read the signs. And, as Hejinian wittily implies throughout, this is no easy matter. When someone says to us "There, just with a few simple words it is possible to say the truth," we surmise the presence of a sensibility that may not be there at all.

But then words like "there" are always suspect in Hejinian's scheme of things, origin and location, whether of speech or event, being all but impossible to define. The line, "People are very aggressive and every week more so," for instance, sounds like a snatch of conversation overheard while waiting on line at the butcher shop. But it may also refer to something quoted from the newspaper or, for that matter, it may record Lyn's own appraisal of her surroundings. Even the stilted Russian constructions of the English language cannot always be attributed to X or Y; often, they may be Hejinian's own, as she tries to make herself understood to those who have schoolbook English. They may even be approximations of Russian syntax, as laboriously translated into English by the poet. The pattern is further complicated by the gaps between statements and/or lines, one perception thus failing to lead, as Charles Olson would have it, immediately (or even remotely) to a further perception.

It is important to notice here that, as in the case of Cage's *Roaratorio*, disjunctiveness does not always accompany an imagistic or filmlike collage surface, or even with the free association of stream-of-consciousness. Language does not represent "thought"; on the contrary, linguistic artifice is emphasized by the embedding of images in a network of abstractions, as in "everything set again in snow," or by the positioning of abstractions in unlikely grammatical constructions, as in the locution "At insomnia, at apathy," on the model of "at school" or "at home." The resulting poem-novel is, as Hejinian puts it in Chapter Two, "something neither invented nor constructed but moving through that time as I experienced it unable to take part personally in the hunting." It is as if the text avoids the requisite distance between subject and object and lets "events" unfold so that the reader feels as if she has come in on a conversation whose participants cannot be located.

In cyberspace, Marcos Novak explains, "the identity of objects does not have to be manifested physically; it can be hidden in a small difference in an attribute that is not displayed."[36] And again, "Cybserspace offers the opportunity of maximizing the benefits of separating *data*, *information*, and *form*."[37] This seems to me precisely what occurs in Hejinian's cyberversion of Leningrad. Forms are no longer symbolic, yielding such and such information and data; rather everything happens in an unspecifiable space/time realm of "minimal restriction."[38] "Being there," as in the *Roaratorio*, is the special pleasure of this dematerialized universe, but where is there?

The "new urbanism," it seems, has penetrated not only the culture of built environments but also the seemingly very different culture of poetic discourse. The question is not just whether Cage's "Dublin" or Hejinian's "Leningrad" can be conventionally located and mapped but whether, in the larger sense, poetry can continue to operate under the old rules of versification, stanza form, justified margins — all attributes, after all, of a confined and recognizable space. Or is it possible that poetic territory is becoming, in Benedikt's description of cyberspace, "billowing, glittering, humming, coursing, a Borgesian library, a city; intimate, immense, firm, liquid, recognizable and unrecognizable at once"?[39]

---

[36]   Novak, 'Liquid', p. 239.
[37]   Novak, p. 225.
[38]   Novak, p. 234.
[39]   Benedikt, 'Introduction', p. 2.

María Eugenia Díaz Sánchez

Coda

Even the casual observer of academic frontiers would be seduced by a path of exploration in new systems of thought. In this collection of essays, what was easily assumed may be now fully faced with its complexity, by discovering strategies that challenge previous order and explore new experimental procedures. Setting literature next to architecture, the divergences and similarities between them renew interest in aspects not anticipated when looked at separately. Many see contemporary poetry as a reaction to modernism's monotonous universal world vision and its values of individuality, progress, and human self-determination. Architecture has suffered a less radical confrontation with modernism but it still moved from a serious, formally experimental structure to a parodic and carnivalesque attitude. Both poetry and architecture are now based on the notion not of the limits intrinsic in the idea of art but in the inexhaustible development of an artistic celebration.

An example of interaction between these separate arts is architect Aldo Rossi, usually defined as a poet who happens to be an architect. He is the creator of models for a historical city where beauty consists of mixing residences and monuments, past and present: the rules of construction are both safeguards and limitation. He proposed a progressive dialogue where his projects would be the outcome of his observations. With the experience of years of constant reduction, he finally wanted to do away with the means of representation: a poetic aim inspired, as he mentioned, by his master of architecture, the poet Raymond Roussel. A way the architect can allow his personal memory to mingle with collective traditions or rather chose to erase traditions and create new nonreferential forms. The building thus seems pure theatre, the theatre of life, and the global media upon which he captures the literary reflections of his native Lombardy, through the literature of Pavese.

Architectures of Poetry is the outcome of a reflection on connections between poetry and architecture suggested at the conference that took place at Universidad de Salamanca the year 2000. I deeply thank Prof. Marjorie Perloff, whose presence at Salamanca as a Visiting Professor was most stimulating, and triggered a web of contacts among scholars in both Europe and United States. To her and her enormous generosity only present in scholars of authentic academic vocation, we owe the outcome of this book.

Architectures of Poetry includes published essays from senior scholars and original essays from outstanding younger critics. Each one presents a distinct point of view, and together they constitute a forum of interpretative methods with new ideas on each text.

It is the hope of the editors that this volume shares the vitality of current critical work in American Poetry. We also expect it will generate new insights and excitement for students and inspire new essays on the subject.